Advanced ABAP®
Programming for
SAP™

Send Us Your Comments:

To comment on this book or any other PRIMA TECH title, visit PRIMA TECH's reader response page on the Web at **www.prima-tech.com/comments**.

How to Order:

For information on quantity discounts, contact the publisher: Prima Publishing, P.O. Box 1260BK, Rocklin, CA 95677-1260; (916) 632-4400. On your letterhead, include information concerning the intended use of the books and the number of books you wish to purchase. For individual orders, visit PRIMA TECH's Web site at **www.prima-tech.com.**

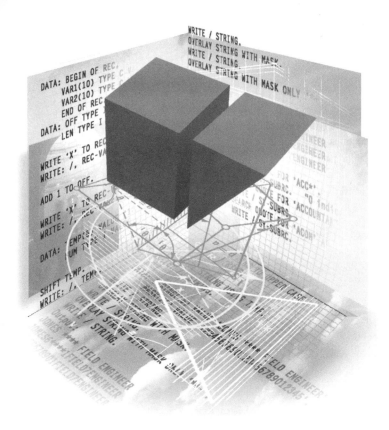

Advanced ABAP®
Programming for
SAP™

Gareth M. de Bruyn
Robert Lyfareff

Certified SAP R/3
Application Consultants

Ken Kroes

A Division of Prima Publishing

A Division of Prima Publishing

Prima Publishing and colophon are registered trademarks of Prima Communications, Inc. PRIMA TECH is a trademark of Prima Communications, Inc., Rocklin, California 95765.

"SAP" is a registered trademark of SAP Aktiengesellschaft, Systems, Applications and Products in Data Processing, Neurottstrasse 16, 69190 Walldorf, Germany. The publisher gratefully acknowledges SAP's kind permission to use its trademark in this publication. SAP AG is not the publisher of this book and is not responsible for it under any aspect of press law.

ABAP, ABAP/4, BAPI, ALE/WEB, Management Cockpit, R/2, R/3, SAP (Logo), SAP (Word), SAP ArchiveLink, SAP Business Workflow, SAP EarlyWatch, SAPPHIRE, and TeamSAP are trademarks or registered trademarks of SAP Aktiengesellschaft, Walldorf, Germany.

Windows, Windows Explorer, and Microsoft are registered trademarks of Microsoft Corporation.

Prima Publishing and the authors have attempted throughout this book to distinguish proprietary trademarks from descriptive terms by following the capitalization style used by the manufacturers.

Information contained in this book has been obtained by Prima Publishing from sources believed to be reliable. However, because of the possibility of human or mechanical error by our sources, Prima Publishing, or others, the Publisher does not guarantee the accuracy, adequacy, or completeness of any information and is not responsible for any errors or omissions or the results obtained from the use of such information. Readers should be particularly aware of the fact that the Internet is an ever-changing entity. Some facts may have changed since this book went to press.

ISBN: 0-7615-1798-7

Library of Congress Catalog Card Number: 98-67614

Printed in the United States of America

99 00 01 02 03 HH 10 9 8 7 6 5 4 3 2 1

Publisher:
Stacy L. Hiquet

Associate Publisher:
Nancy Stevenson

Managing Editor:
Dan J. Foster

Sr. Acquisitions Editor:
Deborah F. Abshier

Project Editor:
Kevin Harreld

Copy Editor:
Gabrielle Nemes

Technical Editors:
Jon Reed, Ken Kroes, and Robert Lyfareff

Interior Layout:
Joyce Black

Cover Design:
Prima Design Team

Indexer:
Katherine Stimson

Dedications

To my brother Jason. You have an excellent perspective on life.

*To the Morgan crew back home. Ian, Grant, Matthew, Nona, Nadine, Uncle Bruce,
Aunty Jas, Stephen, Erica, Bernice, Peter, and Andre. DWMWD*

—GMD

*To my wife Donna and my children, Megan and Jarid, thanks for your support
for the past several months.*

—KK

To Claudia, for more reasons than I can remember.

—RL

Contents at a Glance

Contents

Acknowledgments

We wish to acknowledge and thank the following people for their help in writing this text: Matt Carleson, for your continued support and vision in the process of writing this book and throughout the entire series; Kevin Harreld, for your project management and all your editing behind the scenes; Debbie Abshier, for your patience and moral support throughout the writing process; Robert Parkinson and Sunil Menon, for your answers to technical questions.

Finally, we wish to thank SAP America.

About the Authors

Gareth M. de Bruyn is an independent SAP consultant and a technical lead for a Fortune 50 company. With many years of experience in the IT industry and over four years in the growing SAP arena, he is a veteran of multiple SAP implementations and most modules of R/3. As a Certified SAP R/3 Application Consultant through SAP America, de Bruyn's current projects include build-to-order manufacturing and emerging Web technologies on SAP. A native of South Africa but raised and educated in the United States, de Bruyn believes SAP technology is revolutionizing international business. He can be contacted at **gmdebruyn@bigfoot.com**.

Ken Kroes specializes in implementing SAP for clients with build-to-order (configurable) products and Internet applications for SAP. He received an engineering degree at the University of Calgary, Canada, and now has over 15 years of programming and consulting experience. Ken has worked as an independent SAP consultant in both R/2 and R/3 for many large clients. He can be contacted at **kenkroes@bigfoot.com**.

Robert Lyfareff is a Certified SAP R/3 Application Consultant through SAP America and a veteran of several successful SAP installation teams over the past five years. Coupled with his formal training in computer science and electrical engineering, this unique SAP experience enables him to write about real-world business situations and issues. What excites and challenges him about his work is enabling complex business practices through the use of new technology. Currently, he works as an independent SAP consultant and author. Robert's e-mail address is **rlyf@bigfoot.com**.

Introduction

R/3 is an example of an ERP (Enterprise Resource Planning) system. ERP systems are used by corporations to track all information related to the business including financial, sales, and materials data. R/3 is produced by SAP, a German software company founded in the 70s by a group of former IBM employees. The earlier versions of R/3 were mainframe-based applications offering only a subset of R/3's current functionality. The modern client-server version of R/3 was first introduced in 1992 and has become the most popular ERP system in the world. The most current version of R/3 is version 4.5. It offers a host of improvements over prior versions, including Internet integration, supply chain functionality, and support for the new Euro currency.

R/3 is based on a client/server architecture and uses a relational database to track all information related to a corporation. It's made up of thousands of small programs called transactions. A transaction consists of ABAP code and an associated set of screens that can be used to enter, change, or display data; monitor events within the R/3 system; and change functionality in the R/3 system. R/3 gathers related transactions into groups known as modules. A module is a set of transactions that deal with the same area of business functionality. There are modules for Materials, Financial Data, Human Resources, Sales, and other common business functions.

Throughout this book, the R/3 system is referred to simply as SAP. SAP runs on several operating systems, including UNIX, Windows NT, and AS/300, and can use several different databases, including Oracle, Informix, and SQL Server. Within the SAP application, the operating system and database are normally invisible to both users and programmers.

Programming in R/3

ABAP is the programming language used by SAP's developers to build the transactions that make up the R/3 application and also by corporations to customize the R/3 application. In general, ABAP isn't used by customers of SAP to develop complex applications from scratch, but instead to provide additional business functionality. For example, it's not necessary for a customer to write a program in ABAP to manage inventory levels, because SAP has already written transactions to accomplish this objective.

NOTE

You may have seen ABAP referred to as ABAP/4 in the past. As of version 4.0 of R/3, SAP officially changed the name to ABAP.

The two most common uses for ABAP are for producing custom reports and developing custom interfaces for SAP. In this context, a report is an ABAP program that reads specific data from SAP's database and then displays the data using a computer screen or a printed page. An interface, on the other hand, is an ABAP program that moves data into SAP, or reads data from SAP, and then writes it out to a system file to be transferred to an external computer system, such as a legacy mainframe. Other uses for ABAP include conversion programs that change data into a format usable by SAP, and custom transactions similar to the SAP transactions that make up the R/3 application but are written by users to fulfill some business function not provided by SAP.

As an experienced SAP programmer, you may have produced programs and reports using ABAP, but you may never have developed a custom transaction. Programs and reports are written entirely in ABAP and require no additional tools to develop. Transactions use ABAP and several other tools to perform operations you are familiar with, such as reading from or writing to the database, performing mathematical operations, and calling on system resources. A transaction may have multiple screens that interact with the user, such as a screen to search for a material, a screen to display information about a material, and a final screen to maintain information about a material. These screens are developed using a tool called Screen Painter, and can execute ABAP code through a special language called Flow Logic. Another tool, Menu Painter, allows the programmer to create custom menus and titles for the screens in a transaction. The nice thing about transaction development is that all of the skills you have mastered writing ABAP programs can immediately be used in developing transactions—you simply need to learn a few additional tools and techniques.

How to Use This Book

This book will deal with advanced topics in ABAP development, and so it assumes you have a basic understanding of the language, including defining variables and internal tables, using SAP SQL to access database tables, and performing other basic ABAP operations. However, you do not need to have any prior experience developing transactions with Screen Painter or Menu Painter. This book will provide the information you need to develop your first custom transaction.

TIP

If you feel you are lacking in any of the basic aspects of ABAP programming, please see PRIMA TECH's *Introduction to ABAP/4 Programming for SAP.*

This book is divided into three sections: Advanced ABAP, Data Dictionary Development, and SAP Transaction Development. The first section covers some advanced ABAP topics you may not have previously encountered, such as function modules and global memory. The second section explains how to create your own custom data dictionary objects, such as database tables and lock objects. The third section explains the basics behind developing custom transactions.

Part I: Advanced ABAP

In this section, advanced ABAP commands not discussed in PRIMA TECH's *Introduction to ABAP/4 Programming for SAP* are covered. You will learn these commands, their syntax, and how to use them in your coding. In addition, an introduction to transaction processing is included in Chapter 4.

Chapter 1, "Selection Screen Controls," covers the commands you can utilize in regular programs (reports). You will learn to format your selection screens similar to those created using the Screen Builder.

Chapter 2, "Creating Function Modules," navigates the reader through the Function Builder portion of the ABAP Workbench. How to build a function module is described. Finally, you'll learn how to incorporate a function module in your ABAP code.

Chapter 3, "Remote Function Calls and BAPIs," discusses the differences between RFCs and regular function modules, and how they can be used to communicate between two systems. BAPIs are perfect examples of RFCs in use, and are explained with real-world examples to give the reader a clear vision of how RFCs should work.

Chapter 4, "SAP Transaction Processing," introduces the reader to the SAP transaction model, as well as the locking procedures SAP utilizes at the database and transaction level.

Chapter 5, "Working with Global Memory," discusses how SAP global memory and ABAP memory are utilized in ABAP programs. New memory transport commands are introduced that can be used in future transactions as well as in current reports.

Chapter 6, "Macros," is dedicated to explaining the code behind macros as well as presenting practical applications using the scripting command.

Part II: Data Dictionary Development

This section covers all of the advanced features of the ABAP Dictionary. Included are chapters covering the use, explanation, and creation of Data Dictionary objects—from those as simple as fields to objects as complex as logical databases.

Chapter 7, "Working with Domains, Data Elements, and Fields," covers domains and data elements as well as the steps to creating Dictionary objects.

Chapter 8, "Creating Tables," discusses the definition of fields, how they are comprised of data elements and domains, and how the fields define a table.

Chapter 9, "Creating Views," defines the Dictionary object and discusses the steps needed to create such objects.

Chapter 10, "Lock Objects," discusses the Dictionary objects previously introduced and how to create and use the objects.

Chapter 11, "Creating Search Helps (Matchcodes)," discusses what a matchcode (now called a Search Help in 4.x) is, how to create a Search Help, and how to utilize them in your tables.

Chapter 12, "Creating Logical Databases," shows how to create a Dictionary object and how to utilize the object within your code.

Part III: SAP Transaction Development

In this section, you will learn the basics of transaction development. You will learn how to create and control screens, add menus and titles to your screens, and how to call ABAP code to perform various actions.

Chapter 13, "Transaction Development," introduces you to the process of creating a custom transaction.

Chapter 14, "Creating a Transaction," offers a step-by-step tutorial for creating a simple transaction.

Chapter 15, "Using the Screen Painter," presents a detailed look at using Screen Painter to develop custom screens by creating fields, buttons, and text.

Chapter 16, "Using the Menu Painter," offers a detailed look at using Menu Painter to create GUI statuses and titles for use in custom transactions.

Chapter 17, "Using Flow Logic to Develop a Transaction," provides an explanation of how to use flow logic to control screen functions and execute ABAP code.

Chapter 18, "Using ABAP to Control Transaction Logic," gives examples of using ABAP to perform functions, control screen flow, and perform list processing.

Chapter 19, "Screen Loops," is an explanation of how to further enhance screens by allowing multiple rows or loops of data to be displayed. Both the Step Loop and table control method are discussed, with examples of both.

Chapter 20, "Advanced Techniques," covers the not-so-pretty world of locking data records while ensuring the data integrity. Some of the newer features of Screen Painter are also explained, such as the use of subscreens and tabs.

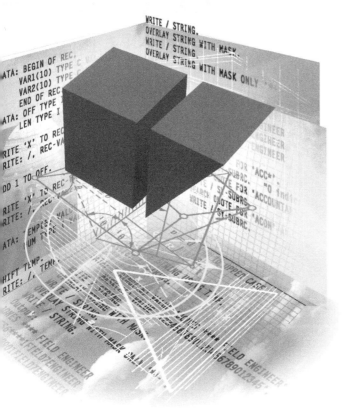

PART I

ADVANCED ABAP

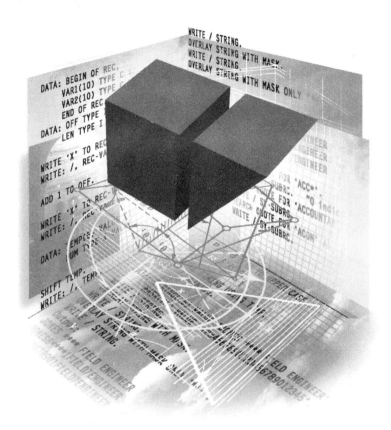

Chapter 1

Selection Screen Controls

In This Chapter

◆ Formatting selection screens using boxes, parameters, and comments

◆ Grouping and boxing selection screen objects

This chapter will cover the initial formatting of reports written in the ABAP editor. While you are probably familiar with the selection screen generated by the SELECT OPTION command and the PARAMETERS command, you may not be aware of other commands that allow a greater degree of control when developing the selection screens of reports.

Have you ever wondered how you could put a particular section in a box of its own, or perhaps add a comment in between inputs for parameters? This chapter will show you. In later chapters, screen formatting using the Screen Painter will be covered, but this chapter will introduce you to such formatting in basic reporting programs.

Certain screen formatting applies to logical databases as well. So that you are presented with new techniques in an ordered format, the steps used for logical databases are discussed in Chapter 12, "Creating Logical Databases."

Formatting the Selection Screen

Using the SELECTION-SCREEN command along with its various additions, you can control the format (appearance) of your selection screen in a report (a program of type 1 in its attributes) or in the initial selection screen of a logical database. The commands introduced in the next section will allow you to create blocks, combine input fields (parameters/pushbuttons/comments) onto a single line, create push buttons, define function keys, and add aesthetic elements (underlines, spaces, extra lines) on your selection screen.

In the definition of a selection screen for a logical database, other options are available in addition to those mentioned in this chapter. These extra options will be described in Chapter 12 when the intricacies and details of logical databases, as well as the additional features of the commands referenced here, are covered in detail.

Boxes and Titles

You may be aware of the presence of graphic boxes surrounding text, parameters, and select options in SAP reports and transactions. Sometimes these boxes have titles or a label associated with the information inside the box. Figure 1-1 displays an example of such a screen and describes each portion of the screen. Refer first, however, to the syntax of the command set, and then match it up to the figure.

The syntax of the command to generate the titles and boxes is:

```
SELECTION-SCREEN BEGIN OF BLOCK block <WITH FRAME> <TITLE title> <NO INTERVALS>.
selection screen statements (PARAMETERS, SELECT-OPTIONS, etc.)
SELECTION-SCREEN END OF BLOCK block.
```

The additions are explained in subsequent paragraphs. Now look at Figure 1-1 and review the labels associated with each portion of the screen.

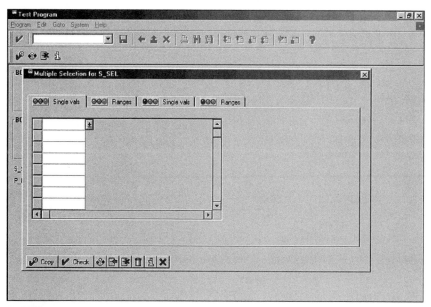

FIGURE 1-1

Sample selection screen showing boxes and titles

The code generating this screen is as follows:

```
REPORT ZTESTABAP .


* BOX 1
SELECTION-SCREEN BEGIN OF BLOCK BOX1
                         WITH FRAME
                         TITLE BOX1 NO INTERVALS.


SELECT-OPTIONS: S_SEL FOR SY-DATUM.
PARAMETERS:     P_PARAM(20).


SELECTION-SCREEN END OF BLOCK BOX1.


* BOX 2
SELECTION-SCREEN BEGIN OF BLOCK BOX2
                         WITH FRAME
                         TITLE BOX2.


SELECT-OPTIONS: S_SEL2 FOR SY-DATUM.
PARAMETERS:     P_PARAM2(20).


SELECTION-SCREEN END OF BLOCK BOX2.


* BOX 3
SELECTION-SCREEN BEGIN OF BLOCK BOX3.


SELECT-OPTIONS: S_SEL3 FOR SY-DATUM.
PARAMETERS:     P_PARAM3(20).


SELECTION-SCREEN END OF BLOCK BOX3.


INITIALIZATION.
MOVE 'BOX 1' TO BOX1.
MOVE 'BOX 2' TO BOX2.
```

The box is generated around the code enclosed by the BEGIN OF BLOCK block command by the WITH FRAME addition. The title listed in the block is generated by the TITLE title command. The title cannot exceed 8 characters. The TITLE addition can only be used if the WITH FRAME addition has been used as well. The third block has no title, and the grouping of parameters after this untitled box does not have the WITH FRAME command.

The effect of the additional command NO INTERVALS can be seen in the box titled BOX 1. In BOX 2, the NO INTERVALS addition is not used. From looking at the example code above and the screen in Figure 1-1, notice that the effect of NO INTERVALS is that the TO range generated by the select-options statement is not present. The effect of the NO INTERVALS addition on the user's choices is that the user can only enter a list of single values. This effect can be seen in Figure 1-2, which shows that the additional list of choices can be reached by clicking the arrow button to the right of the first input field in BOX 1.

In BOX 2, if the NO INTERVALS command is included, the result is different than if the drop-down arrow is clicked. A TO value is now present as shown in Figure 1-3. This TO value allows the user to enter a range of numbers rather than a single value.

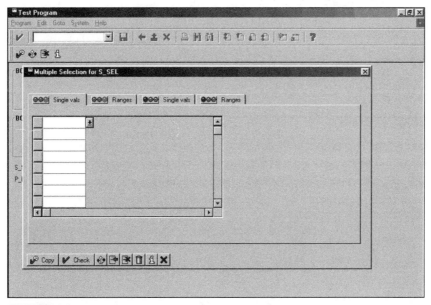

FIGURE 1-2

A list of single values displayed for one of the SELECT-OPTIONS *commands*

FIGURE 1-3

A selection screen with three parameters on the same line

 NOTE

For an overview of SELECT-OPTIONS, please refer to the book *Introduction to ABAP/4 Programming for SAP*, published by Prima Publishing.

There are two limitations and features of this command. Blocks can only be nested five levels deep, and the NO INTERVALS addition is inherited by the nested blocks only if the WITH FRAME option is used. Essentially, this means that the screen size diminishes fairly quickly with the "boxes within boxes" leading to no room for the TO fields generated by the SELECT-OPTIONS statements.

Grouping Items

Have you ever wanted to group parameters or text on the same line of a selection screen? You can do so with additions to the SELECTION-SCREEN command, namely the BEGIN OF LINE and END OF LINE additions. The syntax is as follows:

```
SELECTION-SCREEN BEGIN OF LINE.

<parameters / text>

SELECTION-SCREEN END OF LINE.
```

The effect of including the BEGIN OF LINE / END OF LINE options with the SELECTION-SCREEN command is seen in Figure 1-4, which is based upon the following code:

```
REPORT ZTESTABAP2.
```

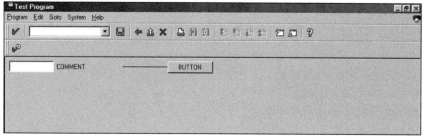

FIGURE 1-4

The selection screen is generated.

```
SELECTION-SCREEN BEGIN OF LINE.
PARAMETERS:    PARAM1(8),
               PARAM2(8),
               PARAM3(8).


SELECTION-SCREEN END OF LINE.
```

You can include parameters, push buttons, comments, or underline blocks as input fields between the BEGIN OF LINE and END OF LINE options. Select options are not allowed between BEGIN OF LINE and END OF LINE since the nature of the SELECT-OPTION is to create multiple objects on one line (high range and low range). The result of a SELECT-OPTION and something else on one line would be a very cramped, and possibly confusing, line. However, since ABAP does not allow for this combination, it does not happen.

The commands allowed between the BEGIN OF LINE and END OF LINE options are:

1. PARAMETERS

2. SELECTION-SCREEN COMMENT <format> <name>.

3. SELECTION-SCREEN ULINE.

4. SELECTION-SCREEN PUSHBUTTON <format> <name>
   USER-COMMAND <ucom>.

The first command should be very familiar to you. If not, then you should probably review a beginning text before continuing with this book. Commands 2 through 4 are explained in subsequent sections of this chapter. In any case, an example of this type of code and its results is displayed in this section. <format> has the form '/pos(len)', '/pos(len)', or '(len)' (pos denotes position, and len denotes length).

```
REPORT ZTESTABAP3.


SELECTION-SCREEN BEGIN OF LINE.


PARAMETERS: P_PARAM1(10).
SELECTION-SCREEN COMMENT (15) W_NAME.
SELECTION-SCREEN ULINE (10).
SELECTION-SCREEN PUSHBUTTON (10) W_BUTTON USER-COMMAND 'UCOM'.


SELECTION-SCREEN END OF LINE.


INITIALIZATION.
W_NAME = 'COMMENT'.
W_BUTTON = 'BUTTON'.
```

Positioning Items

The BEGIN OF LINE and END OF LINE command sequence has an option within its own command set. The syntax of this option is:

```
SELECTION-SCREEN POSITION <position>.
```

This option is used to position objects on the line defined by the BEGIN OF LINE and END OF LINE commands. For example, let's say you have five parameters you want to appear on a single report line. To do so, you place those parameters using values that would place them across the screen. This code example and Figure 1-5 display an example that may make it easier for you to make sense of this command.

```
REPORT ZTESTABAP2.


SELECTION-SCREEN BEGIN OF LINE.
PARAMETERS: PARAM1(8).
SELECTION-SCREEN POSITION 20.
PARAMETERS: PARAM2(8).
```

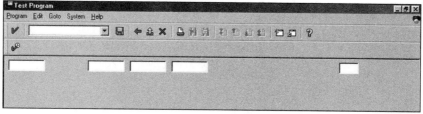

FIGURE 1–5

The result of the code example and the use of the POSITION addition

```
SELECTION-SCREEN POSITION 30.
PARAMETERS: PARAM3(8).
SELECTION-SCREEN POSITION 40.
PARAMETERS: PARAM4(8).
SELECTION-SCREEN POSITION 80.
PARAMETERS: PARAM5(8).


SELECTION-SCREEN END OF LINE.
```

Underlines

Underlines can be generated on selection screens just as they are in ABAP reports. However, there are a few differences in command syntax that will be explained in this section. The syntax for the underline command is:

```
SELECTION-SCREEN ULINE <format>.
```

First of all, consider just typing in:

```
REPORT ZTESTABAP5.


SELECTION-SCREEN BEGIN OF LINE.

PARAMETERS: P_PARAM1(10).
```

CAUTION

ULINE must be used in conjunction with another command, otherwise the selection screen will not generate.

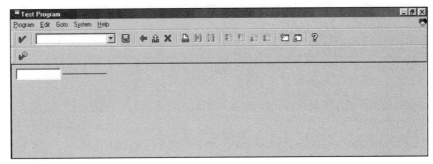

FIGURE 1-6

The effects of the ULINE addition

```
SELECTION-SCREEN ULINE (10).

SELECTION-SCREEN END OF LINE.
```

This code produces the result shown in Figure 1-6. By specifying the format after the ULINE command, you can control length, position, and new lines on the screen. <format> has the form '/pos(len)', '/pos(len)', or '(len)'. The syntax for the formatting is as follows:

```
REPORT ZTESTABAP6.


SELECTION-SCREEN BEGIN OF LINE.
PARAMETERS: P_PARAM1(10).
SELECTION-SCREEN ULINE 10(1).
PARAMETERS: P_PARAM2(10).
SELECTION-SCREEN ULINE 20(1).
PARAMETERS: P_PARAM3(10).


SELECTION-SCREEN END OF LINE.
```

The output of this example is displayed in Figure 1-7.

Comments

You can also generate comments on the selection screen. The command to do this is:

```
SELECTION-SCREEN COMMENT <format> <name>
                FOR FIELD <field>
```

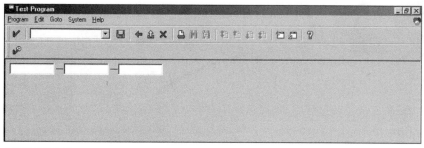

FIGURE 1-7

The formatting options coded by specifying the format after the unline *command*

```
MODIF ID <modification id>
VISIBLE LENGTH <length>.
```

You must always specify a format when using the COMMENT command. There are quite a few additions to this command, so they'll be discussed one by one. Start by analyzing this simple code and then you can add options:

```
REPORT ZTESTABAP3.


SELECTION-SCREEN BEGIN OF LINE.


SELECTION-SCREEN COMMENT (15) W_NAME.
PARAMETERS: P_PARAM1(10).
SELECTION-SCREEN END OF LINE.


INITIALIZATION.
W_NAME = 'COMMENT'.
```

This example generates the selection screen shown in Figure 1-8. Just as with the ULINE command, an input field must be declared or the selection-screen will not generate.

If the FOR FIELD parameter is included as shown in Example 1-9, notice that the comment is now officially tied to the parameter mentioned after FIELD:

```
REPORT ZTESTABAP3.

SELECTION-SCREEN BEGIN OF LINE.
```

FIGURE 1-8

The COMMENT command in its simplest form

FIGURE 1-9

The parameter with comment *tied directly to parameter field*

```
SELECTION-SCREEN COMMENT (15) W_NAME FOR FIELD P_PARAM1.
PARAMETERS: P_PARAM1(10).
SELECTION-SCREEN END OF LINE.

INITIALIZATION.
W_NAME = 'COMMENT'.
```

The output screen looks like Figure 1-9.

Push Buttons

Push buttons can be generated on the actual screen. Push buttons are described in more detail in Section 3 of the book. Push buttons are used to trigger user functions within the code to make the code dynamically interactive with the user. The syntax is:

```
SELECTION-SCREEN BEGIN OF LINE.
```

```
SELECTION-SCREEN PUSHBUTTON fmt name USER-COMMAND ucom.
```

```
SELECTION-SCREEN END OF LINE.
```

If you look back at the previous example and isolate the push button code you'll see this code:

```
REPORT ZTESTABAP3.


SELECTION-SCREEN BEGIN OF LINE.
SELECTION-SCREEN PUSHBUTTON (10) W_BUTTON USER-COMMAND 'UCOM'.
SELECTION-SCREEN END OF LINE.


INITIALIZATION.
W_BUTTON = 'BUTTON'.


AT SELECTION-SCREEN.
IF SSCRFIELDS-UCOMM = 'UCOM'.
WRITE:/ 'You pressed the BUTTON button'.
ENDIF.
```

Notice in this example that the PUSHBUTTON command can exist on its own since it also is an input field. When a button is clicked, the system field SSCRFIELDS-UCOMM is populated with the value listed after the USER-COMMAND notation. An IFÉENDIF statement at the AT SELECTION-SCREEN event allows the program to determine whether the button was clicked and to execute the appropriate code.

The screen that is generated from this code is shown in Figure 1-10.

Generating Blank Lines

Blank lines allow space in the selection screen that can make it easier to read. To skip blank lines on the selection screen, use the command SKIP in the same way you would in a regular ABAP report. The syntax for skipping blank lines is as follows:

```
SELECTION-SCREEN SKIP <number of blank lines>.
```

The number of blank lines can be from 1 to 9. If you want to insert only one blank line, you can omit the number. Here's an example that skips nine lines, the results of which are shown in Figure 1-11:

FIGURE 1-10

The push button feature of the SELECTION-SCREEN *command*

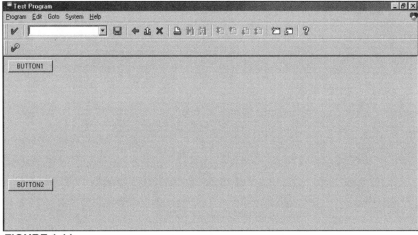

FIGURE 1-11

The effects of the SKIP command, generating blank lines on a selection–screen

```
REPORT ZTESTABAP3.


SELECTION-SCREEN BEGIN OF LINE.


SELECTION-SCREEN PUSHBUTTON (10) W_BUTTON USER-COMMAND 'UCOM'.


SELECTION-SCREEN END OF LINE.


SELECTION-SCREEN SKIP 9.


SELECTION-SCREEN BEGIN OF LINE.
```

```
SELECTION-SCREEN PUSHBUTTON (10) W_BUTTO2 USER-COMMAND 'UCOW'.


SELECTION-SCREEN END OF LINE.


INITIALIZATION.
W_BUTTON = 'BUTTON1'.
W_BUTTO2 = 'BUTTON2'.
```

Push Buttons on the Toolbar

Have you ever noticed that on some SAP reports there are push buttons on the application toolbar in addition to the Execute button? These push buttons are available for you as well, but you need to know how to activate them. At the time the selection screen is generated, you can create up to five push buttons at the application toolbar level. In order to do this, you must use another command that is utilized with the SELECTION-SCREEN command set. The syntax is:

```
SELECTION-SCREEN FUNCTION KEY <number>.
```

The parameter <number> can be a value from 1 to 5. Here's an example using the value 1:

```
REPORT ZTESTABAP3.


TABLES: SSCRFIELDS.


SELECTION-SCREEN FUNCTION KEY 1.


SELECTION-SCREEN BEGIN OF LINE.
SELECTION-SCREEN PUSHBUTTON (10) W_BUTTON USER-COMMAND 'UCOM'.


SELECTION-SCREEN END OF LINE.


SELECTION-SCREEN SKIP 9.


SELECTION-SCREEN BEGIN OF LINE.
SELECTION-SCREEN PUSHBUTTON (10) W_BUTTO2 USER-COMMAND 'UCOW'.
```

```
SELECTION-SCREEN END OF LINE.

INITIALIZATION.
MOVE 'Application Button' TO SSCRFIELDS-FUNCTXT_01.
W_BUTTON = 'BUTTON1'.
W_BUTTO2 = 'BUTTON2'.
```

Figure 1-12 shows the results of this code. When the program is run, the field SSCRFIELDS-FUNCTXT_01 is set for button 1 at the INITIALIZATION event. This value is then displayed on the button at run time. You would set field SSCRFIELDS-FUNCTXT_02 for button 2, and so on. Be sure to declare the table SSCRFIELDS in your program, otherwise your program will not generate.

Certain system variables are set when this command is used. The system field SSCRFIELDS-UCOMM is set to FC01 for FUNCTION KEY 1, FC02 for FUNCTION KEY 2, and so forth.

The system variable's value is set once the button is pressed. You can determine the value at the event AT SELECTION-SCREEN.

In this example, if button 1 is pressed, then the value FC01 is assigned to the SSCRFIELDS-UCOMM field. Then, at the event, the value of the system field is determined and the data analyzed in the fashion assigned by the button. This analysis is determined at the event AT SELECTION-SCREEN.

If you want to assign text to the push button you are creating (a very common action), then be sure to assign text to the field SSCRFIELDS-FUNCTXT_01 for FUNCTION KEY 1, to the field SSCRFIELDS-FUNCTXT_02 for FUNCTION KEY 2, and so forth. The time to assign the text is at the INITIALIZATION event.

Summary

This chapter has been your first step in learning how to create screens in SAP, and has aspired to sharpen your basic ABAP skills so that you have more options than ever before when creating reports.

You have reviewed how to create boxes—and boxes within boxes—with the BEGIN OF BLOCK / END OF BLOCK commands, as well as how to place multiple parameters on one line. You can control where those parameters lie on that line

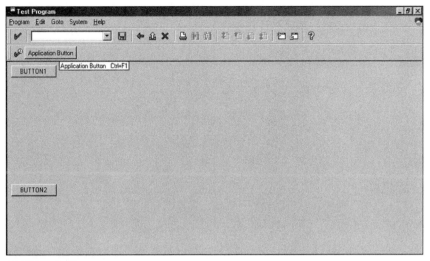

FIGURE 1-12

The presence of an application toolbar button

with the POSITION addition. You can insert underlines on the screen using the ULINE command, text using the COMMENT command, and blank lines using the SKIP command. You can create push buttons on the screen as well as on the application toolbar.

This chapter has demonstrated the limits to which you can push your ABAP report writing skills, at least via the selection screen. Later in this book, you will find that these options and many more are available when developing screens. As you continue, you will learn more about the most important and complex part of screen creation–the code that governs the logic behind it.

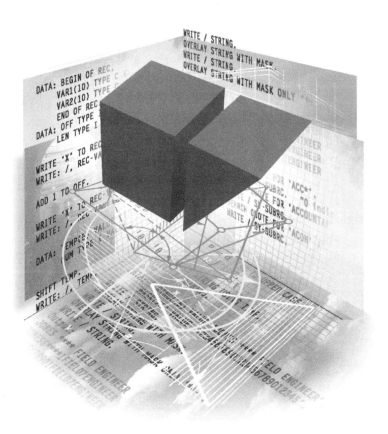

Chapter 2

Creating Function Modules

In This Chapter

◆ Creating the function module (defining characteristics)

◆ Coding the function module

◆ Memory issues

This chapter will cover the topic of function modules and their role in R/3, from creating a function module to designing the function module around the function group. Since utilizing function modules requires a great deal of system overhead, the topic of efficient memory management within the function module will also be discussed. Finally, the concept of remote function calls is introduced, but will be covered extensively in Chapter 3.

What Is a Function Module?

A function module is code that can be called from any ABAP program, therefore making it a globally accessible object. While similar to a subroutine, a function module differs in that the code is completely separate from the program calling it, and is invisible to the programmer using the functionality of the function module. A function module is generally defined with parameters and internal tables that are inbound and outbound. The function module receives data from a program, processes the information in its own code, and then sends back information in the output parameters or internal tables. In addition, the input parameters can have default values assigned to them, or can be made optional, whereas in a subroutine such options do not exist.

SAP comes with many pre-defined function modules that are very helpful in writing code. The functionality of these function modules ranges from defining a factory calendar date to communicating remotely with other SAP instances, especially in database updates.

While the comprehensive library SAP provides is very helpful and quite extensive, sometimes the need to create your own function module arises. In this case you need to use SAP's Function Builder, which allows you to create your own function module step by step. A description of how to create a function using the Function Builder will be described in the next section.

Function modules have exception handling capability that allows program feedback with regard to the happenings within the internal code. Certain errors can be accounted for, thus avoiding short dumps in the programs calling the function.

Function modules also use their own memory area. This avoids the overwriting of memory in a shared memory area (which happens quite often in poorly written code with subroutines). However, communication between the function module and the program must happen via the interface defined in the function module, or through the use of ABAP memory (import/export).

Creating the Interface

If you are quite familiar with function modules, you can skip this beginning section covering how to create a function module from start to finish. It might benefit you to read through this section, however, to make sure you have a thorough understanding of this task.

Function Builder Screens

First of all, to create your own function module you must navigate to the Function Builder. Type /nse37 in the command box in the SAP R/3 toolbar and press F8 (see Figures 2-1 and 2-2).

Once you follow the menu path or type in the transaction you will be navigated to the initial screen of the Function Builder (see Figure 2-3).

In addition to the input field for the function module name, a group of four option buttons appears on this screen: Interface, Source code, Global data, and Main program. To initially create the interface, select Interface, then click Create. Remember to type a name for your function module as Zyour function module name. A dialog box will appear asking you to which function group you want to assign

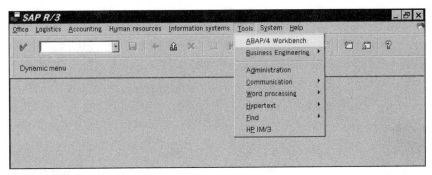

FIGURE 2-1

Menu path to Function Builder

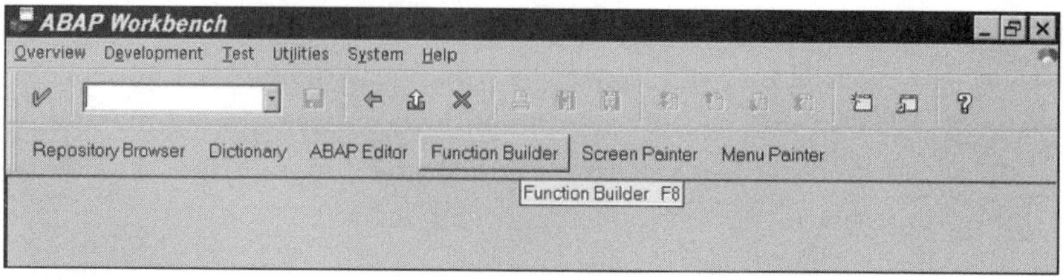

FIGURE 2-2

Menu path to Function Builder

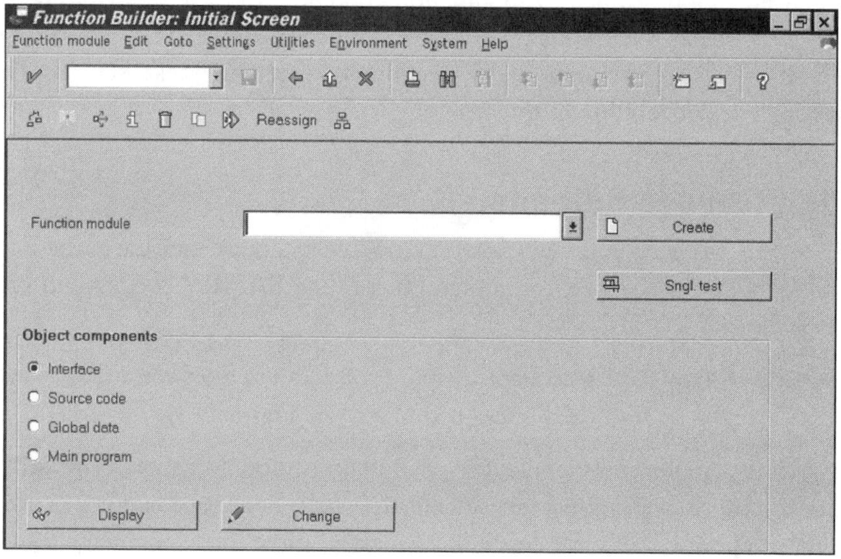

FIGURE 2-3

Initial Screen of the Function Builder

your function module. If you are unfamiliar with function groups, please skip ahead to the "Function Groups and Memory Scope" section of this chapter, and, after reviewing that material, return to this section. Type an existing function group name, or one you've just created, and then continue. The Function Module Create: screen for your initial function module appears, as shown in Figure 2-4.

Administration

In the Short text field, type a brief description for your function module. Next, if your function module is application-specific, type or select the appropriate code in the Application field. If the function module is not application-specific,

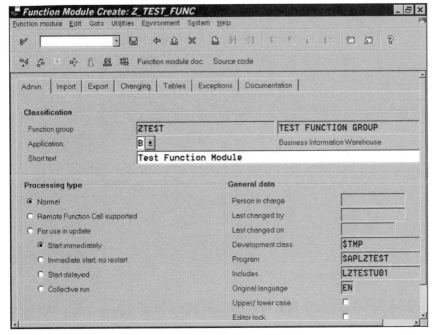

FIGURE 2-4

The Function Module Create: Z_TEST_FUNC screen

then leave the Application field blank. Table 2-1 contains a list of codes and associated applications.

Finally, select the processing type Normal (it's the default choice, so usually no effort is necessary). In the following chapter, you will learn how to create RFCs (remote function calls) that require you to select an alternate processing type. Click the save button. Your function module is now created.

Import/Export Parameters

From the Function Module Create screen, click the Import tab (see Figure 2-5). From the Import tab, you define the parameters that will be imported from ABAP into the function module. The import parameter can be any name of your choosing. You must specify either a variable and structure for the parameter in the Ref.field/Structure column, or a variable type in the Reference type column. In this example, use the variable NAME, similar to the system name, SY-UNAME. To choose a reference type, you can choose a type that exists in the global type pool of the

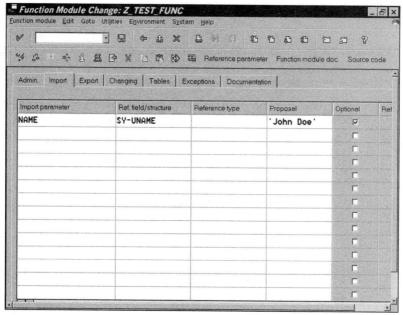

FIGURE 2-5

The Import page of the Function Module Change screen

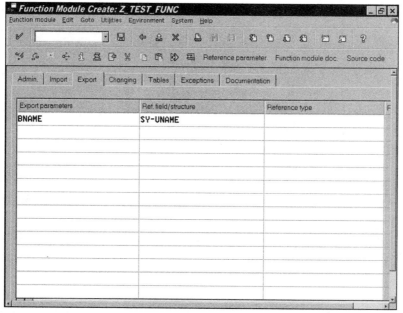

FIGURE 2-6

The Function Module Create: Z_TEST_FUNC Export page

Table 2-1

Application Codes for ABAP Programs and Function Modules

Code	Application
A	Asset Accounting
B	Business Information Warehouse
C	PPC
D	DASS (control station)
E	RIVA
F	Financial Accounting
G	General Ledger
H	Personnel Planning
I	Plant Maintenance
J	Publishing
K	Cost Accounting
L	Inventory Management
M	Materials Management
N	Hospital
P	Human Resources
Q	QSS (Quality Assurance)
S	Basis
U	Enterprise Model
V	Sales
W	MMS (Merchandise Mgmt. System)
Y	Customer Head Office
Z	Customer Branch
*	Cross Application

function group, or the internal ABAP types C, I, N, X, P, D, T, or F. Finally, you can specify a default value in the Proposal column. Specifying the variable as optional dictates whether the user has the choice to specify it. Finally, if you select the reference box, the function module then works with the original parameter and can alter it. When used with large tables, this option saves memory and increases speed.

Note that the figure does not capture all of the columns. In a true SAP screen the resolution of the screen will be such that all the data appears on the screen. Click the Export tab to see a screen very similar to the Import tab (see Figure 2-6). Completing the Export page is much like completing the Import page, with the

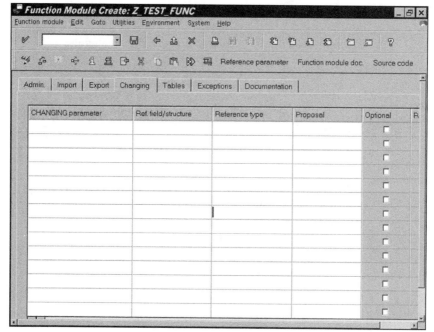

FIGURE 2-7

The Function Module Create: Z_TEST_FUNC Changing page

exception of the Optional checkbox. The Export page identifies information, based on the variables, to be returned to the ABAP program that called this function module.

Clicking the Changing tab opens another very similar page (see Figure 2-7). However, changing parameters contain fields, or field strings, that are passed to the function module and back to the calling program when leaving the function module. Changing parameters must always be assigned values when called.

Tables

The Tables tab is used to pass internal tables back and forth between the program and the function module. Unlike import and export parameters, tables are always passed by reference to some structure. You can flag tables as optional (see Figure 2-8).

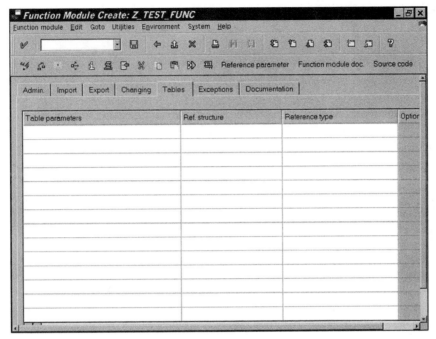

FIGURE 2-8

The Tables page on the Function Module Create: Z_TEST_FUNC screen

Exceptions

Click the Exceptions tab to write down exceptions that might occur (see Figure 2-9). If they occur, these exceptions will be raised by the ABAP source code. The system variable, SY-SUBRC, will then be set to a certain value if the exception occurs as defined by the function module. Two exceptions are defined here.

Documentation

Finally click the Documentation tab to open the Documentation page (see Figure 2-10) where you should add labels to the input/output parameters and any exceptions you have defined.

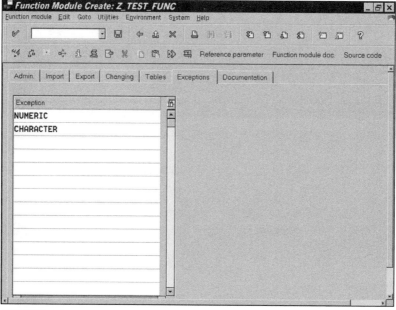

FIGURE 2-9

The Exceptions definition page on the Function Module Create: Z_TEST_FUNC screen

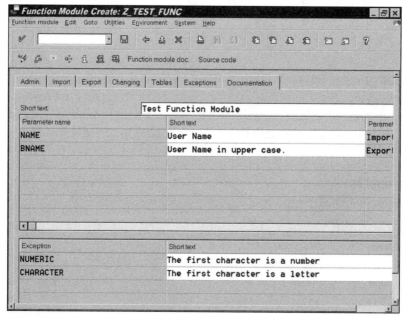

FIGURE 2-10

The Documentation page of the Function Module Create: Z_TEST_FUNC screen

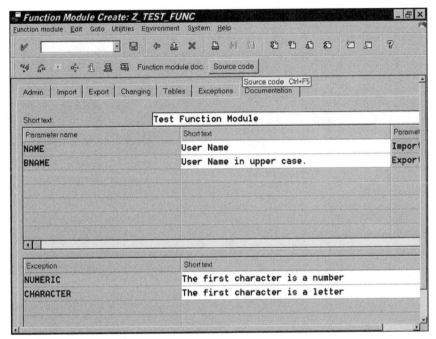

FIGURE 2-11

Source Code Navigation

Coding the Function

From the Documentation page, click save to preserve your work, and then click
Source code to navigate to the next screen (see Figure 2-11).

You are now at the ABAP editor where you can code the functionality of your
function module. In this function module, a user name from a program in the
variable name will be imported. Then the function module moves the value stored
in name into another variable called bname where the value is translated to
all uppercase. Then in a final pass, the function module code checks the
first character of bname to see if it is numeric or a character, and raises the
appropriate exception.

Here's the code:

```
FUNCTION Z_TEST_FUNC.
*"----------------------------------------------
*"*"Local interface:
*"          IMPORTING
```

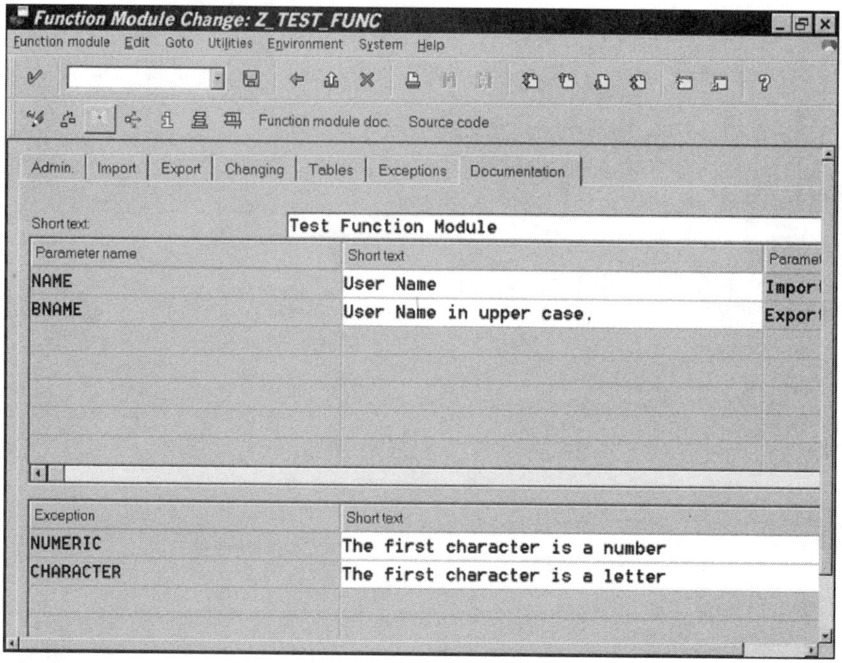

FIGURE 2-12

Activation button of function module

```
*"               VALUE(NAME) LIKE  SY-UNAME DEFAULT JOHNDOE
*"       EXPORTING
*"               VALUE(BNAME) LIKE  SY-UNAME
*"       EXCEPTIONS
*"               NUMERIC
*"               CHARACTER
*"-------------------------------------------------------


  MOVE NAME TO BNAME.
  TRANSLATE BNAME TO UPPER CASE.

  IF BNAME+0(1) CA '0123456789'.
    RAISE NUMERIC.
  ELSEIF BNAME+0(1) CA 'ABCDEFGHIJKLMNOPQRSTUVWXYZ'.
    RAISE CHARACTER.
  ENDIF.
```

Finally, save the code, press the green back arrow button to navigate back to the Documentation page, and then activate the function module by pressing the magic wand button (see Figure 2-12). With the successful activation of your function module, you can use it in a program.

Transferring Data From Main Programs

Create the ABAP program ZTEST with the following code:

```
REPORT ZTESTABAP .


PARAMETERS: P_USER LIKE SY-UNAME LOWER CASE.


DATA: W_UNAME LIKE SY-UNAME.


CALL FUNCTION 'Z_TEST_FUNC'
      EXPORTING
            NAME        = P_USER
      IMPORTING
            BNAME       = W_UNAME
      EXCEPTIONS
            NUMERIC   = 1
            CHARACTER = 2
            OTHERS    = 3.


CASE SY-SUBRC.
   WHEN 1.
     WRITE: / 'The user name is numeric.'.
   WHEN 2.
     WRITE: / 'The user name is character based.'.
   WHEN OTHERS.
     WRITE: / 'The user name is neither character based nor numeric.'.
ENDCASE.


WRITE:/ W_UNAME.
```

If the code is run and Robert is typed as the user name, the results shown in

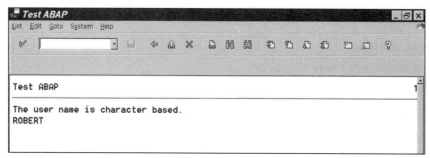

FIGURE 2-13

Results of ZTEST program using 'Robert' as the value for P_USER

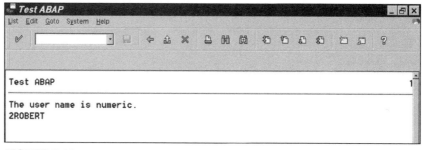

FIGURE 2-14

Results of ZTEST program using '2Robert' as the value for P_USER

Figure 2-13 are obtained. If the same code is run again with 2Robert as the user name, you'll see the results shown in Figure 2-14.

You can see the first effect of the function module is the desired one, which is to translate the user name into uppercase. Then determine whether the name is numeric or character based. That check is performed inside the program using an IF..ENDIF statement, and depending on the result, to RAISE the desired Exception. The syntax for the RAISE command is RAISE exception with exception being the exception you defined in the function module itself. Then, notice in the actual ABAP code that values are assigned to SY-SUBRC based upon which exception is raised. A simple CASE statement at the end of the ABAP program determines which exception was raised and processes the desired logic accordingly.

Function Modules Versus Programs

Function modules share attributes with both programs and subroutines. However, they are much different. Function modules run in their own memory space, as do programs; however, function modules cannot exist on their own, or run by themselves. Function modules must be called by a program.

Function Groups and Memory Scope

A function group is a container for function modules. When a function module is called, the entire function group is loaded into the session of the program. A function group is not an executable program, but rather all of the function modules of a particular area put together along with any includes and global data that they share. There are certain naming conventions and structures that are common to all function groups.

Function modules in the function group share memory space. For example, one function module can initialize data, another function module can update the data, and finally you can have a function module which reports the data. As long as each is called from the same program, the data will be kept in memory. Be sure to note that a DATA statement in the source code of a function group is local to that function module. A DATA statement in the global memory of a function group is shared by all the function modules that belong to that function group.

Generally, a function group is named SAPLfunction group where function group can be any name up to 22 characters long. If the function group is a customer-developed solution, then the letters Y or Z must precede that name. Inside the main program, SAPLfunction group, certain INCLUDE programs exist. Please refer to the example code shown below from the function group Surl, the SAP Internet function group:

```
************************************************************************
*    System-defined Include-files.                                   *
************************************************************************
     INCLUDE LSURLTOP.      " Global Data
     INCLUDE LSURLUXX.      " Function Modules


************************************************************************
*    User-defined Include-files (if necessary).                      *
```

```
********************************************************************
* INCLUDE LSWWWF        " Subprograms
* INCLUDE LSWWWO        " PBO-Modules
* INCLUDE LSWWWI        " PAI-Modules


INCLUDE LSURLF01.
INCLUDE LSURLF02.
INCLUDE LSURLF03.
INCLUDE LSURLF04.
INCLUDE LSURLF05.       "Selection-Screen
INCLUDE LSURLF06.       "Subroutines BOR
```

Lfunction groupTOP is the program containing the global data definitions shared between the function modules. In addition to the data definitions, the FUNCTION-POOL statement is included in this portion of the code. Here, inside the LSURLTOP program, lies the code:

```
FUNCTION-POOL SURL MESSAGE-ID SWWW.


TABLES: VARI, TFDIR, T100.
TABLES: WWWREPS, WWWFUNC.              " security check
* Constants for HTML
INCLUDE LSURLHTM.
* Flags Selection-screen.
INCLUDE RSDBCOM2.
INCLUDE RSDBCOM4.
* URLs in lists
INCLUDE <%_LIST>.
TYPE-POOLS: SLIST.                     "wg. Transport nach W3B  rk


* Typen fŸr HTML-Merger
TYPE-POOLS: SWWW.


* Varianten
TYPE-POOLS SYLDB.


DEFINE APPENDHTMLRESULT.
  &1-LINE = &2.
```

```
    &1-LEN  = &3.
    APPEND &1.
END-OF-DEFINITION.


TABLES: SREPOLIST, SERPLISTS, D020S, TRDIR, TSTC.
TABLES: SERPTREE, SERPT, SREPOVARI, SREPORTEXT.
TABLES: WWWDATA, WWWPARAMS, W3TREES.


DATA:       G_INTERACTIVE_REPORT LIKE SY-REPID,
            G_LISTINDEX         LIKE SY-LSIND,
            G_BROWSER_NAME      LIKE W3QUERY-VALUE,
            G_BROWSER_VERSION   LIKE W3QUERY-VALUE,
            G_PICK_ACTIVE,
            G_BACKGROUND_COLORS,
            G_DISABLE_BG_COLORS,
            G_HTML40_DISABLED.


* url und url_tail werden intern fÿr WebReporting benutzt
DATA: URL LIKE W3PARAM-URL_PREFIX.
DATA: URL_TAIL(150).


* globale Daten
DATA: URL_PREFIX_SINGLE LIKE W3PARAM-URL_PREFIX.
DATA: URL_PREFIX_MULTI  LIKE W3PARAM-URL_PREFIX.
DATA: URL_GATE LIKE W3PARAM-URL_PREFIX.
DATA: URL_EXIT LIKE W3PARAM-URL_PREFIX.
DATA: URL_PREFIX_IMAGES LIKE W3PARAM-URL_PREFIX.
DATA: TEMPLATE_SET TYPE SWWW_T_TEMPLATE_NAME.
DATA: TEMPLATE_NAME TYPE SWWW_T_TEMPLATE_NAME.


DATA:       TARGETNAME(30),
            SESSIONNAME(30),
            SERVICENAME(14).
 MORE GENERAL DATA STATEMENTS
DATA: BEGIN OF TABLE_GRP4 OCCURS 10,
```

```
        GRP4 LIKE F-GRP4,
            END OF TABLE_GRP4.
DATA: BEGIN OF TABLE_AUTH OCCURS 10,
        AUTH LIKE F-AUTH,
            END OF TABLE_AUTH.
```

Lfunction groupUXX is the container for the entire function module coding. Each function module is encapsulated in its own INCLUDE within Lfunction groupUXX in the format, Lfunction groupU01. The numbers increment as the function modules progress (01, 02, 03, etc.). In the real world, sometimes function modules are deleted or added, so the numbering might be out of sequence. Consider the following code, again taken from the SURL function group:

```
********************************************************************
*    THIS FILE IS GENERATED BY THE FUNCTION LIBRARY.          *
*    NEVER CHANGE IT MANUALLY, PLEASE!                        *
********************************************************************
INCLUDE LSURLU01.    "WWW_DISPATCH_REQUEST
INCLUDE LSURLU03.    "WWW_GET_REPORT
INCLUDE LSURLU04.    "WWW_GET_SELSCREEN
INCLUDE LSURLU06.    "WWW_HTML_ECHO
INCLUDE LSURLU07.    "WWW_HTML_FROM_LISTOBJECT
INCLUDE LSURLU09.    "WWW_GET_MIME_OBJECT
INCLUDE LSURLU10.    "WWW_SET_URL
INCLUDE LSURLU11.    "WWW_GET_URL
INCLUDE LSURLU12.    "WWW_HTML_MERGER
INCLUDE LSURLU13.    "WWW_GET_TREE_LIST
INCLUDE LSURLU14.    "WWW_GET_TREE_NODE
INCLUDE LSURLU20.    "WWW_MODEL_MODULE
INCLUDE LSURLU21.    "WWW_LIST_TO_HTML
INCLUDE LSURLU16.    "WWW_GET_NODE_LIST
INCLUDE LSURLU17.    "WWW_GET_HTML_OBJECT
INCLUDE LSURLU08.    "WWW_URL_PREFIX
INCLUDE LSURLU23.    "WWW_SET_RETURN_CODE
INCLUDE LSURLU24.    "WWW_GET_RETURN_CODE
INCLUDE LSURLU26.    "WWW_ITAB_TO_HTML
INCLUDE LSURLU27.    "WWW_ITAB_TO_HTML_LAYOUT
```

```
INCLUDE LSURLU28.    "WWW_ITAB_TO_HTML_HEADERS
INCLUDE LSURLU31.    "WWW_LOAD_TEMPLATE_ATTRIBUTES
INCLUDE LSURLU32.    "WWW_LOAD_OBJECT_ATTRIBUTES
INCLUDE LSURLU05.    "WWW_L_MERGE_LIST_WITH_TEMPLATE
INCLUDE LSURLU30.    "WWW_DRILL_DOWN
INCLUDE LSURLU34.    "WWW_LIST_BACK
INCLUDE LSURLU35.    "WWW_L_HTML_LIST_BUTTONS
INCLUDE LSURLU36.    "WWW_PROCESS_EVENT
INCLUDE LSURLU18.    "WWW_GET_SCRIPT
INCLUDE LSURLU19.    "WWW_PACK_TABLE
INCLUDE LSURLU02.    "WWW_SCREEN_TO_HTML
INCLUDE LSURLU15.    "WWW_ERROR_MESSAGE
```

Finally, in the SAPLfunction group group program exist programs called Lfunction groupF01, numbered consecutively (01, 02, 03, etc.), that contain the shared subroutine calls of the function modules within this particular function group. Refer to the code first introduced in this section and also refer to the piece of code from LSURLF01 below showing the contents of such a program:

```
*_____.
***INCLUDE LSWWWF01 .
*_____.
FORM RUN_REPORT TABLES P_SELTAB STRUCTURE RSPARAMS
                  P_HTML STRUCTURE W3HTML
             USING P_REPORTNAME
                   P_VARIANT_NAME
                   P_TEMPLATE_NAME
                   P_INTERACTIVE_DISABLED
                   P_LISTINDEX  LIKE SY-LSIND
                   P_ROW_COL    TYPE SWWW_T_ROW_COL
                   P_EVENT      LIKE RTRIG-NAME
                   P_UCOMM      LIKE SY-UCOMM.

   DATA:     L_RC LIKE SY-SUBRC,
             L_DRILL_DOWN.
   DATA:     L_LIST      TYPE SLIST_LIST_TAB,
             L_FMBS      TYPE SLIST_FMBS_TAB,
```

```abap
            L_FMBX          TYPE SLIST_FMBS_TAB,
            L_TAGS          TYPE SLIST_HYPERTAGS_TAB,
            L_RET_C LIKE W3PARAM-RET_CODE VALUE 1,
            L_VERSION TYPE I.


TEMPLATE_NAME = P_TEMPLATE_NAME.


IF G_BROWSER_VERSION(1) CO '1234567890'.
  L_VERSION = G_BROWSER_VERSION(1).
ENDIF.


CASE G_BROWSER_NAME(1).
  WHEN 'n' OR 'N'.                             "Netscape
    P_INTERACTIVE_DISABLED = 'x'.
    G_DISABLE_BG_COLORS = 'x'.
  WHEN 'm' OR 'M'.                             "MS IE4
    IF L_VERSION LT 4.
      P_INTERACTIVE_DISABLED = 'x'.
      G_HTML40_DISABLED      = 'x'.
    ELSE.
      P_INTERACTIVE_DISABLED = ' '.
      G_HTML40_DISABLED      = ' '.
    ENDIF.
    CLEAR G_DISABLE_BG_COLORS.


<GENERAL ABAP CODING FOR SUBROUTINES>


    ENDIF.
  ENDIF.
  IF G_SCREEN_CALLED IS INITIAL.


    PERFORM HTML_LIST_TEMPLATE TABLES P_HTML
                                      LISTOBJECT
                               USING  P_REPORTNAME
                                      P_TEMPLATE_NAME
                                      L_DRILL_DOWN.
```

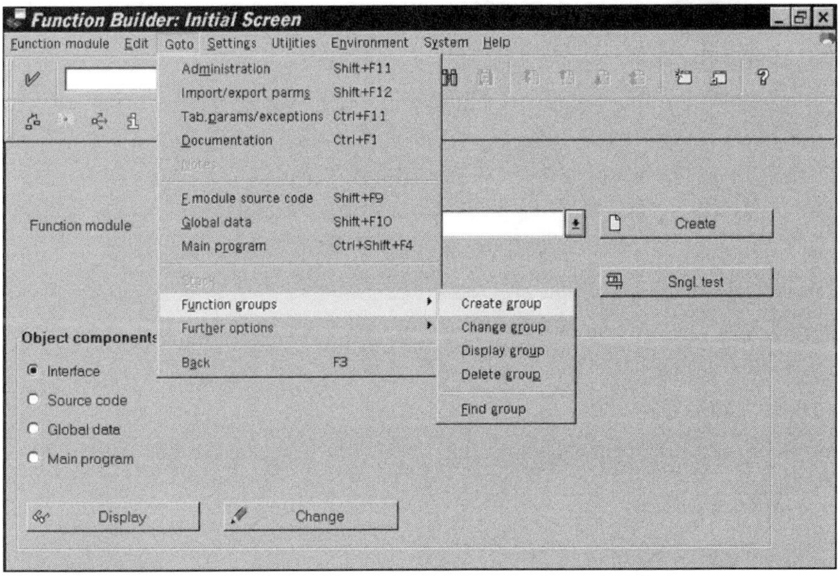

FIGURE 2-15

Menu path to create your own function group

```
   ENDIF.

ENDFORM.




*_____*
*                                         *
*      FORM HTML_SELSCREEN_TEMPLATE        *
*_____*
*                                         *
*      ........                           *
*_____*
*  ->  SOURCE                             *
*  ->  TARGET                             *
*  ->  REPORTTITLE                        *
*_____*
FORM HTML_SELSCREEN_TEMPLATE TABLES P_HTML
                  USING  P_REPORTNAME
                         P_TEMPLATE_NAME.
```

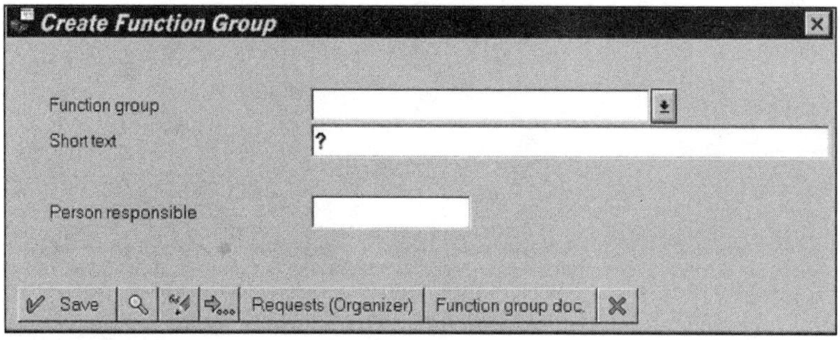

FIGURE 2-16

Create Function Group screen

To create a function group is a very simple task. Navigate to the Function Builder screen (transaction se37), then choose Goto | Function groups | Create group (see Figure 2-15).

A new screen will appear. From there, type the name of your function group (Zname or Yname) and a short description of the function group. Then click Save. Figure 2-16 shows the screen you will enter this information into.

Once you click Save, the system automatically creates the program SAPLyour new function group as well as its respective INCLUDE programs.

Organizing Your Programs

You should place all function modules that use the same data in a function group. The reason for this logic is that all of the function modules in that function group can access the global data of that group. Once you have all of your function modules in the same function group, you should organize your programs according to the guidelines presented earlier in "Function Groups and Memory Scope." All global data should be in the L<function group>TOP include. All subroutines should be in a Lfunction groupFNN INCLUDE program where NN is an incrementing number starting with 01.

Transport Issues

Transport can be a very tricky part of function module and function group development. Generally if you are developing the first function module of a function group, there are no issues to consider. Once you release the function group to the general populace of developers and they start to add to the function group or modify some function modules, some serious issues can arise when transporting these objects. Generally, these complications can also arise when changing existing function modules in existing function groups.

First, remember that in order for a function module to execute, the entire function module must be loaded into the session that is currently running. The entire function group must also be generated and free of syntax errors, otherwise the program will abort. Here begin the complications. Imagine you are developing new functionality for a function module. You check it for syntax, and it passes. Very excited, you transport the function group up into production where the new functionality can be utilized. However, your friend down the hall was halfway through developing a change on another function module in the same function group. They went home early the day you transported, and left their code halfway done and syntactically incorrect. Well, now you have a function group that will not generate, and whichever programs utilize that function group by using any individual function module from that group will not compile either. Steps must be taken to ensure that the entire function group compiles before transport out of development.

However, now you are wondering why you do not just transport the function module code itself. Well, in addition to the function module code, you must also transport the `Lfunction moduleTOP` program with all the data declarations, and any includes you have modified. While this sounds simple, in fact it is not. SAP does not handle transports of individual function modules very well. When you transport a function module, you must transport the entire function group, and in doing so, must be very careful to transport an object that can be generated. The BASIS team will be the people you will interact with if you have transport issues.

NOTE

"If you are planning to do an extensive transport that will impact a large number of function groups or function modules in the target system, it is advisable to create a transport and release and export the original objects in the target system before performing the import. By impact, I mean overwriting and replacing the original objects that should not have been overwritten.

It is not recommended to use unconditional modes on the tp import command unless you are sure you want to overwrite the objects on the target system. There is no real SAP utility available to actually reverse a transport once it has been imported into the system. Version management will allow you to retrieve a previous version if one exists—but if you have a lot of objects spread across multiple transports, this task can be very difficult, if not impossible. In extreme cases, a restore of the database from a backup may be necessary. You also may want to think about breaking up an extensive function module or function group transport into several smaller transports, so if some parts fail, you don't have to reverse the entire thing. If all parts of the transport are dependent upon each other, however, there may not be any way to break the transport up into smaller transports. To be safe, export the original objects in the target system first before transporting function groups or function modules."

Robert E. Parkinson

Prima Tech's _Basis Administration for SAP_

Summary

The effective use of function modules in SAP is a very important lesson to learn. For the most part, if you utilize pre-existing function modules created by SAP, you not only standardize functionality in your code, but you avoid rewriting functionality that could take you days, if not months, of development time.

In addition to utilizing function modules, the capability of developing your own is a great skill. Not only can you share functionality across development teams, but you also create code that can be utilized over and over again by numerous programs.

All in all, function modules are a very important part of the R/3 system. SAP AG utilizes function modules throughout their code, so a good understanding of function modules and their respective groups is essential to your growth as a good developer.

When developing function modules, follow these steps:

1. Check whether a function module already exists. If it does not, then move on to step 2.
2. Create a function group, if no appropriate group exists.
3. Create the function module (administration screen).
4. Define the function module interface by entering its parameters and exceptions.
5. Write the actual ABAP code for the function module, adding any relevant global data declarations to the TOP include.
6. Activate the function module.
7. Test the module.
8. Document the module and its parameters for your peers.
9. Transport the function module to production.

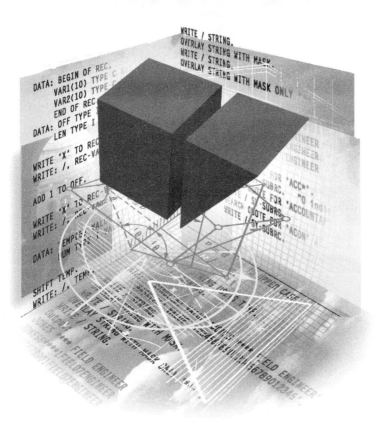

Chapter 3

Remote Function Calls and BAPIs

In This Chapter:

◆ Basics of Remote Function Calls

◆ Calling remote function modules in ABAP/4

◆ Writing remote function modules in ABAP/4

◆ Introduction to BAPIs

◆ RFC examples using BAPIs

◆ Destination setup and maintenance (Table RFCDES)

Basics of Remote Function Calls

A *Remote Function Call (RFC)* is simply a call to a function in one system (server) from another system (client). The communication can be between two SAP systems or between an SAP and a non-SAP system. RFCs in SAP are implemented through the DESTINATION parameter on the CALL FUNCTION statement and through configuration of a table named RFCDES.

There is always confusion when reading through SAP literature or talking with SAP consultants about the terms "client" and "server" with regards to RFCs. They are defined as follows:

◆ Client–The system which originates the RFC

◆ Server–The system that is being called by the client

This is not just a semantic argument because the code can be different depending on what side of the call you are on. This is especially true for RFCs to or from non-SAP systems.

Calling Remote Function Modules from ABAP/4

Calling a remote function module from ABAP/4 is accomplished using the DESTINATION parameter of the CALL FUNCTION ABAP statement. The general syntax is:

```
CALL FUNCTION 'REMOTE_FUNCTION'
            DESTINATION 'DESTINATION_NAME'
            EXPORTING          ...
            IMPORTING          ...
            TABLES             ...
            EXCEPTIONS         ...
```

All of the rules for calling normal function modules apply to calling a remote function. The destination name can be either a literal value (enclosed in single quotation marks) or a variable. The destination must be predefined in the RFCDES table, which is usually done by the system administrator of your SAP system. More information on the RFCDES table can be found later in this chapter in "Destination Setup and Maintenance (Table RFCDES)."

There is a special type of destination labeled `'BACK'`, as shown in the example below. This is used when you want the server to execute a function module on the client. When you use the `'BACK'` function, the same RFC connection is used as the original RFC call.

```
CALL FUNCTION 'REMOTE_FUNCTION'
           DESTINATION 'BACK'
           EXPORTING          ...
           IMPORTING          ...
           TABLES             ...
           EXCEPTIONS         ...
```

Using the `'BACK'` destination enables you to set up a continuous communication session between two systems that is not terminated until the original server function ends or the calling program on the client terminates.

Parameter Passing

When you set up a call to a remote function, parameters are not passed as they would be if you were making a normal function call. Most function modules set up their parameters to be passed by reference. This is more efficient because only the pointer to the variable needs to be moved around when the function module is called. With RFCs, parameters cannot be passed by reference because two different environments are involved; therefore the value of the parameter must be passed.

Tables are also dealt with differently. Because two different environments are involved, the entire content of the table is passed during the initial call to the remote function. This creates a local copy of the table on the server. The original table on the client is not updated until the RFC is finished.

Calling the Remote Function

Remote functions can be called just like normal function modules, and they will behave similarly to normal synchronous function module calls. This means that you make the RFC and wait for the RFC to finish. Your program will then continue to process.

In addition, remote functions can be called in two other ways. The first method is asynchronously using the following syntax:

```
CALL 'REMOTE_FUNCTION'
            STARTING NEW TASK     'TASKNAME'
            DESTINATION           'PLUTO'
            PERFORMING            'FORM_NAME' ON END OF TASK
            EXPORTING                 ...
            TABLES                    ...
```

This starts up an RFC on the server. After the RFC has started, your program will continue. For example, an RFC can start a task on the client displaying a new screen that connects the user to the server. To get values back from an asynchronous call, you must program your form like this:

```
FORM FORM_NAME USING TASKNAME.
            RECEIVE RESULTS FROM FUNCTION 'REMOTE_FUNCTION'
                        IMPORTING          ...
                        EXCEPTIONS         ...
ENDFORM.
```

The other way to call a remote function is with *update processing* (sometimes referred to as *transactional processing*). With this method, you make a call to the remote function that is not immediately performed. Instead, the parameters and function name are logged, and they are performed when a COMMIT WORK is encountered. The syntax for this type of RFC is as follows:

```
CALL FUNCTION 'REMOTE_FUNCTION' IN BACKGROUNDTASK
            DESTINATION 'PLUTO'
            EXPORTING ...
            TABLES   ...
```

Before using an update process RFC, make sure you fully understand how the COMMIT WORK process works and how all events are handled after a COMMIT is performed. Details for using COMMIT WORK are found in Chapter 20.

One important RFC feature is that a function module designed as a remote function can be called as a normal function module by an ABAP program on the same system. This can be very handy for writing programs, as discussed in "Introduction to BAPIs" later on in this chapter.

Exception Handling

There are two exceptions specific to RFC interfaces. These are related to system and communication errors that can occur with the RFC itself. The exceptions are:

SYSTEM_FAILURE –This exception is raised if there is a problem on the server system

COMMUNICATION_FAILURE –This exception is raised if there is a problem in communication between the client and the server hardware

If you want more details on specifically why an exception was raised, you can use the following syntax:

```
CALL FUNCTION 'REMOTE_FUNCTION'
          DESTINATION 'PLUTO'
          EXPORTING          ...
          IMPORTING          ...
          TABLES             ...
          EXCEPTIONS    SYSTEM_FAILURE = return code
                        MESSAGE WS_MESS1
                        COMMUNICATIONS_FAILURE = return code
                        MESSAGE WS_MESS2.
```

In the example above, the return codes are values that you define for the system return code SY-SUBRC. The variables WS_MESS1 and WS_MESS2 are character strings and will contain a textual description of the exception.

The only other difference with RFC exception handling occurs if an RFC executes in the background. As explained in more detail in Chapter 20, this type of RFC cannot return exception codes since the function module is not executed until after the calling program has performed a COMMIT WORK statement, and may already be finished.

Calling RFCs from Non-SAP Systems

If you write an ABAP program that calls a function module on a non-SAP system, you need to define the function module's attributes, parameters, and tables. After the function module is created and generated, be sure that the

RFCDES entries are set up for the system to be called. You may require a separate logical connection for each RFC, depending on the exact nature of the RFC and the system on which it is running.

Once completed, call the function module in the same manner as you would any other RFC.

TIP

If you are part of a team that is developing both the ABAP code and the external RFC, it's helpful to set up the function module fairly early in the project. After setting up the function, develop the RFC Stub (discussed later in this chapter). Having a tested code sample to work with will eliminate a great deal of confusion.

Writing Remote Function Modules in ABAP/4

Writing a function module that will be used as an RFC is not too much different than writing a normal function module. You must use common sense when coding these; for instance, you cannot return parameters in a function module that will be used asynchronously, nor can you raise exceptions in a function module that will be used as a transactional RFC.

Parameter Declaration

When creating a normal function module, you do not have to define what an input parameter's data structure is. If you leave the reference field blank, the parameter will take on the characteristics of the variable passed by the calling program. However, if called remotely, this information is not available to your RFC because it only receives the value of the parameter. Therefore, you must define the characteristics for every parameter for a function module that will be used as an RFC.

TIP

The lengths of the parameters do not have to match exactly those of the calling variable. If you declare a parameter as 100 characters long and the calling program passes a 30-character variable, the remaining 70 characters will be padded with spaces. You must make sure, however, that your parameters are at least as long as those that will be passed to them.

Setting the REMOTE Status and Configuration

To enable a function module to be called as an RFC, two things must be done in addition to the actual ABAP coding. The first is done in the attributes section of the function module configuration, as shown in Figure 3-1. In this screen, make sure you check that the module can be called using a REMOTE CALL.

Secondly, make sure that the system calling your function module is entered in the RFCDES table. The system administrator usually completes this step.

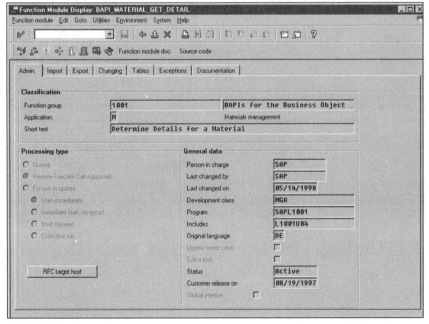

FIGURE 3-1

Attributes for a function module that can be used as an RFC

Generating RFC Stubs

If you write a function module to be used as a remote function from a system other than SAP, you should provide the RFC Stub. The RFC Stub is a skeleton program that defines how the function module should be called. Currently SAP provides the capabilities to generate a Stub using ANSI C or Microsoft Visual Basic.

To generate a Stub, set up the parameters for your function module and then define it as callable from a remote system. When complete, select Utilities | RFC Interface | Generate. The screen shown in Figure 3-2 will appear.

From this screen, you can define exactly what is to be generated. Remember that if you are writing code where SAP calls an external system, SAP will be the client and you will generate code for the server. If you are writing code where SAP is called by an external system, SAP is the server and you will generate code for the client.

When generating RFC Stubs, the clearing of the destination output files is not automatic unless you so specify in the setting screen shown in Figure 3-2. In this way, you can generate one set of files for many different function modules.

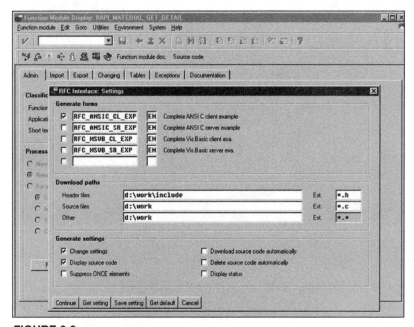

FIGURE 3-2

Screen used to generate RFC Stubs

Introduction to BAPIs

Business Application Programming Interfaces (BAPIs) are core building blocks of SAP's Business Object Repository (BOR). BAPIs were introduced to ABAP in R/3 version 3.*x* but they really have increased in number and functionality in the version 4.*x* SAP release.

SAP implemented BAPIs through RFCs. BAPIs are a perfect example of how powerful RFCs are. Understanding BAPIs will become more and more important to programmers as the integration of SAP with other systems becomes more common.

Definition of a BAPI

A BAPI is defined as a method of an SAP Business Object. BAPIs allow a common method of access to SAP's data and functions from both external and internal programs.

The calling program does not require knowledge of how SAP stores data or the intricate functionality of SAP; it only needs to know how to interface with the BAPI. This involves knowing the meaning and configuration of the parameters and tables being exported and imported from the BAPI.

SAP has based its current BAPI technology on RFCs. A few differences exist between a normal RFC function module and a BAPI RFC function module. They are as follows:

- BAPI RFCs are registered as methods in the BOR.
- BAPI RFCs cannot contain screens or dialog modules.
- BAPI RFCs cannot contain the ABAP statement COMMIT WORK.
- BAPI RFCs must follow a strict set of rules that govern the names of the BAPI itself, the names of the parameters, the parameter structures, and the BAPI documentation. This forces consistency among all BAPIs.

How BAPIs are Integrated In SAP

BAPIs are integrated in SAP through the BOR. This definition can be found in the transaction code BAPI. You will see a screen similar to Figure 3-3. From this transaction screen, drill down to the business area you want to see. Then double-click that specific object to reach a screen similar to that shown in Figure 3-4.

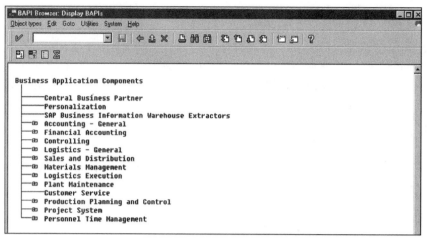

FIGURE 3-3

Start of the transaction BAPI

Expanding the tree structure for both the key fields and methods will lead you to the associated BAPIs and their associated parameters, as shown in Figure 3-5. In this example, the associated function module is named `BAPI_MATERIAL_GET_DETAIL`.

Resources for Additional Information About BAPIs

The world of BAPIs is changing very quickly. SAP, in addition to third-party vendors, is very quickly changing the BAPI landscape. One of the best ways to keep up with the latest information is to use the Internet and technical magazines. The following sections briefly describe two resources we've found to be informative.

SAP's BAPI Network Home Page

SAP America's Web site, http://www.sap.com/products/techno/bapis/bapi.htm, lists many documents related to BAPIs, including introductory and advanced material on writing and using them. You can also sign up for the OPEN BAPI network; this puts you on an e-mail mailing list that will keep you informed of things that are happening in the SAP BAPI world.

SAP Tech Journal

The SAP Tech Journal, located at http://www.saptechjournal.com/, is a quarterly magazine by SAP Labs and Miller Freeman, Inc. It contains a great deal of high-quality technical information.

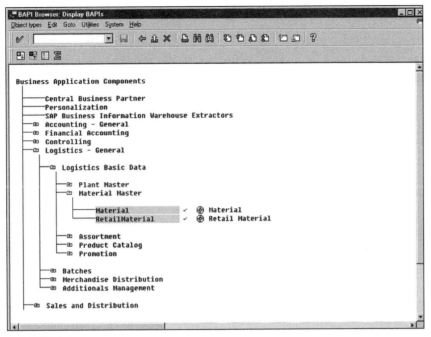

FIGURE 3-4

Attributes of a Business Object (in this case the material master)

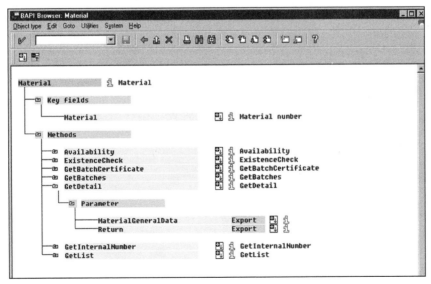

FIGURE 3-5

Detail key field and parameters for BAPIs

RFC Examples Using BAPIs

The following are examples of calls made to BAPI remote functions. One of the neat features about BAPI RFCs is that they do not need to be used as RFCs. If you want to perform a business function that has a built BAPI call, you can use that BAPI call directly in your ABAP code on the same system.

Get Data From Material Master

This example retrieves data for a specific material number:

```
DATA: WS_MATNR     LIKE BAPIMATDET-MATNR,
    STR_RETVAL     LIKE BAPIMATDOA,
    BAPI_RC        LIKE BAPIRETURN,
    WS_MESS(255).
WS_MATNR = 'TSTMAT'.
CALL FUNCTION 'BAPI_MATERIAL_GET_DETAIL'
DESTINATION    'PLUTO'
    EXPORTING
            MATERIAL                        = WS_MATNR
    IMPORTING
            MATERIAL_GENERAL_DATA          = STR_RETVAL
            RETURN                          = BAPI_RC
    EXCEPTIONS
    SYSTEM_FAILURE = 1
                                      MESSAGE WS_MESS
    COMMUNICATIONS_FAILURE = 2
                                      MESSAGE WS_MESS.
* Handle exceptions
IF SY-SUBRC EQ 1.
    WRITE: /001 'RFC System Error',
          /001 WS_MESS.
    EXIT.
ENDIF.
IF SY-SUBRC EQ 2.
    WRITE: /001 'RFC Communications Error',
          /001 WS_MESS.
    EXIT.
```

```
ENDIF.
* Write out material detail.
Write: /001 STR_RETVAL-MATNR,
        020 STR_RETVAL-SPART,
        025 STR_RETVAL-MAKTX.
```

Get List of Materials

```
DATA:
  INT_MATLST  LIKE BAPIMATLST OCCURS 50 WITH HEADER LINE,
  INT_MATSEL  LIKE BAPIMATRAM OCCURS 10 WITH HEADER LINE,
  INT_BAPI_RET LIKE BAPIRET2 OCCURS 10 WITH HEADER LINE,
  WS_MESS(255).


* Select materials that start with 'B'
INT_MATSEL-LOW = 'B*'.
INT_MATSEL-SIGN = 'I'.
INT_MATSEL-OPTION = 'CP'.
APPEND INT_MATSEL.
* Perform BAPI RFC and get first 20 materials
CALL FUNCTION 'BAPI_MATERIAL_GETLIST'
DESTINATION   'PLUTO'
   EXPORTING
           MAXROWS          = '20'
   TABLES
           MATNRSELECTION   = INT_MATSEL
           MATNRLIST        = INT_MATLST
           RETURN           = INT_BAPI_RET
   EXCEPTIONS
           SYSTEM_FAILURE = 1
                           MESSAGE WS_MESS
   COMMUNICATIONS_FAILURE = 2
                            MESSAGE WS_MESS.
* Handle exceptions
IF SY-SUBRC EQ 1.
   WRITE: /001 'RFC System Error',
          /001 WS_MESS.
```

```
  EXIT.
ENDIF.
IF SY-SUBRC EQ 2.
  WRITE: /001 'RFC Communications Error',
         /001 WS_MESS.
  EXIT.
ENDIF.
* Write out the returned materials
LOOP at INT_MATLST.
  WRITE: /001 INT_MATLST-MATNR,
         020 INT_MATLST-MAKTX.
ENDLOOP.
* Write out any returned messages
LOOP AT INT_BAPI_RET.
  WRITE: /001 INT_BAPI_RET-MESSAGE.
ENDLOOP.
```

Destination Setup and Maintenance (Table RFCDES)

In a typical SAP installation, the ABAP programmer is not concerned about how the configuration is done for RFCs. Either the people who take care of the SAP environment or the people who take care of customization in general typically handle configuration. There are times, however, when it is good to know more about the configuration, especially when trying to establish a connection to a new system.

Purpose of RFCDES

The SAP table RFCDES contains information of the remote destinations and is maintained through transaction SM59. When you make a call to a remote system, such as in the example that follows, the SAP system goes to the RFCDES table to determine the communication parameters, system parameters, and login information required to make the call to the remote system.

```
CALL FUNCTION 'RFC_GET_YTRACK_TOTREC' DESTINATION 'PLUTO'
              EXPORTING
```

```
                    TABLE = 'YTRACK'

            IMPORTING

                    NUMBER = WC_RECS.
```

TIP

Remember that for an RFC function to work for SAP to SAP calls, the correct entries need to be in the RFCDES table on both the client and the server.

A screen similar to Figure 3-6 appears when you make transaction SM59. This screen shows the possible types of destinations that can be configured. Depending on your system configuration, not all types may be shown; for instance the screen in Figure 3-6 does not have a type "2" connection that refers to an R2 destination. Table 3-1 lists the types of possible connections.

Table 3-1 RFCDES Destination Types

Type	Description
2	R/2 System
3	R/3 System
I	R/3 System connected to the same database as the current system
L	Logical Entries can refer to each other and are typically used to define login information. With type 'L' entries you can define logical names for other RFCDES entries and then add other data (such as user ID and password)
X	Systems where device drivers in ABAP have been installed
S	An R/2 connection with the destination as an SNA or APPC
T	Type T destinations are for external programs that use the RFC APIs to receive RFCs
M	Asynchronous RFC connections to other R/3 system via CMC

Details of the RFCDES Entries

When you drill down through the menu shown in Figure 3-6 or create a new destination, you come to a screen similar to that shown in Figure 3-7. The fields that you are shown vary depending on the RFC type. The example shown here is for an R/3 connection.

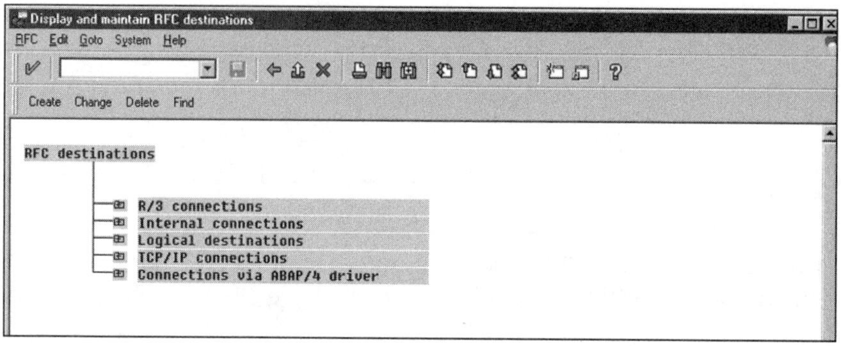

FIGURE 3-6

RFC overview from transaction SM59

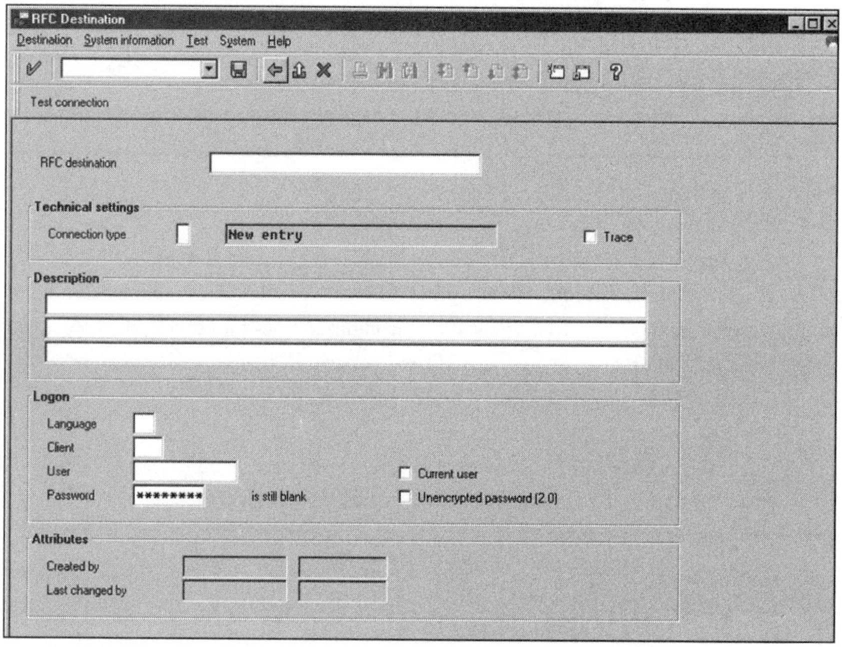

FIGURE 3-7

Detail view of an RFC destination screen

Summary

Remote Function Calls are becoming more and more popular in SAP. Fundamentally, there is very little difference between writing and calling an RFC, and calling a regular function module. It is important to understand how RFCs work–especially transactional RFCs. Before attempting to use transactional RFCs, be sure to read Chapter 20.

SAP's BOR and its connection with BAPIs provides a standard method for accessing both SAP data and functionality. BAPIs are based on RFCs. The transaction BAPI can be used to determine the currently available BAPIs and their calling parameters.

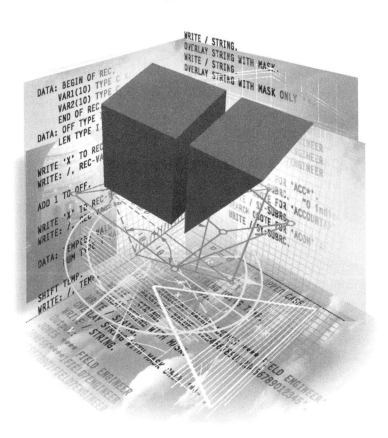

Chapter 4

SAP Transaction Processing

In This Chapter

- Transactions vs. Reports
- Logical Units of Work (LUWs)
- Database Locking Techniques
- Jobs/Background Processes
- BDC Sessions vs. Transactions

This chapter provides an overview of transaction processing, how tables are locked in SAP, as well as an introduction to job monitoring and BDC sessions. All of these general understandings are very important, as they represent the bulk of the background workings of SAP. This book teaches you to design screens and update tables through transactions in later chapters. For a comprehensive attack on these types of issues, one must understand how SAP works in the background with the database on such transactions.

The SAP Transaction Model

SAP transactions consist of nothing more than a quick command to execute a certain set of code called a screen. A screen then can lead to other screens, and finally to a command which updates the database.

If you read PRIMA TECH's *Introduction to ABAP/4 Programming for SAP*, you are quite familiar with the type 1 program, or report. Then the question arises, "What is the difference between a report and a transaction?"

Reports vs. Transactions

A transaction is a code entered in the command box of any SAP screen. See Figure 4-1 for a graphic of where to enter a transaction code. A transaction code can also be called by a system command, executed by pressing a button or selecting a menu option.

A transaction usually refers to a series of screens, which end in a database update. The truth is that the transaction is a code that calls these screens. The transaction code can also call a report. So, the loose definition of a transaction is any set of screens that are executed after the transaction code is executed.

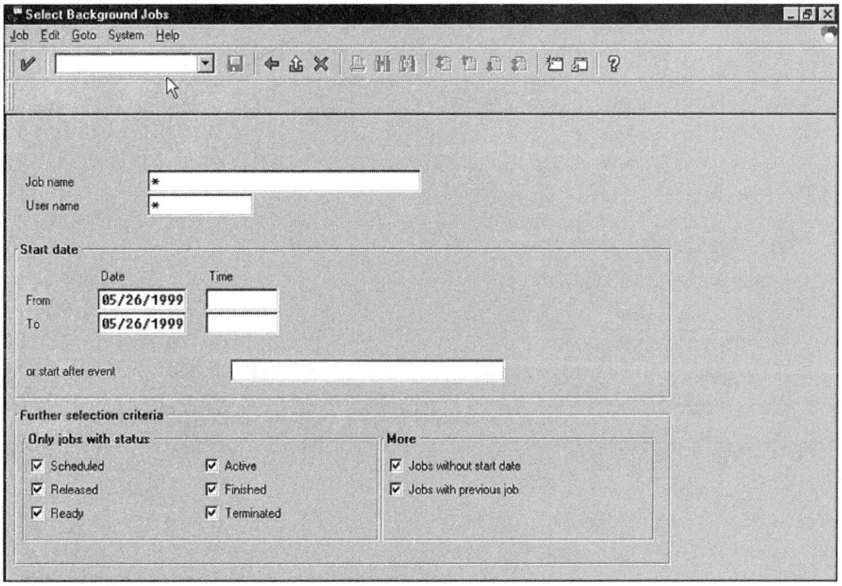

FIGURE 4-1

Sample SAP Screen with an arrow pointing at the command box

A report is an executable program that can be started without a transaction code, either directly or in background mode. These programs are controlled by an invisible system program. This invisible system program calls processing blocks in the program in a specified order. The selection screen is displayed first, and the output list is displayed in the end. The final criteria are that these programs allow you to use logical databases. Programs of this nature are referred to as Type 1 programs (executable programs).

Type M programs, or module pools, contain code that defines screen painter screens. These screens are defined by two sections: a PAI (process after input) and PBO (process before output). In each section modules are called to execute certain pieces of code to display data or process data before it is displayed in the current or a later screen. The module pools contain processing steps for a screen. They can only be executed by a transaction code. For these screens defined within the type M programs, you must design the output screen, the PAI/PBO (or flow logic) code, and finally the fields (usually declarations are stored in yet another INCLUDE program). In addition to defining the screen, you must also define a GUI-STATUS, which defines how the menu bar behaves. Essentially the GUI-STATUS turns buttons on/off, creates new buttons, and controls all the menus and submenus. Each screen must call an independent GUI-STATUS.

In summary, a report is an independent program that can be run on its own. A transaction is a group of screens and/or reports which are grouped together to execute sequentially after the transaction code is called.

Security Issues

An advantage for transactions is that you can assign authorization objects directly to the transaction, along with the values needed to execute the transaction.

Look at the transaction code C103, the transaction code to display classes in SAP. First, navigate to the screen where the transaction code is defined via the transaction code SE93. You can also follow the menu path, shown in Figure 4-2. Navigate to the ABAP workbench (from the initial logon screen, follow the menu path Tools | ABAP Workbench). Then follow the menu path Development | Other Tools | Transactions.

At the new screen (see Figure 4-3), enter the transaction code C103, and click display (the button with the pair of eyeglasses on it) (see Figure 4-4).

You can define the transaction if you were in create mode or edit mode. To be in either of these modes, click the create button or edit button on the previous screen.

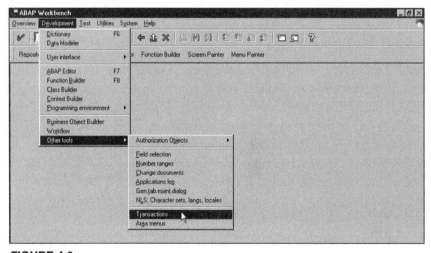

FIGURE 4-2

Menu path to the transaction definition screens

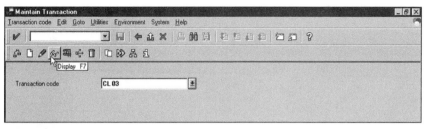

FIGURE 4-3

Initial screen of the transaction definition

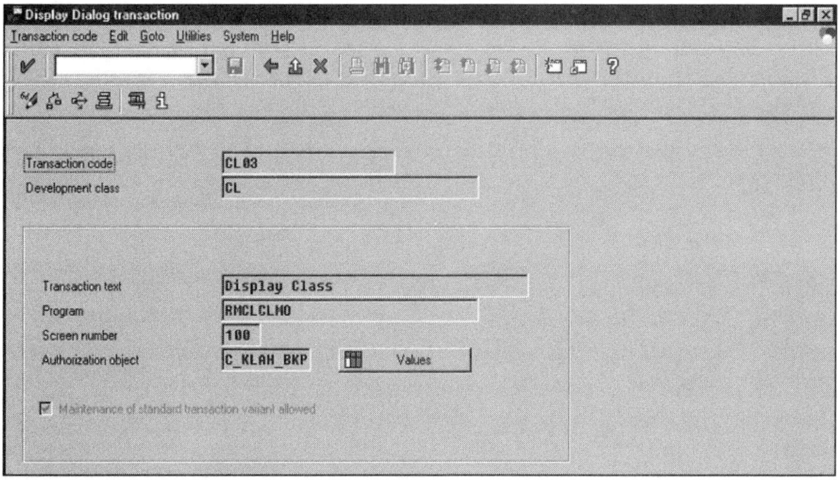

FIGURE 4-4

Definition screen of the transaction definition

When you create a transaction, you enter the transaction code initially, click create, and navigate to this screen. At this point, you would enter a description of the transaction, the main program which has the screen defined in it, and the initial screen of the transaction. This definition will be discussed in detail in Part 3, "SAP Transaction Development." The last box is the one that concerns us. Here, at the authorization object box, you can enter a pre-defined authorization object, and define values that are acceptable for the authorization check.

For example, with this transaction, you see that the fields ACTVT must be valid for a value of 3, and the BGRKP field is not assigned. Before any code is called, the user's profile is compared against this object and checked to see if he is able to call this transaction. You can also check for this authorization object in a report; however, you will need to use the AUTHORITY-CHECK command. This command is explained in depth in PRIMA TECH's *Introduction to ABAP/4 Programming for SAP*. However, if a programmer can have the code run, he could potentially debug his way around the authority check. To debug past an authority check in the transaction is next to impossible, as no code (none the user can debug) is called to check the authority of that user.

Transaction Naming Conventions

There are certain naming conventions that SAP uses in its transactions. To maintain consistency, it becomes necessary to adhere to these standards when creating your own custom transactions.

Just as with your own customer-based ABAP solutions, you should always start your transactions with the letter Z. Secondly, the transactions can be up to 20 characters total in length. The transactions are stored in the table TSTC, in the field TCODE.

Finally, there are numbering conventions to attach to the transactions. 01 denotes a transaction that creates (i.e. va01, create sales order, cu01, create dependency rule, cv01, create document, etc.). 02 denotes a transaction that changes or modifies (i.e. va02, change sales order, cu02, change dependency rule, cv02, change document, etc.). 03 denotes a transaction that displays (va03, display sales order, cu03, display dependency rule, cv03, display document).

Beyond those naming conventions, you are free to choose the names for your transactions; however, be sure to pick transaction names that your users will have no trouble remembering. It is necessary to "protect" the data being inspected and modified from other parallel transactions attempting to manipulate it.

Database Locking Techniques

Imagine that you have 10 widgets in your warehouse. Two phone calls come in to place orders for widgets to separate salesmen. One customer wants seven and the other wants eight. To prevent your company from promising immediate delivery to both customers, the database takes the order from the salesman who enters it first, reserves those eight for shipment, and thereafter considers two to be left in the warehouse. Then, the slower salesman can promise two for immediate delivery to the customer and give an estimated ship date for the remaining widgets based on production schedules or incoming shipments.

Database locking prevents one or more records from being simultaneously updated by more than one user. It prevents overlapping updates in a large-scale operation (which includes most companies that use R/3).

The database automatically sets database locks when it receives INSERT, UPDATE, MODIFY, or DELETE statements from a program, screen, or function module. These locks place flags next to the entries that are being changed, and prevent other users or programs from modifying these entries. An entry can only be locked once it is in the database, not if it is waiting in the queue to be added later. These flags are automatically deleted during each database commit (when the database is actually updated). This means that database locks can never be set for longer than a single database logical unit of work (LUW); in other words, a single dialog step in an R/3 application program.

A database LUW is a sequence of database operations that ends with a database commit. The database LUW is either fully executed by the database system or not executed at all. Just as nerve cells build up energy and fire only in an all or none response once a specific threshold is reached, database LUWs complete a number of database operations all at once, or not at all. If the update to the database is successful, then the database is sound and ready for more updates. If the LUW brings about an error, then all of the updates to the database are reversed immediately and an error code is returned to the calling program. By doing this quick reversal, the database is left unchanged, without any blemish or error.

While the LUW is occurring, the database can be changed. Updates within the LUW are not fully updated to the database until a compete database commit has occurred. Up to this point, all updates in the LUW can be reversed using a database rollback. Sometimes the database, sensing errors, will roll back on its own, but specific commands also can be issued to the database to reach this state. Speak to people in your Basis team in regards to that issue. Also, refer to PRIMA TECH's *Basis Administration for SAP*.

In Figure 4-5, a graphic depicts the bundling of Database locks into an entire LUW, right until the save command.

 NOTE

It is very rare that you have reason to explicitly force the database to roll back.

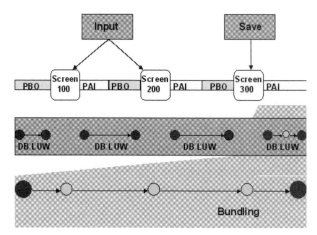

FIGURE 4-5

SAP graphic depicting how a LUW bundles DB locks

Directly from ABAP, you can cause a rollback by using the command ROLLBACK WORK. Indirectly, a rollback occurs when there is a runtime error or a fatal error (divide by zero error, etc.), or a termination message of type A or X is generated by the ABAP MESSAGE command.

Database commits can be performed indirectly or directly. Directly, you can commit the database in ABAP through the command COMMIT WORK, which explicitly commits the database. Another way to directly commit the database is by using the function module DB_COMMIT. Both methods finish a LUW and commit the data to the database.

Indirectly, a commit can occur when any of the following actions have occurred in SAP:

◆ A dialog step completes

◆ Control changes from the work process on the application server back to the SAP GUI

◆ A function module is called in another work process

◆ Control passes to another work process (another transaction is called within a transaction)

The locks performed on the tables are only available for the update task at hand, specifically when you wish to update the database. Let's say that you access a sales order and are navigating through the screens to change different items, or are just looking in change mode. A physical lock on the database is not present at this time, and theoretically another user can come along and modify those pieces of data in the tables you are navigating through. So, the physical locking is insufficient for your purposes in SAP, and another locking mechanism must be used which can lock the specific records for many dialog steps until you have left the transaction. The locks must be represented on all application servers.

To satisfy this additional need, SAP introduces lock objects. Lock objects allow you to set a "lock" (often called an SAP lock) which lasts several dialog steps. I use the word "lock" loosely because the data is not necessarily locked at the database level. Rather, a tracking system in SAP has locked those records. Any program not checking the tracking system can update those records directly.

Programs can check the tracking system by checking the lock object through function modules ENQUEUE and DEQUEUE which lock and unlock the records in the tracking system.

Enqueue/Dequeue and Lock Objects

The SAP lock utilizes data dictionary objects called lock objects, discussed in depth in Chapter 10. Lock objects create a relationship between tables using foreign key relationships, which lock an entire table or set of transactional data, rather than just records at the database level. So, when modifying an entire sales order, all the entries in the sales order tables—VBAK, VBAP, and VBEP—for that particular order are locked, but so are the other corresponding table entries in other tables which relate to that order.

Jobs/Background Processes on SAP

While online transactions occur during an R/3 system, other applications, or jobs, are running behind the scenes. These jobs are a series of programs, which can be run in background mode, including ABAP reports or queries, and even transactions, if executed through a BDC session (see the next section). On any R/3 system, follow the SM51 transaction to see a list of the application servers along with the database server. Double-click on a server to see a list of sessions idle or running on that server. The server will be configured to handle a combination of dialog (DIA) and batch (BTC) sessions. Only a certain number are configured for batch sessions and others for dialog processes. If an additional process is needed to run a program in a certain mode, and none are available, then the program is put in queue until one becomes available.

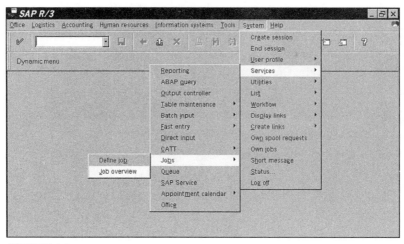

FIGURE 4-6

Menu path to the Jobs Overview Screen

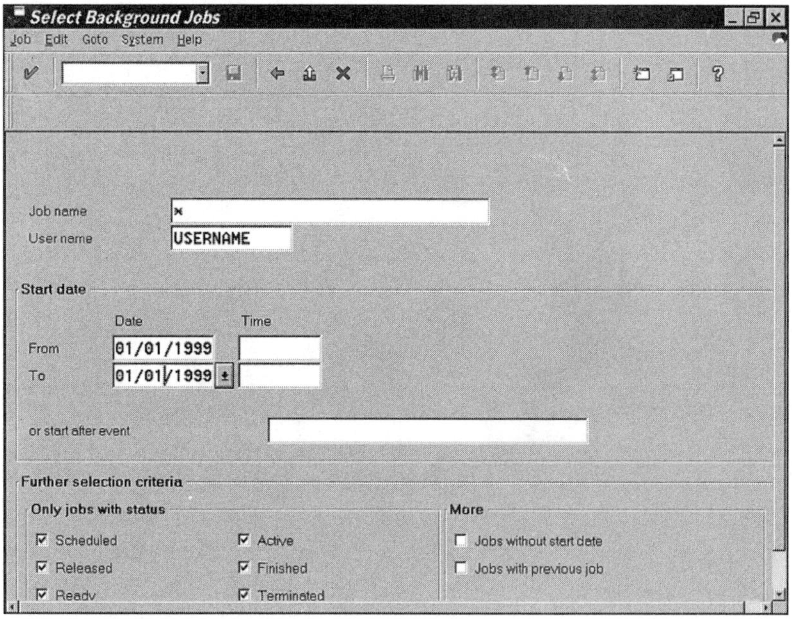

FIGURE 4-7

Initial jobs overview screen

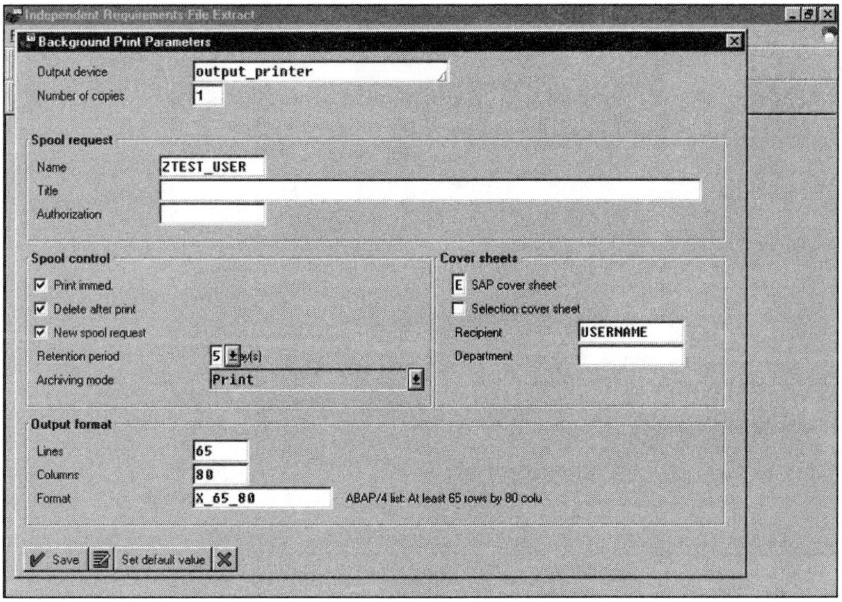

FIGURE 4-8

Printing Options for a Background Job

To check the status of a job, as well as to monitor your jobs, you can follow transaction SM37 to the job monitor screen. Here you can view, schedule, and manipulate jobs. Alternatively, you can follow the menu path System | Services | Jobs | Jobs Overview, as shown in Figure 4-6.

Figure 4-7 shows the initial screen of the jobs overview transaction. From this screen, enter the attributes of the job you are searching for, and press Enter. The next screen shows you a list of jobs that meet your criteria, along with buttons to analyze those jobs.

To execute a report in background mode, simply execute the program as you would from the ABAP editor, in SE38. Also remember that you can use the alternate transaction, SA38, to execute the transaction. This transaction will execute reports as well, but it has much less overhead than SE38. However, in either screen, at the initial selection screen, choose Program | Execute In Background. The program will then be executed as a job, rather than as an online dialog process.

When executing a program in background, you will be prompted for printing options before you release it to background (see Figure 4-8).

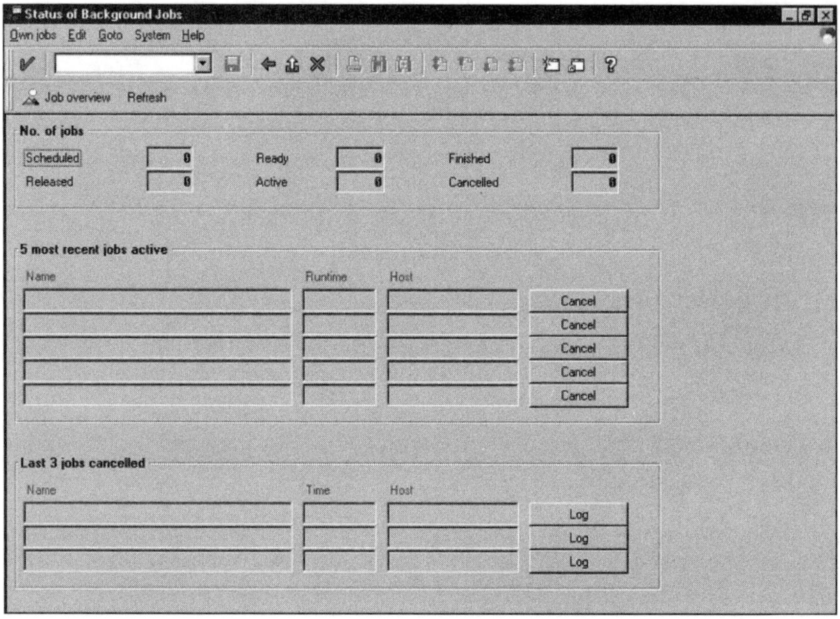

FIGURE 4-9

SMX Status of Background Jobs Screen

Specify the printer to which you want any output printed. Enter a title of that output. For spool control, determine whether the printer must immediately print the output, or if it can wait in queue and print when another spool job is kicked off to that printer. Check the "delete after print" box if you do not wish to have a copy of the output saved in the spool control log. Finally, check the "create new spool" box if you wish to have a spool file that is independent of other spool files (I recommend this because you would rather have a separate file than a set of spool files all appended together). Determine how long you wish the spool file to be saved (Retention Period). Then specify the print format (column vs. rows) and click Save to launch the job in background mode. All background jobs executed in such a fashion are of job class C. Job class C is the lowest priority in background processing.

To see your background process running (or the status of it), execute the transaction SMX (see Figure 4-9). SMX displays your background processes. Click on the refresh button to obtain the current status of those jobs. Click on Job Overview to get a more specific view of jobs or jobs running under another user ID than your own.

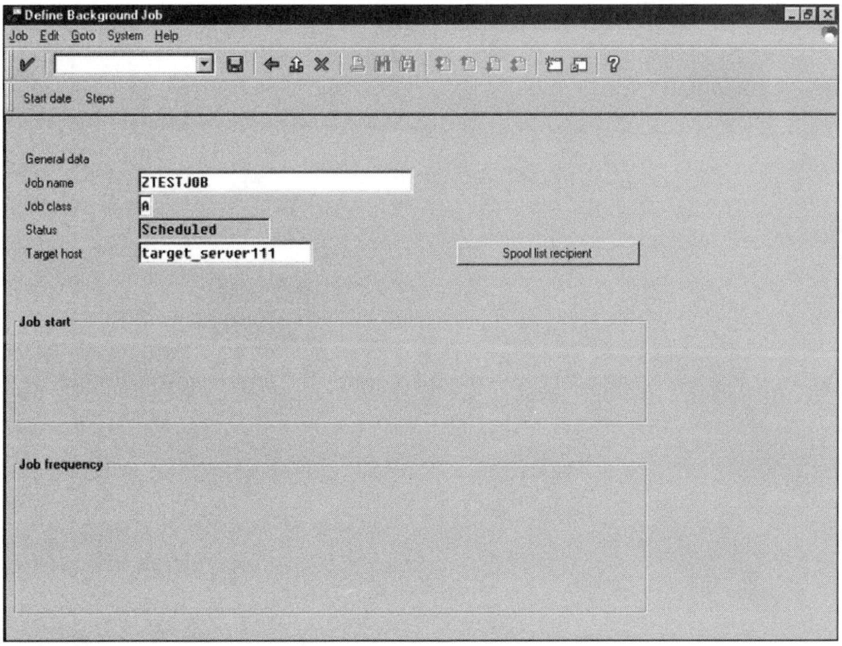

FIGURE 4-10

Initial screen for job creation

Another way to run a job is to create an actual job to be scheduled using transaction SM36 (see Figure 4-10). From here, specify your job name, job class (see Table 4-1), and the schedule you wish to run it on. Also, most importantly, you would include the programs you wish to run (a job can be scheduled to run several programs one after each other).

Table 4-1

Job Classes Used When Scheduling Jobs

Job Class	Description
A	Immediate; will supercede all jobs with class B or C
B	Medium priority; can only be bypassed by a class A job
C	Lowest priority; class A and B jobs both take precedence over class C jobs. Any background processes kicked off from SA38 or SE38 are considered to be class C by default.

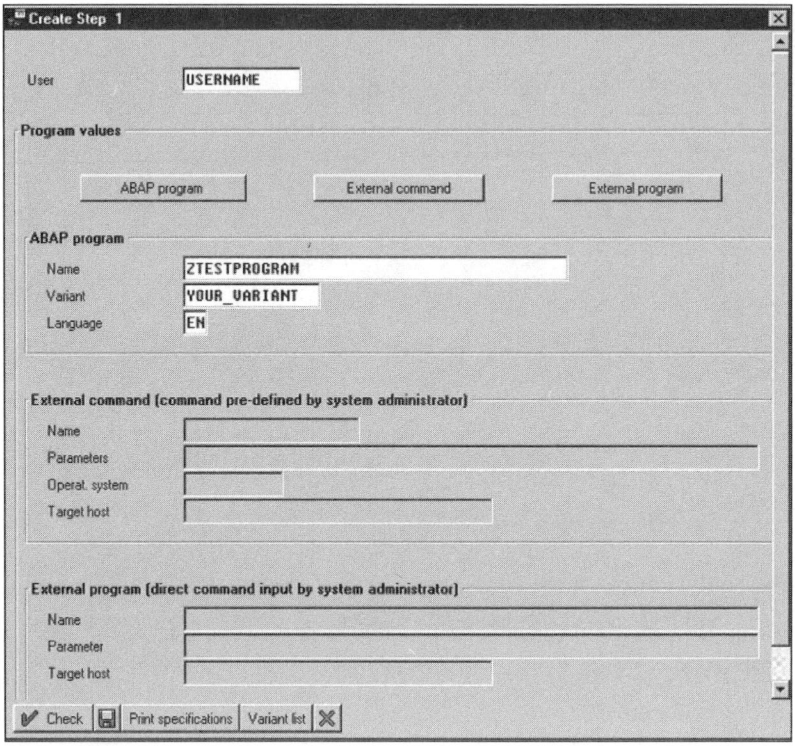

FIGURE 4-11

Defining steps for your job

The target host determines which application server the job will run on. This is important because many performance-tuned systems have one application server dedicated to background processes. Rather than let your background job run on any application server, you would want to specify the server, which has been configured for exactly that.

By clicking the Steps button, you can create individual steps in the job. A job consists of many programs (internal SAP programs as well as external programs) (see Figure 4-11).

Here, you must specify the name, variant you wish to use, and language of your ABAP program, or the other parameters for external programs if you choose those options (generally, these are not chosen). You can create multiple steps.

Once you have defined all your steps, it is time to specify the start date (and periodic nature) of your job. Click start date and navigate to the screen shown in Figure 4-12.

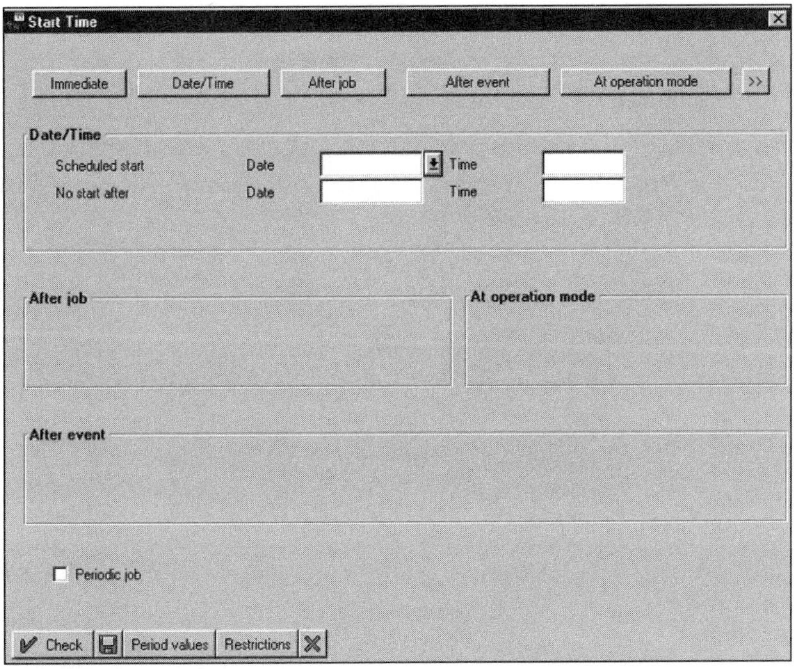

FIGURE 4-12

Defining the timing of your job

Here, you can specify your job as immediate if you want the job to execute right away, or date and time to determine when the job will run, or after another job, or after an event. Finally, you can have the job run at operation mode. Date and time is easy to understand. You specify the exact date and time you wish the job to run. After another job means that once another job finishes, this job will start. After an event means that if an event is triggered on the system, this job will start. An event is a signal stating that a predefined status in the system has been reached. The background processing system receives events and then starts the background jobs that are linked to an event. Events are defined in the system and triggered by programs or manually by users. Operation mode is, for example, normal operation mode (in the day or at night).

For the date, event, and operation mode, you can specify the periodic job check box. If you check this box, once the job finishes, it will reschedule itself in the future to start either on a certain date/time, after an event, or at a certain operation mode. This is convenient, especially if you are on the support team because you will not want to spend your days scheduling these jobs over and over again. One important note is that to delete a periodic job, you must search for jobs without start date in the job overview screen to bring up these jobs that have not run. Then delete the job that is in a released or scheduled status.

If you want to really have some clever ABAPs, you can actually define and submit jobs in your ABAP code. The function modules, JOB_OPEN, JOB_SUBMIT, and JOB_CLOSE, make this possible. Let's look at the calls to these functions in ABAP, and you can see from previous definitions how to do this.

```
CALL FUNCTION 'JOB_OPEN'
      EXPORTING
*             DELANFREP                 = ' '
*             JOBGROUP                  = ' '
              JOBNAME                   =
*             SDLSTRTDT                 = NO_DATE
*             SDLSTRTTM                 = NO_TIME
*     IMPORTING
*             JOBCOUNT                  =
*     EXCEPTIONS
*             CANT_CREATE_JOB           = 1
*             INVALID_JOB_DATA          = 2
*             JOBNAME_MISSING           = 3
*             OTHERS                    = 4
            .
```

DELANFREP is a flag. If it is set, the job is deleted after processing. JOBGROUP defines a summary of jobs for a group. The JOBNAME is intuitive. The next two fields define Start Date and Start Time. The IMPORT field gives the job number. Finally, the exceptions tell what happened when the program tried to create the job definition.

```
CALL FUNCTION 'JOB_SUBMIT'
      EXPORTING
*             ARCPARAMS                 = ' '
              AUTHCKNAM                 =
*             COMMANDNAME               = ' '
*             OPERATINGSYSTEM           = ' '
*             EXTPGM_NAME               = ' '
*             EXTPGM_PARAM              = ' '
*             EXTPGM_SET_TRACE_ON       = ' '
*             EXTPGM_STDERR_IN_JOBLOG   = 'X'
```

```
*          EXTPGM_STDOUT_IN_JOBLOG      = 'X'
*          EXTPGM_SYSTEM                = ' '
*          EXTPGM_RFCDEST               = ' '
*          EXTPGM_WAIT_FOR_TERMINATION  = 'X'
           JOBCOUNT                     =
           JOBNAME                      =
*          LANGUAGE                     = SY-LANGU
*          PRIPARAMS                    = ' '
*          REPORT                       = ' '
*          VARIANT                      = ' '
*     IMPORTING
*          STEP_NUMBER                  =
*     EXCEPTIONS
*          BAD_PRIPARAMS                = 1
*          BAD_XPGFLAGS                 = 2
*          INVALID_JOBDATA              = 3
*          JOBNAME_MISSING              = 4
*          JOB_NOTEX                    = 5
*          JOB_SUBMIT_FAILED            = 6
*          LOCK_FAILED                   = 7
*          PROGRAM_MISSING              = 8
*          PROG_ABAP_AND_EXTPG_SET      = 9
*          OTHERS                       = 10
           .
```

The function module, JOB_SUBMIT, submits the steps of the job to be created, while the first JOB_OPEN creates the job definition. For this function module, the following parameters are defined:

ARC_PARAMS	Structure	Contains SAP Archiving Data (not necessary)
AUTHCKNAM	Field	Background user name for authorization check
COMMANDNAME	Field	Logical command name
OPERATINGSYSTEM	Field	System: Operating system
EXTPGM_NAME	Field	Program name in internal step list
EXTPGM_PARAM	Field	Parameters of external program (string)
EXTPGM_SET_TRACE_ON	Field	Flag

EXTPGM_STDERR_IN_JOBLOG	Field	Flag (standard error reporting in job log?)
EXTPGM_STDOUT_IN_JOBLOG	Field	Flag (standard output in job log?)
EXTPGM_SYSTEM	Field	Target system to run background job
EXTPGM_RFCDEST	Field	Logical destination (specified in function call)
EXTPGM_WAIT_FOR_TERMINATION	Field	
JOBCOUNT	Field	Batch job number
JOBNAME	Field	Job Name
LANGUAGE	Field	Language
PRIPARAMS	Field	Print: Output device
REPORT	Field	Report Name
VARIANT	Field	Variant to Use

All of the fields are optional, except for JOBNAME, JOBCOUNT, and AUTHCKNAM. All of the rest of the optional fields add features to the job submission process.

```
CALL FUNCTION 'JOB_CLOSE'
        EXPORTING
*           AT_OPMODE                        = ' '
*           AT_OPMODE_PERIODIC               = ' '
*           CALENDAR_ID                      = ' '
*           EVENT_ID                         = ' '
*           EVENT_PARAM                      = ' '
*           EVENT_PERIODIC                   = ' '
            JOBCOUNT                         =
            JOBNAME                          =
*           LASTSTRTDT                       = NO_DATE
*           LASTSTRTTM                       = NO_TIME
*           PRDDAYS                          = 0
*           PRDHOURS                         = 0
*           PRDMINS                          = 0
*           PRDMONTHS                        = 0
*           PRDWEEKS                         = 0
*           PREDJOB_CHECKSTAT                = ' '
*           PRED_JOBCOUNT                    = ' '
*           PRED_JOBNAME                     = ' '
*           SDLSTRTDT                        = NO_DATE
*           SDLSTRTTM                        = NO_TIME
```

```
*         STARTDATE_RESTRICTION              = BTC_PROCESS_ALWAYS
*         STRTIMMED                          = ' '
*         TARGETSYSTEM                       = ' '
*         START_ON_WORKDAY_NOT_BEFORE        = SY-DATUM
*         START_ON_WORKDAY_NR                = 0
*         WORKDAY_COUNT_DIRECTION            = 0
*         RECIPIENT_OBJ                      =
*         TARGETSERVER                       = ' '
*    IMPORTING
*         JOB_WAS_RELEASED                   =
*    EXCEPTIONS
*         CANT_START_IMMEDIATE               = 1
*         INVALID_STARTDATE                  = 2
*         JOBNAME_MISSING                    = 3
*         JOB_CLOSE_FAILED                   = 4
*         JOB_NOSTEPS                        = 5
*         JOB_NOTEX                          = 6
*         LOCK_FAILED                        = 7
*         OTHERS                             = 8
```

Finally, the JOB_CLOSE function module saves the definition of the job, along with the definition of the steps and schedules it is to run. For this function module, JOBNAME and JOBCOUNT are the mandatory fields that must be specified. The rest of the fields are optional. The optional export fields match up very easily with options on the job schedule creation screen, so as you create the schedule for a job, these options will become well defined to you. You can then specify in your ABAP program as you would manually create the schedule for this job.

The benefit of these function modules allows you to create master ABAP routines, which can spawn off small batch jobs to run independently of the master program in parallel.

BDC Sessions versus Transactions

BDC sessions are covered extensively in PRIMA TECH's *Introduction to ABAP/4 Programming for SAP*. Here, however, we want to consider how BDC sessions compare to actual transactions.

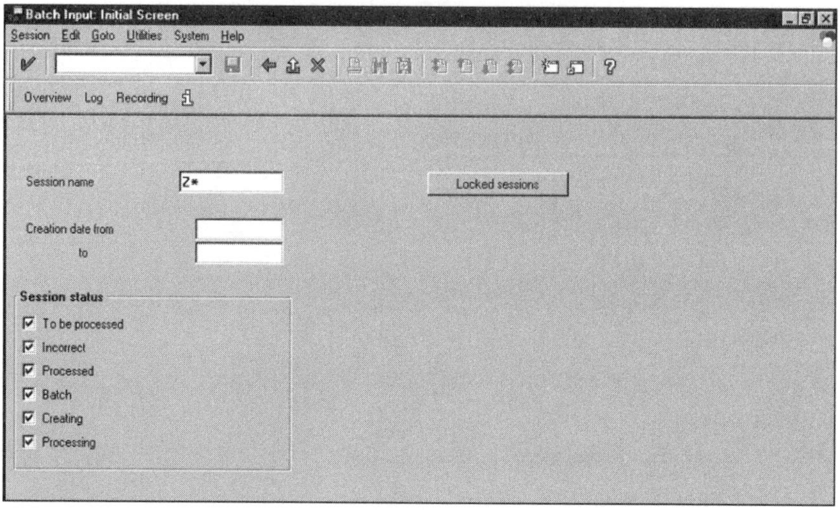

FIGURE 4-13

Initial screen of the BDC overview

A BDC session emulates a user running numerous transactions. While a transaction can be performed online through the GUI, a BDC session runs in the background as a job. While the option does exist to run the BDC session in the foreground, this option is only exercised generally when users are checking errors in sessions or when the developer is debugging the BDC session. For the most part, BDC sessions run in the background.

In summary, a BDC session is written in ABAP, and an input file is provided to the ABAP, which then creates a BDC session, which is slowly processed in background by the R/3 system. The BDC session can be run in a CALL transaction mode, which executes the transaction almost instantaneously, or as a BDC session that creates a BDC process, which the user can either trigger to be loaded into the system or automatically load.

To see an overview of which BDC sessions exist, follow transaction SM35, which will take you to the initial BDC overview screen, as shown in Figure 4-13.

From this screen, you can view the BDC sessions that have already been processed, the ones that are being processed, and the ones that have been processed but still have errors in the session.

Here, at this screen, you can manually trigger these BDC sessions. By double-clicking on the session name, or selecting the session and pressing execute, you trigger the BDC session. A pop-up window appears, asking you which run mode

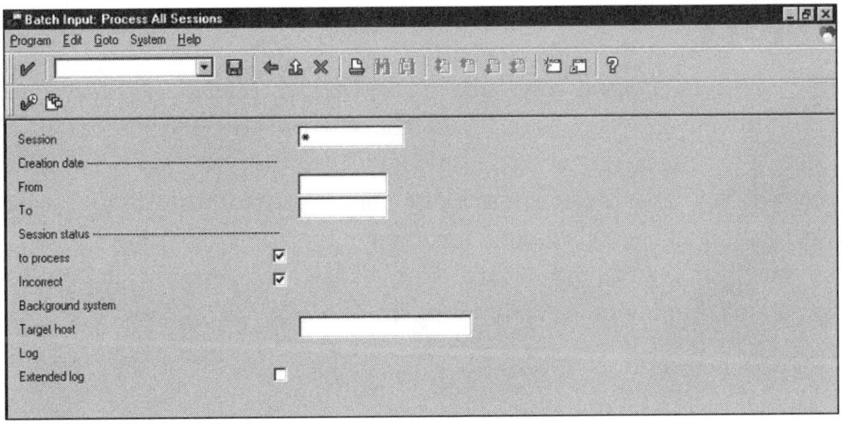

FIGURE 4-14

Selection Screen of RSBDCSUB

you would like to specify, the destination of the BDC session (target host), and some optional features that you can turn off or on. The run modes include Process/Foreground, Display Errors Only, and Background (only for this option do you need to specify a target host). If you pick the first run mode, every screen of the BDC session will appear, after which you will need to press Enter to move to the next screen to finally finish the transaction(s). This feature is especially useful when you are debugging BDC sessions. You can follow your transaction and see where the error is made, and then modify your ABAP code to fix the error. An alternative to the first run mode is the second. This run mode will only stop and display the actual screen if an error is encountered. When stepping through the screens, keep in mind that if you type **/n** in the command box, you will skip that record and move to the next one. To exit batch input mode, type the transaction **/bend**. This will exit you from Batch input.

Finally, you can process the BDC in background mode, specifying a target host (application server, just like a job) to run it on.

One option you have to trigger unprocessed BDC sessions is to use the report RSBDCSUB. This program, when executed, comes up with a selection screen, as shown in Figure 4-14.

Here you can specify session names, or leave the asterisk there for all sessions. You can also specify date ranges, and which BDC sessions to process. Once this program is executed, the applicable BDC sessions are triggered. You can also specify a target host on which the BDC session should run. This target host is the same definition as the one defined for background jobs.

Summary

SAP is quite a complicated system, and this chapter offered a high level overview of the different processes available on the system and the repercussions of each process. First the SAP transaction model was introduced, and then locking was discussed. You've learned the difference between actual database locks and SAP locks, which you'll see elaborated in Chapter 10, "Lock Objects." The concept of jobs was introduced and compared to BDC sessions, which are basically transactions running in background mode.

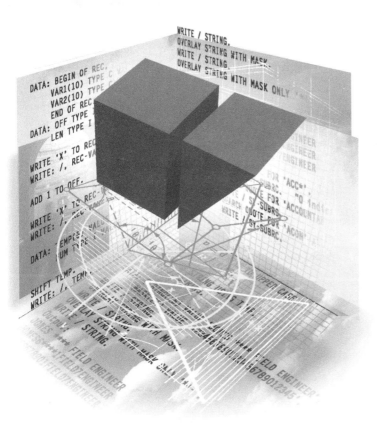

Chapter 5

**Working with
Global Memory**

In This Chapter

◆ ABAP memory

◆ SAP global memory

◆ User-specific parameter IDs

◆ Importing/exporting data between programs

This chapter will cover SAP's memory capabilities. You will learn how to set user specific memory IDs and SAP global memory, and how to transport information (data) between programs.

There are two different memory types in SAP: SAP memory and ABAP memory. SAP memory is global memory, or the memory available to a user during the duration of a terminal session (logon session). ABAP memory, on the other hand, is only available during the lifetime of an external session (duration of program). This memory can be passed across internal sessions.

SAP memory, or global memory, is retained even if a user exits a transaction and enters another transaction. ABAP memory is only retained for the duration of the program's runtime existence. During that runtime, the program might call other screens or programs, which can access this memory, but only while the main program is still running. This memory is all a part of the overall memory structure set up by R/3 (see Figure 5-1).

Importing and Exporting Data

SAP allows certain data to be kept in memory, even though separate programs might be run or several transactions called. By exporting these objects (allowable objects include structures, internal tables, fields, and complex structures) to memory, they are available for access by other separate programs or transactions (reports, transactions, or dialog modules) while the calling program is still running. The benefit is that the data is available across boundaries of programs and transactions. The advanced commands introduced in this chapter relate to ABAP memory that is available only during the transaction. Once the user leaves the transaction, the memory is cleared.

The data, in whatever form it exists, is exported first by one program to a data cluster in ABAP memory. A data cluster is a space where the data is stored. The formal definition for ABAP memory is defined in the introduction of this program.

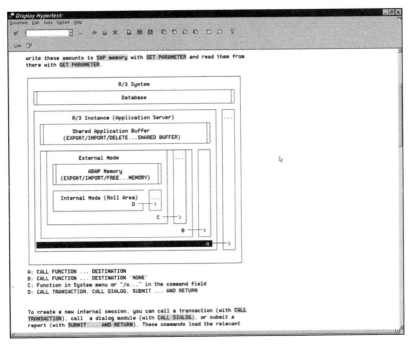

FIGURE 5-1

The memory hierarchy in SAP R/3

Using the EXPORT Command

The EXPORT command enables you to store information in SAP memory for use by other programs later. The syntax for the EXPORT command is:

```
EXPORT object 1 [from placeholder 1]
                TO MEMORY ID key.
```

The statement stores the objects mentioned in `object` in ABAP memory. The data is stored in the area labeled by `key`, which can be up to 32 characters in length. The `[from placeholder 1]` option allows the object to be stored under the name of `placeholder`. If this option is omitted, then the object is stored under its own name.

An object can be a field, parameter, structure, or internal table. In the case of an internal table, you will find that while the table can be exported, the header line in the table cannot, and will be returned as blank upon importing the data back into memory:

```
REPORT TESTABAP.

*DEMONSTRATION OF THE EXPORT COMMAND
```

```
DATA:  BEGIN OF INTTAB OCCURS 10.
DATA:  FIELD_1(10).
DATA:  END OF INTTAB.


DO 10 TIMES.
       MOVE SY-TABIX TO INTTAB-FIELD_1.
       APPEND INTTAB.
       CLEAR INTTAB.
ENDDO.


EXPORT INTTAB TO MEMORY ID 'TESTKEY1'.
```

This program creates a simple internal table, adds 10 entries (the numbers 1 through 10 as individual records), and then exports the table to memory. The internal table is stored in the memory space labeled TESTKEY1.

CAUTION

If data already exists in TESTKEY1, it is automatically overwritten by the new data.

Using the IMPORT Command

Simply put, the IMPORT command is the opposite of the EXPORT command. Whatever has been exported to global memory can be imported back into a program by utilizing the IMPORT command. First, here is the syntax for this command:

```
IMPORT object 1 [from placeholder 1]
                TO MEMORY ID key.
```

The syntax and meanings for the object, placeholder, and key fields are exactly the same as for the EXPORT command. However, in this case, the information is flowing in reverse. Your object will receive information, placeholder still identifies the name for the information, and key still tells where the information is held in memory. You can see how the IMPORT command works by adding to the previous example:

```
REPORT TESTABAP.
*DEMONSTRATION OF THE EXPORT COMMAND
```

```
DATA:    BEGIN OF INTTAB OCCURS 10.
DATA:    FIELD_1(10).
DATA:    END OF INTTAB.



DO 10 TIMES.
        MOVE SY-TABIX TO INTTAB-FIELD_1.
        APPEND INTTAB.
        CLEAR INTTAB.
ENDDO.


EXPORT INTTAB TO MEMORY ID 'TESTKEY1'.


REFRESH INTTAB.


*ILLUSTRATION OF THE IMPORT COMMAND.
IMPORT INTTAB FROM MEMORY ID 'TESTKEY1'.
LOOP AT INTTAB.
        WRITE:/ INTTAB.
ENDLOOP.
```

This program illustrates what happens when you import data from ABAP memory. Note that as long as you do not use the <KEY> addition when you export the data, you can import the data by just using the same structure name. The imported data could be from another program that is running under the same transaction, or it could be inside this same program, as illustrated here. The import command in this example takes the contents of memory ID TESTKEY1 and copies it into the internal table INTTAB. Note that the data structure must be called INTTAB. If the FROM option had been included, an identical structure to INTTAB could have been used that was named something different, as long as it referenced the same FROM location.

The information that you export to memory is retained for the entirety of your logon session and only is wiped clean once you log off. The FREE MEMORY command is commonly used to clear the memory section. Following the same syntax as the EXPORT and IMPORT commands, its functionality only differs in that it clears that memory location or structure.

Using SET and GET with Parameter IDs (PIDs)

You'll find one big similarity and a couple of big differences between utilizing the IMPORT/EXPORT command set and utilizing the IMPORT/EXPORT combination. The similarity is that data can be passed from program to program via both command sets. The differences are that the SET/GET combination can only export/import field data (IMPORT/EXPORT is capable of transporting more complex objects) and that the SET/GET combination is unique to the user and the particular session under which the user has logged on. PIDs are also completely integrated with Screen Painter and Data Dictionary. Default values for PIDs can be set which are unique to each user (such as logon language) through the user default screen.

Using Unique PIDs

SAP has a set of certain PIDs that it utilizes throughout its code. The list of PIDs is stored in the table TPARA along with a brief description of each PID. The PIDs are set and held for a particular user for the duration of a single terminal session. Values assigned to that PID remain set even if a user leaves a program. Only when a new terminal session is opened will another set of PIDs be available with initial values. PIDs can be up to 20 characters long and cannot consist of all spaces. In addition, the value stored in the PID cannot exceed 250 characters and the ID name must consist of a type C or type N character set.

Care must be taken when using PIDs because when you have multiple sessions open (parallel sessions under one logon) they all use a shared memory area. If you open one session of SAP using the SAP GUI logon and another one using the same SAP GUI logon, then those two sessions do not share memory. If you open one session using the SAP GUI logon, and then open another session by typing /o or choosing SYSTEM | NEW SESSION, then the memory space for those two sessions is shared.

 TIP

PID name cannot exceed 20 characters.

PID name cannot be all spaces.

PID value cannot exceed 250 characters.

PID name must consist of only type C or type N values.

Using the SET Command with PIDs

The SET command puts a particular field's value in a particular PID. The syntax is:

```
SET PARAMETER ID parameter id FIELD field name.
```

Remember that parameter id can be any character combination as long as it is 20 characters or less. FIELDfield name identifies a field already declared in the ABAP code containing some value, either numeric or character. If parameter id has already been set by another program, then the value stored in field name will overwrite the old value automatically, so care must be taken to pick unique PIDs. Now consider this example of how the PID setting works:

```
REPORT TESTABAP.
DATA: W_TEXT(80) VALUE 'GARETH'.
SET PARAMETER ID 'GMD' FIELD W_TEXT.
```

Simply put, the PID for the user session labeled GMD now stores the value GARETH, which will remain its value until it is overwritten with another program.

One clever technique is to set PIDs based on specific information only relevant to that program. For instance, if you know that two programs will run on the same day, then you can use the current date as part of the PID. The following example shows such a case:

```
REPORT ZTESTABAP.
PARAMETER: P_UNAME LIKE SY-UNAME.
DATA: W_PID(20).
CONCATENATE SY-REPID SY-DATUM INTO W_PID.
SET PARAMETER ID W_PID FIELD P_UNAME.
```

When this code is run, an initial selection screen (see Figure 5-2) asks for a username entry (parameter P_UNAME).

If TESTUSER is typed as the entry, and today is March 1, 1999 (19990301), then the value TESTUSER is stored in the PID labeled ZTESTABAP19990301. Chances are that this PID is very unique. The data can then be used, either later in the program by recalling the value stored in that PID, or by accessing that PID from another program. To get the data, use the GET command.

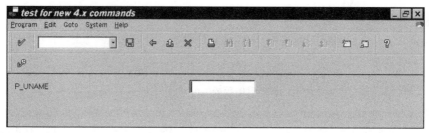

FIGURE 5-2

The selection screen for parameter P_UNAME

Using the GET Command for PIDs

The syntax for the GET command is very similar to the SET command.

```
GET PARAMETER ID parameter id FIELD field name.
```

The only difference in this syntax is the replacement of SET with GET. The functionality does change—essentially it is the SET command in reverse. The GET command takes the data that is stored in PID parameter id and puts the value in the field field name. Here's an example to illustrate this point:

```
REPORT ZTESTABAP2.

DATA: W_UNAME LIKE SY-UNAME.

GET PARAMETER ID 'ZTESTABAP19990301' FIELD W_UNAME.

WRITE:/ W_UNAME.
```

The output of this piece of code, assuming that the last example from the SET was run, would be the value TESTUSER since that was the value stored in the PID by the earlier program.

 NOTE

The restrictions that apply to the SET command also apply to the GET command.

Summary

This chapter covered the memory features of ABAP in SAP—specifically those memory features related to transferring data between programs using SAP global memory and ABAP memory.

The EXPORT/IMPORT command set is used to transport data between programs that are encompassed under one transaction session. This session is held in ABAP memory. The values or data stored by EXPORT/IMPORT are held for the length of that session.

The SET/GET command set is used to transfer data between screens, programs, or transactions using SAP global memory. This memory can be used beyond just the scope of a single transaction. The memory is session- and user-specific. Creative use of these commands can make your ABAP programs much more versatile and efficient.

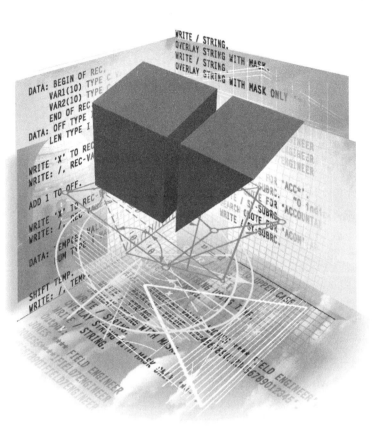

Chapter 6

Macros

In This Chapter

◆ Defining a macro

◆ Calling a macro

◆ Useful macros (SAP-provided and author-defined)

This chapter introduces and covers some very simple topics: how to create a macro, how to use the macros you create, and how to make the most of the macros that are already built into the system.

What Is a Macro?

As defined by SAP Online Help, a macro is an "executable module of the program code within an ABAP program." While this explanation is not the most intuitive, it is a very accurate definition of what a macro is. A macro is several lines of code grouped together under a custom name. Every time this name is called, along with a group of variables, the grouped code is executed. If you want to reuse the same set of statements more than once in a program, you can include them in a macro. For example, this can be useful for long calculations or complex WRITE statements. You can only use a macro within the program in which it is defined, and it can only be called in lines of the program following its definition. Essentially, during the generation of the program you have defined, the system replaces the name, or macro, with the statements and parameters defined by the code under the definition of that macro. So when do you use a macro, and when do you use a subroutine? Well, a macro should be used for short routines of code. By short, I mean tedious coding that can be replaced by a macro. The advantage of a macro is that when a program is generated, it replaces the macro with the actual code of the macro. However, when a subroutine is called by a program, it actually calls a separate program object, thus having more overhead. However, a subroutine should include long complex coding sequences, which macros would not need. For example, one would not use a subroutine for the BREAK macro, to be explained in the next section. It would be equivalent to trying to kill a mosquito with a cannon.

The syntax used to create a macro is:

```
<macro name> [<parameter1> <parameter2> … <parametern>]
```

A simple example for you to consider uses the BREAK-POINT command. The syntax of this command is:

```
BREAK <user name>.
```

Using this code in your program is equivalent to coding an IF..ENDIF statement, like the following:

```
IF SY-UNAME = <user name>.
BREAK-POINT.
ENDIF.
```

Now, consider how this macro would work in an actual program:

EXAMPLE 6-1

```
REPORT ZTESTABAP.


TABLES:      MARA,
             MAKT.


PARAMETERS:  P_MATNR LIKE MARA-MATNR.


SELECT SINGLE FROM MARA WHERE
MATNR = P_MATNR.


BREAK GARETH.


CASE SY-SUBRC.
   WHEN 0.
           SELECT SINGLE * FROM MAKT WHERE
                          MATNR = MARA-MATNR AND
                          LANGU = SY-SPRAS.
           WRITE:/    'Material'
                      MARA-MATNR
                      'is described as'
                      MAKT-MAKTX.
   WHEN OTHERS.
           WRITE:/    'Material' P_MATNR
                      'does not exist in this database'.
ENDCASE.
```

TIP

If you want to test this program, make sure you replace 'GARETH' with your own logon name.

When this program is executed and a material number is typed at the selection screen, the dialog box shown in Figure 6-1 appears.

Rather than completing, this program enters Debug mode at the BREAK GARETH command. There are many times while coding that a hard break point must be inserted in the program. A problem occurs when other people are using the program at the same time. By using the BREAK macro, time is saved by coding only one line of commands rather than three lines of code required by the IF .. ENDIF, BREAK-POINT command sequence. Creating a macro ultimately saves time for you, the programmer. Also, realize that if others execute the code while this line of code is present, it will not enter debug mode because the IF...THEN statement only executes for your user ID.

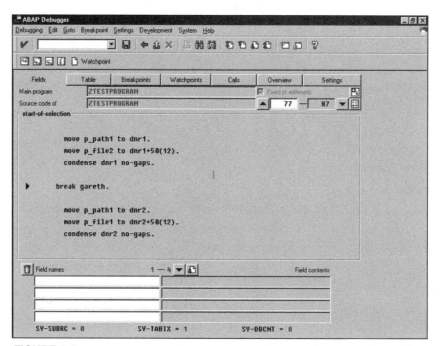

FIGURE 6-1

Upon execution of the Example 6-1 program, the macro starts Debug mode at the BREAK GARETH *statement.*

The next sections explain how to define a macro as well as how to utilize some predefined SAP macros. Included are some add-on macros we have created for your use.

The BREAK macro is an SAP macro from the table TRMAC. Since the macro is defined in the system table TRMAC, it is global to all code in the system.

Defining a Macro

Macros can be defined in two different ways. One way to define a macro is via a **TRMAC** macro. The source code of these modules is stored in the function section of the control table **TRMAC**. This code is grouped under a specific name in the table key. According to conventions, the first two letters of the name must stand for the application. The rest of the name is freely definable.

 NOTE

When you change a macro in the table TRMAC, the reports that use this macro are not regenerated automatically. You must regenerate them manually.

In the other way to define a macro, you must use the DEFINE statement. The syntax is:

```
DEFINE <macro>.
<code>
END-OF-DEFINITION.
```

This book covers how to define a macro through standard ABAP code. The TRMAC method is Human Resources module-specific. This syntax defines what code your new macro executes. The name <macro> is programmer-defined, however, do not name it using any SAP keyword. Complete ABAP statements must replace the <code> section of the previous syntax. These statements process the variables that are passed to the macro code when the macro is called.

 NOTE

The "define" of a macro must occur before the macro is actually called (hence they are usually in the 'TOP' module) and that it is only used after the code has been regenerated.

Placeholders represent the variables using the '&' symbol and a number. A maximum of nine placeholders can be used, with the names &1, &2, &3, &4, &5, &6, &7, &8, &9.

NOTE

You can call one macro from another macro, but a macro cannot call itself.

Examine the following example:

EXAMPLE 6-2

```
REPORT ZTESTABAP2.


PARAMETERS:        P_WORD1(20) lower case,
                   P_WORD2(20) lower case,
                   P_WORD3(20) lower case.


DATA:              W_RESULT(80) TYPE C.


DEFINE OUTPUT.
WRITE: / 'The words &1 &2 &3 make up the sentence:'.
WRITE: / &4.
END-OF-DEFINITION.


DEFINE SENTENCE.
CONCATENATE P_WORD1 P_WORD2 P_WORD3 INTO W_RESULT.
OUTPUT &1 &2 &3 W_RESULT.
END-OF-DEFINITION.
SENTENCE P_WORD1 P_WORD2 P_WORD3.
```

This code asks the user for three words (from the parameter definition). Then the SENTENCE macro concatenates all of the words to form a sentence, which is then stored in the variable W_RESULT. Finally, the three individual words and the sentence are output to the screen via the OUTPUT macro. All of this occurs because the SENTENCE macro is called in the code. In fact, SENTENCE is the only command in the entire program. The rest of the program consists of parameter, variable, and macro definitions.

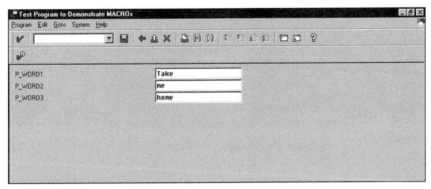

FIGURE 6-2

Initial screen displayed as the program from Example 6-2 executes

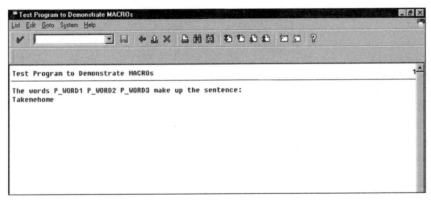

FIGURE 6-3

End result of the program from Example 6-2

Executing this program with the words 'Take', 'me', and 'home,' as shown in Figure 6-2, results in the output shown in Figure 6-3.

The output shows the sentence:

```
The words Take me home make up the sentence:
Take me home
```

More than just values of variables can be stored in placeholders. Operators, as well as variables, can be sent and processed by macros. Look at another example:

EXAMPLE 6-3

```
REPORT ZTESTABAP3.
DATA:       W_RESULT TYPE I,
```

```
                    W_NUM1 TYPE I VALUE 2,
                    W_NUM2 TYPE I VALUE 4.
DEFINE MATH.
RESULT = &1 &2 &3.
OUTPUT &1 &2 &3 W_RESULT.
END-OF-DEFINITION.
DEFINE OUTPUT.
WRITE: / '&1 &2 &3 equals', &4.
END-OF-DEFINITION.
MATH 1 + 1.
MATH 2 * 2.
MATH 10 / 2.
```

The code from Example 6-3 produces the following output:

```
1 + 1 equals 2
2 * 2 equals 4
10 / 2 equals 5
```

In this example, not only are the numbers passed to the macro, but so are the operators. The three pieces of information yield a result that is stored in the W_RESULT variable.

Notice that the first macro called has called another macro. This use of macros within macros illustrates that macros can be called within macros. Be sure to keep in mind that a macro cannot call itself.

Calling a Macro

To call a macro, use the following syntax:

```
<macro name> <info1> <info2> …<info9>.
```

Refer to the previous examples. You will find that the <info> pieces of information can consist of variable values, text, or operators.

Useful Macros (SAP-Provided and Author-Defined)

There are three useful macros in the TRMAC table. They are BREAK, BREAKRC, and COMMIT WORK. We have already discussed BREAK. BREAKRC initiates a breakpoint if the return code (SY-SUBRC) does not equal zero. Finally, COMMIT WORK completes the update task of whatever database updates you have sent over via your ABAP program.

There are hundreds of other macros, but these macros are specific to the HR module.

Summary

Macros are very simple to program; however, they represent a powerful shortcut for more complicated programming if used correctly. In a report, the macro is defined in the topmost portion of the program along with the rest of the variables and parameters. In online programming, the macro is defined globally in the TOP include, allowing all of the screens, modules, forms, or functions to utilize the code in the macro.

Macros allow you to replace repetitive code with a one-line command. Remember that only nine pieces of information can be passed to a macro. Use of macros in your programs can simplify the code and increase the speed at which you generate your programs. One extra benefit occurs when several developers are working on several different screens; macros guarantee consistent results as long as the developers communicate with each other.

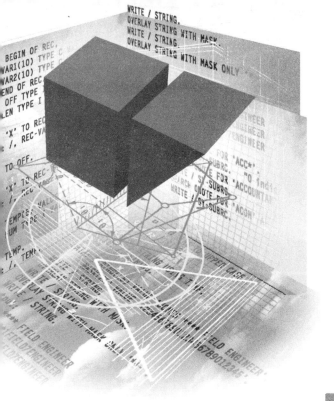

PART II

DATA DICTIONARY DEVELOPMENT

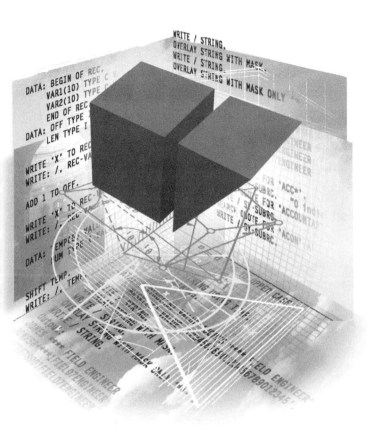

Chapter 7

Working With Domains, Data Elements, and Fields

In This Chapter

◆ Domain definition

◆ Creating conversion routines

◆ Assigning hierarchy

◆ Data element definition

◆ Field definition

This chapter introduces the Dictionary elements, domains, data elements, and fields. Each of these elements will be explained and you will learn the attributes of each, as well as how to create and utilize them.

The Data Dictionary is the skeleton, or base, from which you will build all of your ABAP programs. Most programs are defined from pre-existing structures that come with R/3; as you gain experience in SAP, you will find that it becomes necessary to create, modify, or add to these elements. The rule of thumb when creating structures is to borrow from SAP structures. Look to the current provided SAP Data Dictionary Objects and see if any of them have objects similar to the ones you need to create. If similar objects exist, use the domains and data elements or actual structures themselves in the creation of your object or objects. Chances are that 70 percent of the time you will not need to create your very own objects.

This chapter will also introduce you to the building blocks of tables and views. The domains, data elements, and fields are the core building blocks from which the database tables are built.

Domain Definition

SAP defines domain as a dictionary object that defines a value range describing the valid data values for all the fields referring to the domain.

Fields that are defined with the same domain (via data elements) are changed when the domain attributes are changed. Grouping certain fields under certain domains guarantees consistency among certain fields. An example of such a grouping might be date fields, all grouped with date attributes under a date domain.

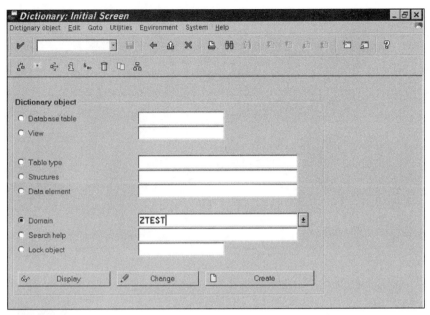

FIGURE 7-1

Initial Data Dictionary screen for domain creation

How to Create a Domain

Create a simple domain in the Data Dictionary:

1. Navigate to the Data Dictionary via the transaction code SE11 (refer to Figure 7-1).

2. Select the Domain option in the Dictionary: Initial Screen, type the name for the domain you are creating, and click Create. The domain maintenance screen appears, as shown in Figure 7-2.

3. In the Short Text field, type a description for the domain.

4. Now, for each field, type its Field Name, Key, Data Element, data type (in the DTyp field), Length, Check Table, and Short Text. For data type, you can use character, number, integer, date, etc. The Length field is used to specify the number of places available for data entry into the domain. Some data types (client, date, etc.) have fixed lengths preassigned to them. If you enter a different number of places, the system will give you an error message.

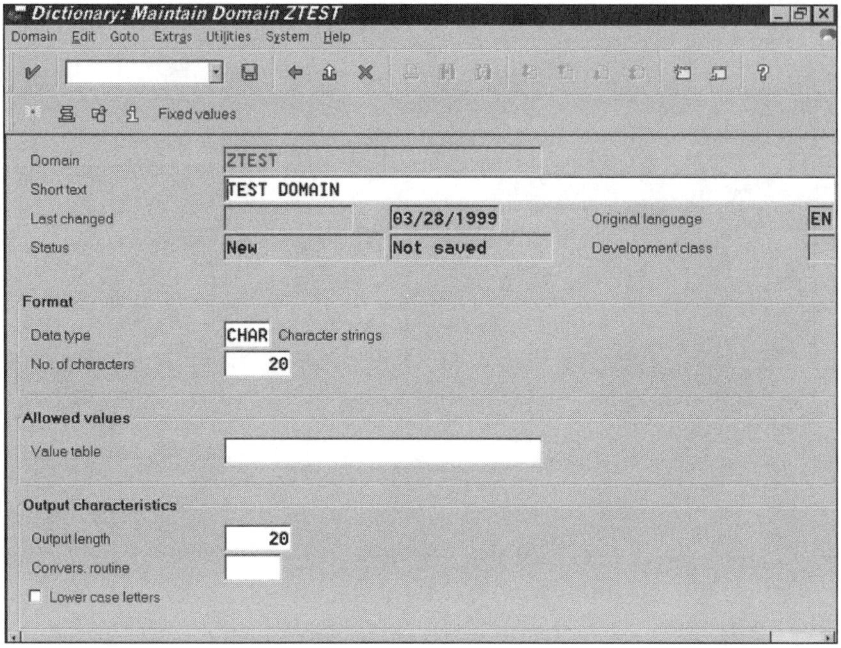

FIGURE 7-2

Domain maintenance screen

5. When complete, click the save button. You will be asked to assign the domain to a development class of your choosing or to make the object a local object. If the object is not local, a correction number will then be assigned to the new domain to log its existence in the system.

6. Activate the domain by clicking the magic wand button. Your domain is now active and can be utilized in creating data elements and fields.

Creating Conversion Routines

A unique attribute of the domain object is that a conversion routine can be attached to the object. The conversion routine box appears in the lower-left corner of the initial domain creation screen (refer to Figure 7-2). It is labeled "Convers. Routine."

Conversion routines are identified by a five-place name and are stored as a group in two function modules. The function modules have a naming convention—the following ABAP function modules are assigned to the conversion routine xxxxx:

```
CONVERSION_EXIT_xxxxx_INPUT
CONVERSION_EXIT_xxxxx_OUTPUT
```

The INPUT module carries out the conversion from display format to internal format, while the OUTPUT module converts from internal format to display format.

These conversion routines are executed whenever a field that is defined by that domain is utilized in a screen definition. For example, if the field name MATNR is utilized in the screen definition, and you want to make sure no one enters a material number beginning with the letter A, then a conversion routine would check for that and modify the user's entry.

A conversion routine is executed every time a field defined by that domain is utilized in a screen definition.

If a screen field refers to a domain with a conversion routine, this conversion routine is executed automatically each time an entry is made or values are displayed in the screen field.

Defining a Conversion Routine

As introduced in the previous section, the conversion routine can be defined in the domain creation screen. To create a conversion routine, create the two function modules listed above with the actual domain name replacing XXXXX and then insert the conversion routine in the domain definition.

How to Code a Conversion Routine

Every time a conversion routine is used, overhead is created in the performance of the program. Conversion routines are also used when the commands WRITE and WRITE TO are used. Therefore, conversion routines can be used in lists quite frequently. The output conversion should, therefore, be programmed to be as efficient as possible.

No external performs should be used in conversion routines because the table work areas of the first calling main program are also used in externally called programs. With conversion routines, this could result in errors that cannot be analyzed because they are sometimes included in the program flow at unexpected times.

Coding a conversion routine is quite simple. Essentially the internal code of the two function modules is an elaborate IF...ENDIF statement or a CASE...ENDCASE statement, with logical routines listed between the beginning and end commands.

Rules for Conversion Routines

Some commands should not be used in the coding of a conversion routine, specifically those commands that result in an interruption of processing. This includes commands such as CALL SCREEN, CALL DIALOG, CALL TRANSACTION, SUBMIT, COMMIT WORK, ROLLBACK WORK, MESSAGE I, and MESSAGE W.

Assigning Hierarchy

While you might find a new skill creating dictionary objects such as domains, data elements, and fields, it is much better to utilize existing objects rather than create new ones. Write down all the attributes of the object you need to create and see if the object is standard in SAP or whether another user has already created it on your system.

Remember that when transporting tables, you will need to transport data elements as well as domain definitions. By using existing elements, therefore, your transport will be much smaller.

Data Element Definition

A data element defines the description and authorization object of certain fields. It also is defined by a domain definition.

How to Create a Data Element

This section describes how to create a data element. By navigating through the creation process, you will become familiar with the existing data elements already defined within SAP and how to understand the various screens. Use these steps:

1. First, as with the domain element, navigate to the Data Dictionary. The transaction code is SE11.

2. Select the Data Element option, and type in a name for the element you are defining. If you type a name that does not start with a Z (Z denotes

a customer object), then you will need an object key from your OSS system. Generally, the rule of thumb is that if you need to modify an existing SAP object, get this key from your Basis team (SAP administration); otherwise name the object starting with a Z. Refer to Figure 7-3.

3. Click the Create button. The data element maintenance screen appears, as shown in Figure 7-4.

4. In the Short Text field, type a phrase to describe the purpose of your new data element. This description is displayed when a field defined by this data element is used in a screen and when the F1 (help) key is pressed.

5. Each data element is defined by a domain. In the Domain Name field, type the domain from which the data element will inherit attributes.

6. Type the short, medium, and long field labels in their appropriate fields. These labels are generally the same as the short text description, although you might need to condense your definition for the short field label. These labels are used by different Data Dictionary screens as field definitions.

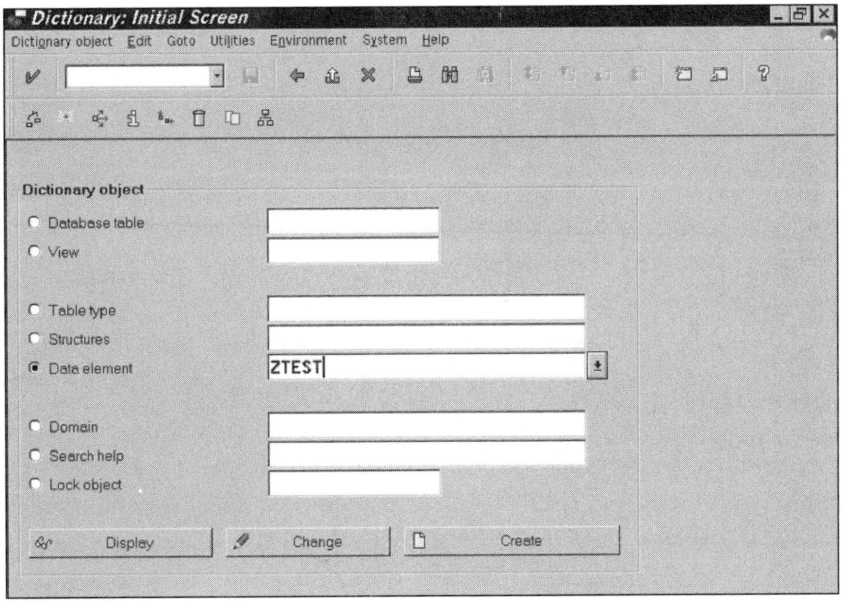

FIGURE 7-3

Initial Data Dictionary screen with data element selected

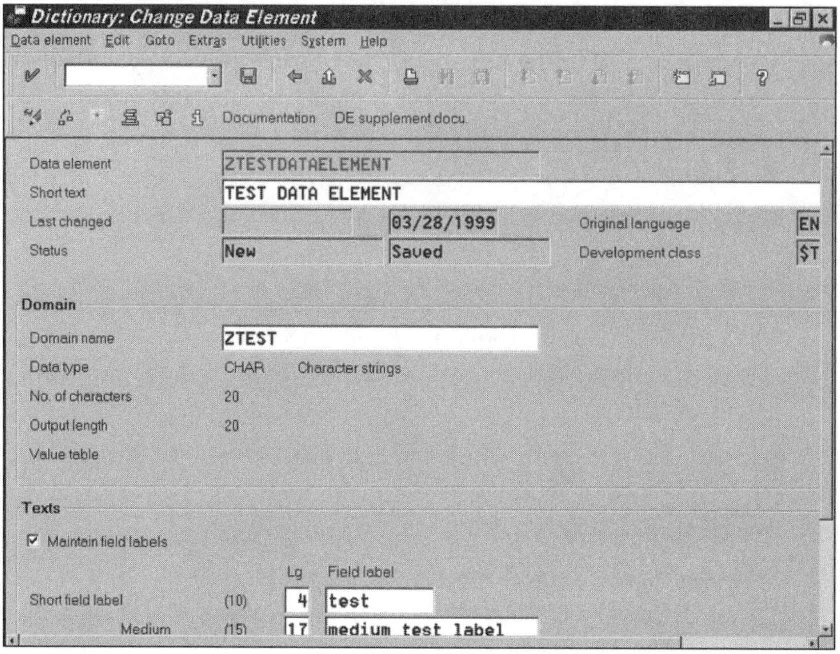

FIGURE 7-4

Maintenance screen of data element

7. Click the Save button or press F11. You will be prompted to assign a development class to the data element. Activate the data element by clicking the activate button (the magic wand button).

Congratulations! You have created a data element that can now be used to define a field. As with all dictionary objects, you can check to see if any errors were recorded in the activation log by choosing Utilities | Activation Log. Generally, if errors occur, then they will be displayed upon activation.

Field Definition

A field is the primary building block of structures and database tables. Each row of a table/structure is defined by a series of fields. Fields are subsequently defined by data elements that are, in turn, partially defined by domains. Creating a field starts at the Data Dictionary screen in SAP using transaction SE11 (see Figure 7-5).

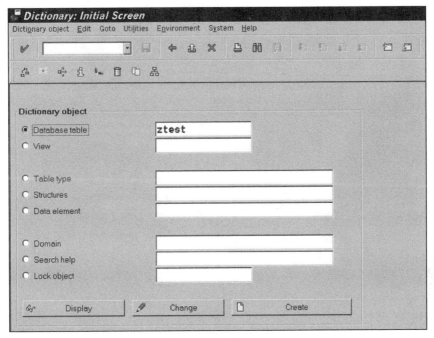

FIGURE 7-5

Initial screen from which you will create fields

A field dictionary object differs from other objects in the Data Dictionary in that a field is unique to a table in which it is defined. To illustrate, fields will be added to an existing table. Use these steps:

1. Choose any table (or structure) that you have previously defined. Alternatively, you can pick a customer table (Z<tablename>) that you can modify in your development environment.

2. In the table field, type the table name, then click Change. The maintenance screen for a table will appear. From the table maintenance screen, you will see other defined fields. (In the next chapter you will create fields in tables where none exist using the same process.)

Continue creating a field using these steps:

1. From the Edit menu, choose New Fields. This enables you to add new fields to the existing structure/table. Below the existing fields, new empty fields appear, with entry boxes for the field name, key, and data element (see Figure 7-6).

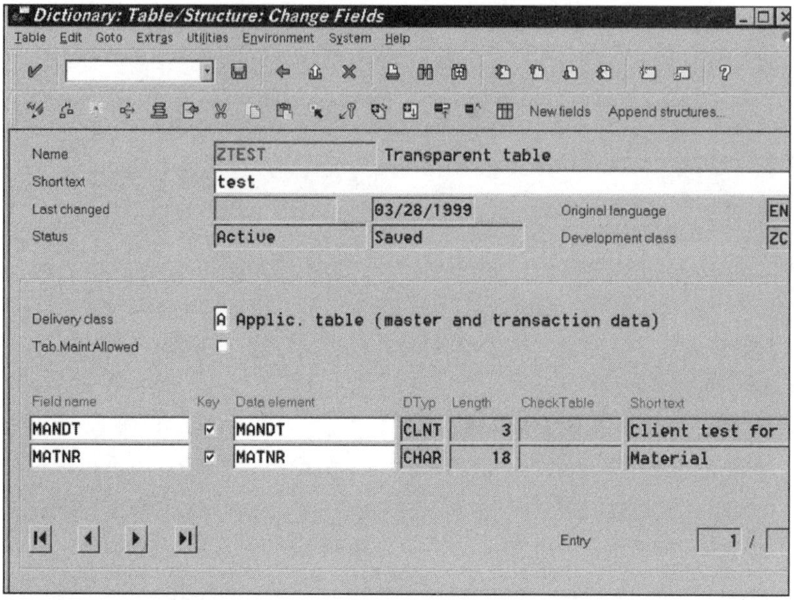

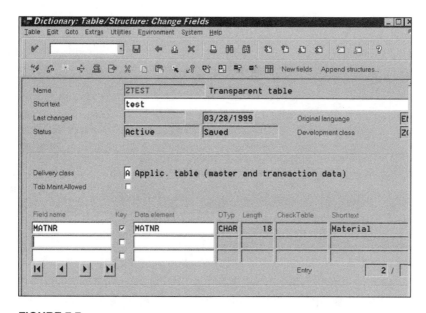

FIGURE 7-6

Menu path to add new fields

FIGURE 7-7

Entries for new fields to be defined

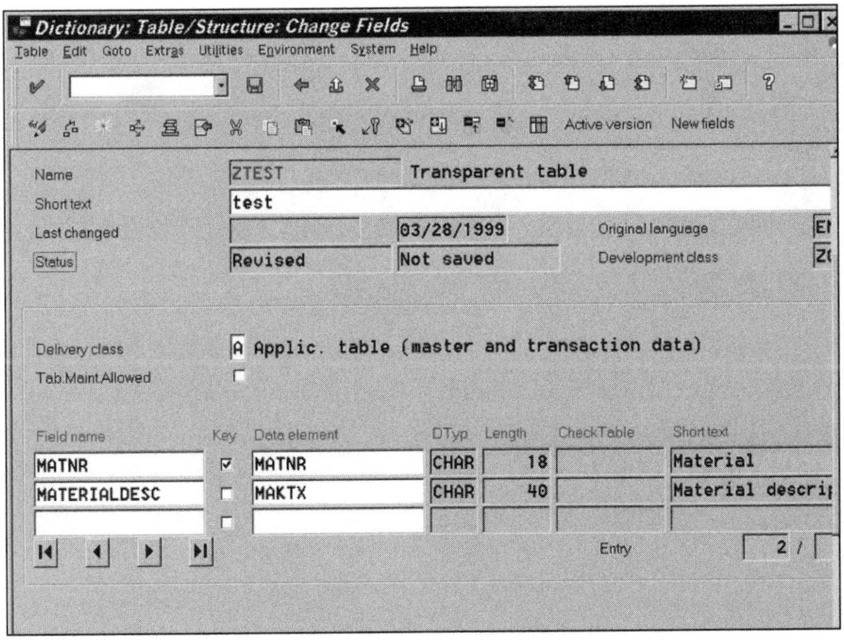

FIGURE 7-8

New field in your ZTEST table

This manipulation will allow you to add new fields to the existing structure/table. Below the existing fields, new empty fields appear, with entry boxes for the field name, key, and data element (see Figure 7-7).

2. Choose Edit | New Fields.

3. Position the cursor on an existing field and click Insert Field. A blank field is created above the existing field.

4. Type a name for the field. The field name can be up to 30 characters in length.

5. Type a data element in the Data Element box to define the attributes of the field. The Dtype, Length, Check Table, and Short Text fields will be defined automatically from the data element definition. Figure 7-8 shows an example of a newly defined field.

6. Click the activate button to activate this table. You will see the REVISED status on the top of the screen. Your table is now modified and has new fields.

NOTE

If you are adding a field to an existing table, you probably will not make it a key field since key fields denote unique entries in that table. To make it a key field would redefine the table (refer to Chapter 8 for details).

Summary

This chapter has been an overview and very simple guide to creating the basic building blocks of the Data Dictionary— domains, data elements, and fields.

Although the steps are quite simple to create these elements, there are some common rules to remember when working with these objects. First, when you can use a pre-existing object to define your element, do so! The less work you have to do, the better. This avoids the potential of having multiple duplicate objects co-existing on the same R/3 system.

When you create objects, make sure you store them in the correct development class, which is common to your solution that you are developing.

It's important that you feel comfortable creating and using these objects, because you will build on these skills in the next chapter as you define structures and tables in the Data Dictionary.

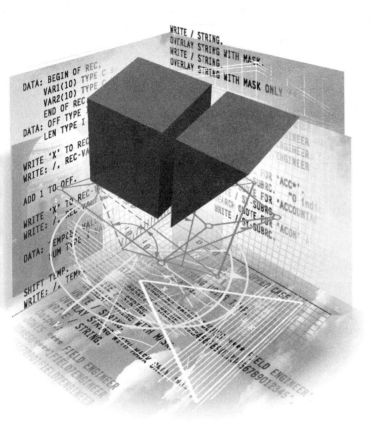

Chapter 8

*Creating
Tables*

In This Chapter

◆ Creating a table definition

◆ Defining a table's attributes

◆ Table maintenance

This chapter will discuss database tables and how to create them. Three types of database tables exist in R/3: transparent, cluster, and pooled, with a transparent table being the most common table type you will set up. Additionally, as you create a table, you will make a few choices that define how a table will be used, such as to store master or transactional data, or perhaps to customize data.

In Chapter 7, you learned how to define a field; this chapter will enhance your knowledge by making sure you understand how field creation defines the structure of a table. Once the structure has been defined, you must also determine if the user can maintain the table directly, or if an ABAP program must be used to add, delete, or modify the records.

Each aspect of table creation and use will be reviewed in this chapter. At the end of this chapter, you will know how to create any type of table in SAP, how to activate it, and then how to add data to it using several methods.

SE11/SE12 Transactions

By now, you are probably quite familiar with the SE11 transaction. Paired with this transaction is the SE12 transaction. SE12 is the same transaction as SE11, except that the Create and Change features have been turned off (display only).

Transaction Overview

SE11 and SE12 should be familiar to you already, but here is a brief overview to refresh your memory. SE11/SE12 are the Data Dictionary maintenance transactions (SE12 is display only). Refer to Figure 8-1 for an image of the initial screen for SE11. Figure 8-2 shows the initial screen for SE12.

An alternative method of going to the Data Dictionary from the initial logon screen is by choosing Tools | ABAP Workbench. Then click the Dictionary button.

Security authorizations are associated with the SE11 and SE12 transactions. The authorizations are usually incorporated in most developer's authority profiles.

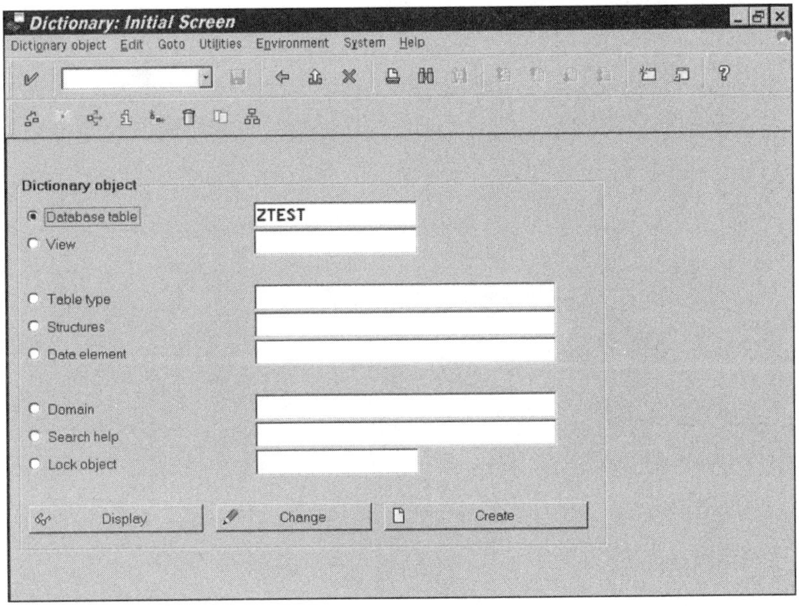

FIGURE 8-1

Initial screen for the SE11 transaction

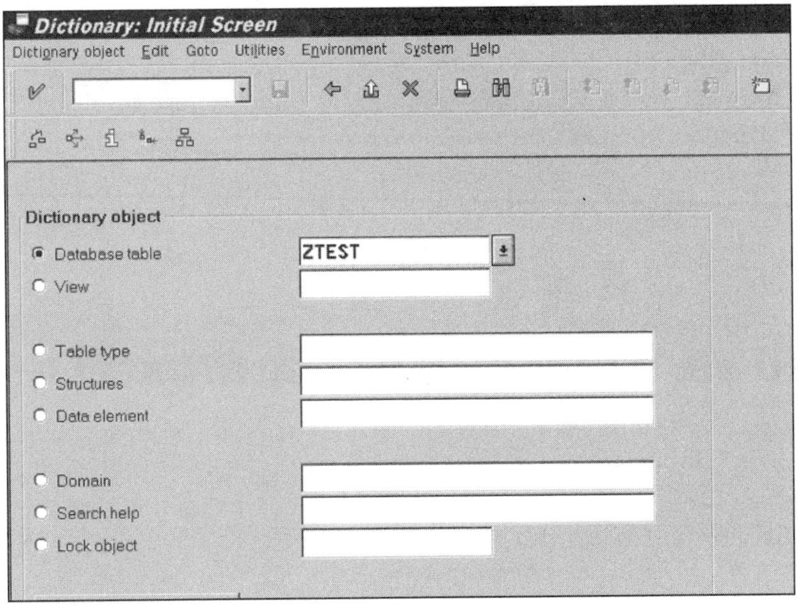

FIGURE 8-2

Initial screen for the SE12 transaction

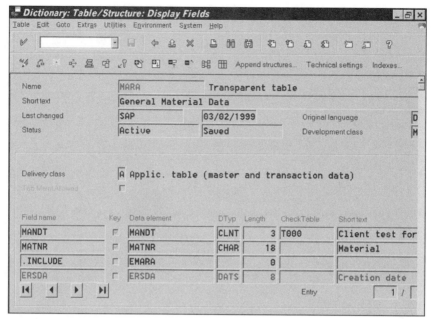

FIGURE 8-3

MARA displayed in the first table maintenance screen

Navigating Through Table Screens

Once you reach the Dictionary Initial Screen, the process used to navigate through the table screens is quite simple. First, select the Database Table option, type the table name, and then finally click the appropriate button to display, create, or change the table. The first of the table maintenance screens will appear. Figure 8-3 displays the table maintenance screen for the SAP standard table MARA.

Pooled vs. Transparent vs. Cluster

When creating a table, you must choose whether it should be a pooled, cluster, or transparent table type. The definition of each type is included below to assist you in selecting the best one for a given task. As a rule of thumb, you should make all your custom tables transparent.

Pooled and Cluster

Data from several database tables can be stored together in a pool or cluster. These tables are then referred to as pooled tables or cluster tables.

Data should only be stored in a pooled or cluster table if the table is used for internal control information (such as temporary data, screen sequences, or text information). All transactional or master data should be stored in a transparent table.

The difference between these table types becomes more apparent as you examine the structure for each type. The definition of a pooled table is that it consists of two key fields, Tabname and Varkey, and a long argument field, Vardata. The structure of a pooled table is as listed in Table 8-1.

Table 8-1

Pooled Table Structure

© SAP AG

Field	Data type	Meaning
Tabname	CHAR(10)	Name of pooled table
Varkey	CHAR (n)	Contains the entries from all key fields of the pooled table record as a string; maximum length for n is 110
Dataln	INT2(5)	Length of the string in Vardata
Vardata	RAW (n)	Contains the entries from all data fields of the pooled table record as a string; maximum length for n depends on the database system used

If a record is saved to a pooled table, then the name of the pooled table is written to the field Tabname; the contents of the key fields are written to the field Varkey; and the contents of all data fields are written to the field Vardata.

Pooled tables have certain restrictions. The name of a pooled table cannot exceed 10 characters. Since Varkey is a character field, all key fields of a pooled table must also have character data types (for example, CHAR, NUMC, CLNT).

On the other hand, a cluster table consists of several logical records from different cluster tables. The structure of a cluster table is very similar to that of a pooled table. However, a cluster table differs in that it has a new field, Pageno. This field defines whether the current record is continued in another record.

The long field Vardata exists just as in a pooled table; however, if the record exceeds the length of the table, then a new continuation record is created and indicated in the Pageno field. The structure of a cluster table is listed in Table 8-2.

Table 8-2

Structure of a Cluster Table

© SAP AG

Field	Data type	Meaning
CLKEY1	*	First key field
CLKEY2	*	Second key field
CLKEYn	*	nth key field
Pageno	INT2(5)	Number of the continuation record
Timestamp	CHAR(14)	Time stamp
Pagelg	INT2(5)	Length of the string in Vardata
Vardata	RAW (n)	Contains the entries from the data fields of the assigned cluster tables as a string; maximum length of n depends on the database system used

Since the majority of tables in R/3 are transparent, this chapter will cover how to define transparent tables. If you wish to create a pooled or cluster table, from the Extras menu of the initial maintenance screen, choose Change Table Type, and then select Pool or Cluster. From here, the general settings of these table types are similar to those of a transparent table. Cluster tables (such as documentation) usually contain continuous text.

Transparent Tables

What differentiates transparent tables from pooled or cluster tables is that a physical database table exists for each transparent table, while none exists for pooled or cluster tables. Pooled or Clusters borrow from transparent or other tables. Transparent tables exist in a namespace at the DB level, along with other transparent tables. Pooled and Cluster tables don't exist by themselves, but rather borrow their definition from multiple tables. Further, there are no shared tables between transparent tables. The name of the physical database table exactly matches the name in the ABAP dictionary. All business data and application data should be stored in transparent tables.

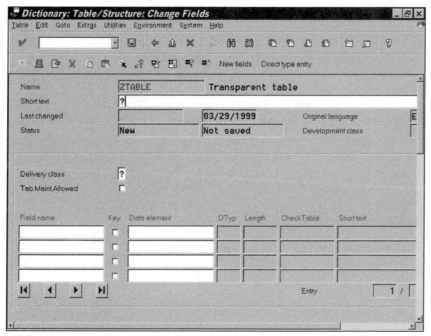

FIGURE 8-4

Initial screen for creating the table ZTABLE

Field / Table Definition

To create a table, go to the initial Data Dictionary screen using transaction SE11. There, type your new table name in the Database Table input field, select the option button next to this box, and click Create. You will navigate to the initial screen for creating a table. This screen is shown in Figure 8-4.

How to Create the Table

You can now define the table and create the fields that determine its structure. From the Data Dictionary Initial Screen, begin by typing a short description of the table in the Short Text field. Next, define the delivery class for the table. Generally, class A should be used since transactional data will be stored; however, other delivery classes are allowed. See Figure 8-5 for a list of delivery classes.

Now determine the structure of the table. First, determine whether the table will be client-dependent. If your table will be maintained on separate clients of your SAP instance, then add the field MANDT with the data element MANDT as your first key field.

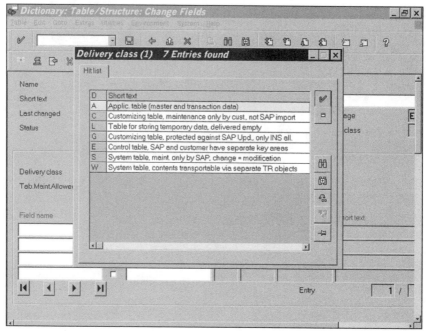

FIGURE 8-5

Delivery classes of tables in R/3

Second, enter the fields that comprise the key fields of the table. Key fields are the fields that define a record as unique. All additional fields provide supporting information about that unique combination.

A maximum of 16 key fields per table is permitted. To identify a key field, type the name of the field, then check the Key box. In the Data Element field, type the name you will use that defines characteristics of the field. If your data element does not exist, R/3 will prompt you to create the new data element. Finally, assign any additional fields to the table.

Note that you can assign a search help to a field by clicking on that field, and then choosing Goto | Search Help for Field. (You can find additional information about creating and using search helps in Chapter 11.) A dialog box will appear in which you enter the search help name and click Continue. Assign the search help parameters you want, or accept the suggested ones from the system.

There is one final step that SAP will guide you to, which is the setting of technical settings of the table. Here you will define the table type (master data, transactional data, or customizing data) as well as the table size (X number of records). Also, you will define buffering attributes of the table.

The last step is determining the technical settings of your table. You must maintain the technical settings of the table by determining the data class and size category of the view. The data class is defined in Table 8-3. The size category determines how many records will be in the view.

Table 8-3

Table Data Classes

© SAP AG

Data Class	Description
APPL0 (master data)	Data which is seldom changed. An example of master data is the data contained in an address file, such as name, address, and telephone number.
APPL1 (transaction data)	Data which is frequently changed. An example of transaction data are the goods in a warehouse, which change after each purchase order.
APPL2 (organizational data)	Customizing data that is defined when the system is installed and seldom changed. An example is the table with country codes.

Determine if the table must be buffered. A buffered table stores copies on application servers, which allows for faster performance, but greater overhead.

Finally, click the save button and assign a development class or make a local object. Click the activate button to complete creation of your table. Click Save here and your table is created and ready for use.

Setting the Correct Data Element

One important task in creating tables is defining the fields. The most important step in creating a field is determining the correct data element.

Check Other Tables

A great source of information for data elements can be found in other tables you work with. Where possible, copy the information from these tables. Find a table you are familiar with that has a field similar to the new one you need, and use that data element.

Choosing between Custom and Existing Data Elements

Occasionally, it is necessary to create new data elements that do not already exist in the Data Dictionary. You should use custom data elements (and create them) only when you have exhausted your search through the standard data dictionary.

Allowing Table Maintenance

Table maintenance is used for customization tables only. Do not allow table maintenance for tables in which master or transactional data is stored.

Table maintenance allowed determines whether you can use the SM30 or SM31 transaction to enter or alter information in this table. The first limitation is that the table name cannot exceed five characters since both the SM31 and transaction only allow a five-character input field for the table to be maintained.

To set table maintenance options, from the System menu, choose Utilities | Table Maintenance. To allow table maintenance, check the table maintenance box and then follow the instructions that are provided when you attempt to activate the table.

How to Generate the Screens

If you have allowed Table Maintenance, then one or two screens must be created so that the SM30 or SM31 transaction will work with that particular table. To create these screens, from the table maintenance screen, choose Environment | Table Maintenance Generator (see Figure 8-6). The table maintenance Initial Screen will appear, as shown in Figure 8-7.

First, type a unique (new) function group for this table's screens. There are several transport issues if you choose to use an existing function group. Until those issues are resolved with SAP, create a new function group and use it only with this table.

 TIP

You may want to start the screen numbering at 9000 because SAP has not yet reached that number in its own screen count. Doing so would denote a custom screen for that function group.

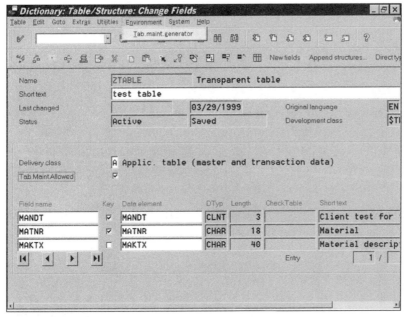

FIGURE 8-6

Choosing the table maintenance generator

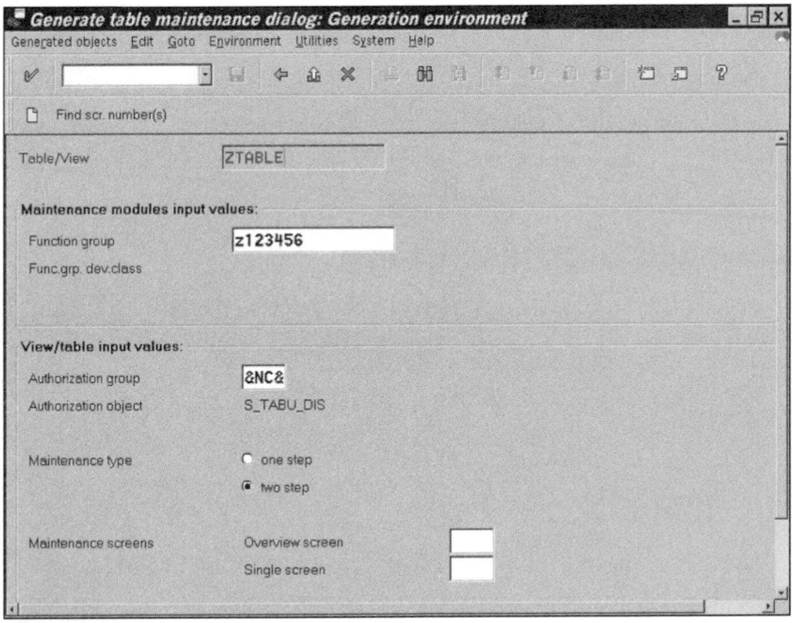

FIGURE 8-7

Initial screen of the table maintenance generator

Second, determine what authorization group must be assigned to the table. If this is a customizing table with sensitive data, then scroll through the authority groups and assign the correct one. The system proposes &NC&, which is the symbol for no authorization group. If security is not an issue, then use this default. Otherwise scroll through the objects and choose the appropriate one.

Now determine if you want this table maintenance to be a one- or two-step process. If two steps are chosen, then two maintenance screens are processed during the table maintenance: the first, or overview, screen, displays multiple entries in list form; the second screen shows only one entry. If the maintenance is a one-step process, only the list format is shown.

If you choose the one-step process, type a single screen number in the Overview Screen field. If you choose the two-step process, then also type a screen number in the Single Screen field.

On the application toolbar, click the Create button. (It looks like a dog-eared piece of paper.) Once again, you will be asked to assign a development class. Finally, click the back arrow twice. Your maintainable table is ready for use.

Database Utility

The database utility is a very useful tool. It is utilized mainly when you maintain tables. To locate the database utility, from the initial table maintenance screen choose Utilities | Database Utility.

When to Use the Database Utility

The database utility adjusts tables. If you add, delete, or modify a field in a table definition, then you need to adjust the data stored in the table at the database level. The database utility locks the entire table and makes the necessary modifications.

Changing a Table

To change a table, choose the SE11 menu, type a table name, and then click the Change button. You will navigate into the screen change screen, with which you are familiar. It is the same screen as the one in which we defined the table earlier on in this chapter.

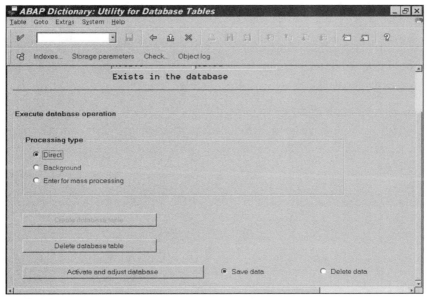

FIGURE 8-8

Database utility

Adding/Modifying Fields in a Table

Once you are in change mode, you can add, modify the data element of a field, or delete a field. When finished, you must activate the table again. In general, the system will prompt you to use the database utility to adjust the table. If it doesn't do so for some reason, choose Utilities | Database Utility. A screen similar to Figure 8-8 appears.

In the Processing Type group, select the option appropriate for your table (Background for large tables, Direct for small tables, or Enter for Mass Processing for very large tables). If desired, you can select the Save Data or Delete Data options depending on what you want to do with your data. Sometimes, especially when testing, you might want to completely dump your existing data and start over. This is a nice feature of the database utility. When your options are complete, click Activate and Adjust Table.

Summary

At the very core of the integrated R/3 system lie the tables which define it. This chapter discussed what types of tables create the system (pooled, cluster or transparent), as well as how to define a table.

Extra features such as assigning search helps or using the database utility to adjust your existing table have been introduced. With the basic table concepts now under your command, the next chapter will move into creating views by utilizing multiple tables.

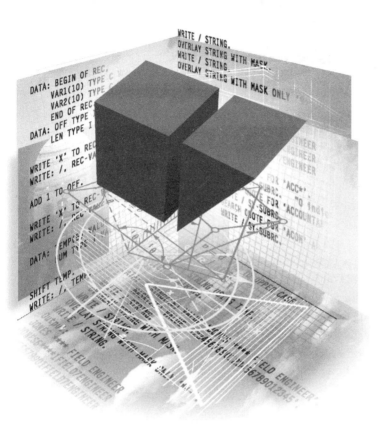

Chapter 9

Creating Views

In This Chapter

♦ Explanation of views

♦ Database views

♦ Projection views

♦ Maintenance views

♦ Help views

This chapter will cover what a view is, and how to create one in SAP R/3. Have you ever had a moment where you wished that two or three tables were combined in one table, so that you would not have to access all of the individual tables to get all your desired information? A carefully defined view can provide the solution. In addition to views that create joins between tables (creating access to multiple tables through one source), other views—such as help views, projection views, and database views—are discussed.

Definition of a View

Data about an application object (transactional data rather than header and item data) is often distributed into several tables. By defining a view, you can create a structure that combines this data into one source. The structure of a view is defined by specifying the tables and fields used in the view. A view can be used in ABAP programs for data selection. There are four types of views:

♦ Help View. A help view is comparable to a search help. With a help view, however, the available entries are shown with associated information from other tables in addition to the root table.

♦ Database View. In a database view, a database table actually exists at the database level. It can be read using ABAP Open SQL and Native SQL. One limitation to a database view is that it can only be defined from transparent tables. Only read-access is allowed in a view constructed from multiple tables; changes are allowed in a single table view changes.

♦ Projection View. Projection views are used to limit the number of fields shown in a particular table. A projection view is comprised only of one table, which, unlike a database view, can be any type of table. Since this view is comprised of one table, both read and write access is allowed.

◆ Maintenance View. Maintenance views provide a business view of internal data. Changes are allowed, but only through the transaction SM30. SM30 enables maintenance of data in all tables that make up the view.

A view can be considered a separate table, but behind the scenes, the view is comprised of many tables or sources. A projection view, for example, is simply a limited set of fields in a single table, while a database view displays the combination of data from multiple tables.

See PRIMA TECH's *Introduction to ABAP/4 Programming for SAP* for an explanation of the JOIN command. Rather than write JOINs between several tables, a view definition has the system define those JOIN statements and gives the ABAP programmer the opportunity to write a SELECT statement to the virtual table or view.

Creating Views

This section defines several views and offers several methods you can use to create each type of view. The first step, of course, is to use the SE11 transaction to navigate to the ABAP Dictionary. Once in this area, a view can be created by selecting the View option and typing a view name. Then click the Create button. In subsequent sections, instructions are provided to take you from these elementary steps to detailed instructions on how to create each type of view.

How to Map Tables

Views are created from a single table or multiple tables. In the latter situation, you must choose how to link the multiple tables together. If tables are completely unrelated, you will not be able to link the tables and the view will be ineffective.

The first step to creating a view begins on paper. Find all the tables you need that contain the pertinent data, and write them down. Then once you have this information, see how the tables link together. You are looking for the common fields between the tables so that if you were to write multiple select statements, all the data would be found. Once you have this hierarchical picture or order by which you select the data, write this down as well, because it will help you once you start creating the actual views.

Help Views

Help views are quite useful when writing screens or reports. When you need to display information that is beyond the normal search help definition, you must create a help view. The search help can then utilize the help view to create the help screen the user desires.

To create a help view, use these steps:

1. In the initial Data Dictionary screen (SE11), select the View option, type the name of your view (help views must start with the prefix H_), and click Create. A dialog box appears (see Figure 9-1) asking you to select the view type you are creating.

2. Select Help View and click Choose. You will be navigated to the help view maintenance screen, shown in Figure 9-2.

There are three input areas. The areas are for tables, join conditions, and view fields. Complete this screen using these steps:

1. Type a description of your new help view in the Short Text box.

2. In the tables area, type the name of the primary table from which the main data will be pulled. Now save your work. When prompted, assign a development class. After saving, the key fields of the primary table are copied over as default values.

3. Add any additional tables you need. However, for help views, realize that these tables must be linked together with foreign keys.

To link tables using foreign keys, use these steps:

1. Select the initial table and click Relationships. All of the existing foreign key relationships will be displayed.

2. Select the foreign keys you need and click Copy. The tables selected will be included in the view. Other tables can also be selected if they are included in the foreign key definition of the currently selected tables. Follow the previous instructions on how to add tables.

You can now select the fields that are to be included in the view using these steps:

1. Select the table containing the fields and click TabFields. The fields of the table will be displayed in a dialog box.

2. Select the fields you want to use and click Copy.

3. Repeat these two steps for all tables that have fields to be included in the view until you have selected all the fields you need.

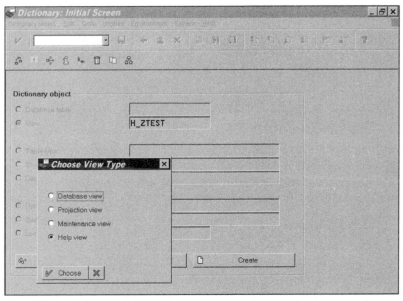

FIGURE 9-1

In this dialog box you specify which view type you want to create.

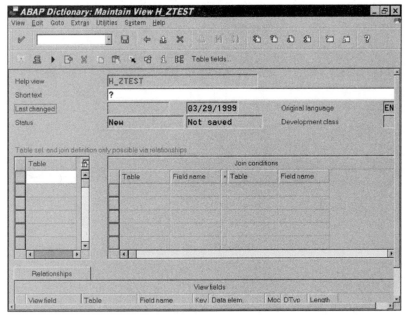

FIGURE 9-2

Help view maintenance screen

Now you must create the selection conditions. Use these steps:

1. From the Goto menu, choose Selection Condition.
2. Define the fields from the tables that must equate to bring back the correct information. Once you have completed this task, click the activate button to activate the view.

Congratulations, you have created a help view.

Database Views

Database views are defined in the ABAP Dictionary. The view defined in the ABAP Dictionary has a view at the database level as well. In ABAP, views of this type can be accessed via simple SELECT commands.

To create a database view, follow the initial steps used to create a help view. Use any name for a database view; however if it is a customer-defined object, it must start with a Z. Once the dialog box appears, choose the database view type, and click Create.

Again, a maintenance screen appears with three input areas for tables, join conditions, and view fields. Define the view using these steps:

1. Similar to creating help views, type a brief description of the view in the Short Text field.
2. Type the names for the tables you want to include in this view in the tables input area.
3. Link these tables in the Join Conditions section. (Fields of one table must equal fields of another table to find the correct data.) As with help views, you can also define these connections via foreign key relationships by clicking the Relationships button. The foreign key relationships will now define the join conditions.
4. Choose the fields for the view by selecting a table and clicking TabFields. For each table, select the fields and click copy.
5. From the Goto menu, choose Selection Condition. At this point, determine the initial selection condition to define the view.
6. Now you must maintain the technical settings of the view (see Figure 9-3).

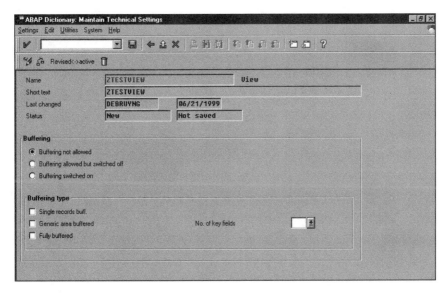

FIGURE 9-3

Technical settings of a view

7. Determine if the view must be buffered. A buffered view stores copies on application servers, which allows for faster performance, but greater overhead.

8. Finally, click Save, determine the development class of the view, and then click the activate button.

Your database view is now ready for use.

Projection Views

For a projection view, start by following the initial steps described in the two previous sections. Then continue using these steps:

1. Name the projection view Z<view name>.

2. When the Choose View Type dialog box appears, choose projection view and then click Choose. As before, you will be directed to the view maintenance screen.

3. Type a short text description for the projection view.

4. Type the name of a base table in the base table field.

5. Select the fields you want to include in the view.

6. As with the other views, select the base table, and click TabFields.

7. Select the fields you need and click Copy.

8. Save your entries, and assign a development class.

9. Click the activate button.

You have a projection view ready to use!

Maintenance Views

For a maintenance view, follow the initial instructions presented in the three previous sections. You can name the maintenance view anything, but if it is a customer-defined object, start the name with a z. When the Choose View Type dialog box appears, select Maintenance View, and then click Choose. Again, you will navigate to the familiar screen of the initial view maintenance where you should start by typing a short text description for the view.

As with all the other views, there are three input areas: tables, join conditions, and view fields. Complete these areas using these steps:

1. In the tables area, type the name of the primary table for the view. You can list more tables if you want to include them; just as with a help view, however, these tables must all be linked together via foreign key relationships.

2. To link the tables, select one table, then click Relationships and choose the foreign key that links it to the next table.

3. Just as with the other views, you must determine the fields of the view. Select the table, and click TabFields. Select the fields you want to use and proceed through all the tables in this fashion to determine the fields defined in the view. In a maintenance view, all key fields must be included.

4. Now create the selection condition by choosing Goto | Selection Condition, and then creating the logical expression to determine the selection condition.

5. Save the view, assign it to a development class and activate the view by clicking the activate button.

6. The final step is to use a new transaction, SE54 (or choose Environment | Tab.maint.generator). This is similar to using the same utility as when creating a table with table maintenance allowed, as was discussed in the previous chapter.

7. Follow the instructions in Chapter 8 to create table maintenance screens so that this view can be accessed via SM30.

When to Create Particular Views

Help, projection, and maintenance views will be created on an as-needed basis. Rather than writing complex ABAP statements or allowing third-party reporting tools, database views are one convenient way to access your data in a more friendly manner.

Create a database view when you feel that the data that is accessible via a join of multiple tables is valuable to numerous members of your development/business team. While you might be able to write very good JOIN statements, other programmers who are just learning ABAP may be unable to write the statements. Further, crudely written code may cause an incredibly intensive performance hit on the database.

Performance Issues

A view's performance is similar to writing select statements for all the tables involved in the view. If you have ten tables in your view, performance will be terrible. You must link the tables as cleverly as possible—utilizing key fields as much as possible—to enable faster reads at the database level.

Summary

This chapter introduces the concept of views, explains the four most common types of views utilized in SAP, and gives instructions on how to use and create these view types in the Data Dictionary.

Views are a great way to access multiple tables via one selection condition. If you need to standardize how these tables are accessed, views are especially helpful in creating efficient table access for everyone on the implementation team.

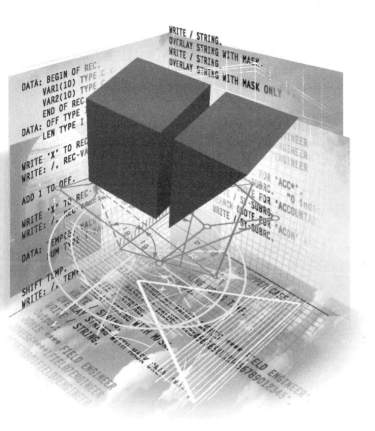

Chapter 10

Lock Objects

In This Chapter

◆ Definition of lock objects

◆ Creating lock objects

◆ Using lock objects in your code

This chapter will explore locking mechanisms and how to create lock objects. In this chapter, you will learn how to set up a lock object for a particular table, the function modules that the lock objects create, and how to utilize these lock objects in a simple fashion. Later in this book (Chapter 20), more elaborate uses of lock objects will be covered.

A lock object allows multiple users to access the same records at the same time, but, at times, only allows access rights to some users. For example, lock objects can prevent multiple users from writing to a database table at the same time, changing the same sales order at the same time, or one user reading data that another user is about to change with new data.

In a multi-transactional interactive environment, locks are set and unset by transactions and programs through lock objects. Lock objects lock entries or entire tables via certain function modules that are set up through the lock objects. When a lock object is generated or created, the function modules that lock and unlock the database table are created.

Lock and unlock are not completely accurate terms since the database tables are not locked at all. However, as long as programs and transactions check the lock objects before accessing the data, then the lock objects system will synchronize access to those tables in the most adequate fashion. Essentially, lock objects are an elaborate communications system between programs and transactions that allow sharing of data between all interested parties. They prevent overwriting of data if all programs and transactions utilize and access the lock objects for the tables.

 NOTE

The locking system described here should be viewed as an elaborate communications system between code. Actual locking would prevent access to the database does not take place. The lock object is only valuable if utilized.

Defining a Lock Object

A lock object is created and maintained in the Data Dictionary. Before discussing the creation and use of a lock object, you should first understand the attributes and structure of the lock object.

Structure of a Lock Object

Lock objects consist of a table or tables in association with their key fields. This association is defined in the Data Dictionary, accessed using transaction SE11. To understand how locking works, you must understand the structure of a lock object.

At the top level of a lock object is a primary table governing the locked record and dictating which records in the secondary tables are locked. Secondary tables are associated with the primary table through foreign key relationships. A foreign key relationship links two tables by assigning the field from the primary table to the keys of the dependent table. Consider Figure 10-1 for the relationship between the primary table and subsequent tables. Figure 10-2 shows how the SAP screen displays the definition of a lock object.

It's necessary to put all of this technical jargon into perspective to truly understand how the locking mechanism works. Imagine that a transaction has been created to modify a sales order in SAP. So that the transaction is effective, no one else can modify the same sales order at the same time, which would result in inconsistent data in the database. Therefore the lock object locks the sales order at the VBAK record level. Since VBAK is the header table of VBAP and VBEP, both of its associated tables are also locked for that sales order. From one record in one table, other records in other tables are locked respectively.

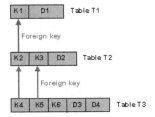

FIGURE 10-1

Relationship between a primary table and secondary tables through foreign keys (Copyright SAP-AG)

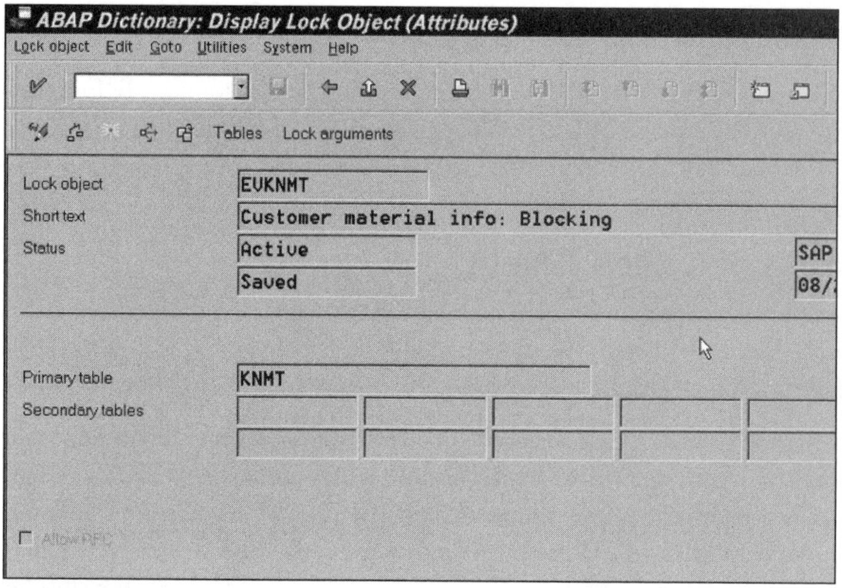

ABAP Dictionary: Display Lock Object (Attributes)

Lock object   Edit   Goto   Utilities   System   Help

Tables   Lock arguments

Lock object	EVKNMT
Short text	Customer material info: Blocking
Status	Active
	Saved

Primary table   KNMT

Secondary tables

FIGURE 10-2

SAP screen definition of the standard SAP lock object, EVKNMT

NOTE

A foreign key links two tables by assigning certain fields of the parent table to the primary key of the dependent table.

A lock object is a relationship defined in the Data Dictionary between a main table and possible secondary tables representing single or multiple pieces of transactional data.

Lock Arguments and Lock Modes

A lock argument of a lock object is the key field of the table that comprises the lock object. Then, to further define what is to be locked, more definitions are created from that record using that lock object. This lock argument is used to lock or unlock any dependent table records. The lock argument is the input to the function modules which lock (enqueue) or unlock (dequeue) the respective table entries.

A lock object consists of a lock argument and the tables that are subsequently affected by that initial lock argument. The values that make up the lock argument define which table rows are to be locked or unlocked by the function modules.

NOTE

A lock argument of a lock object is the key field(s) of that table(s), which make up the lock object. Lock arguments are the parameters that are fed to the function module to lock the primary tables' records, which in turn lock the dependent tables' records.

In addition to locking arguments, which determine the rows to be locked, there are different lock modes that grant certain types of access to the table rows you have locked. The lock mode determines how other users can access the record that your code has locked. These lock modes are defined in Table 10-1.

Table 10-1

Types of Locks

Type	Name	Definition
E	Exclusive	The locked data under an exclusive lock cannot be accessed by more than one user. Therefore, a request for a shared lock or another exclusive lock will be rejected by SAP.
S	Shared	The locked data under a shared lock can be viewed by other users, but any exclusive lock by another user will be rejected. Edits can only come from one source.
X	Exclusive, but not cumulative	An exclusive, but not cumulative, lock can be called only once in a transaction, as contrasted to an exclusive lock (E) that can be called several times in one transaction. This lock has the same restrictions as a type E lock.

 NOTE

A lock mode defines the access by which multiple users can access the same records of tables at the same time. Refer to Table 10-1 for a complete definition of the three lock modes (E, S, and X).

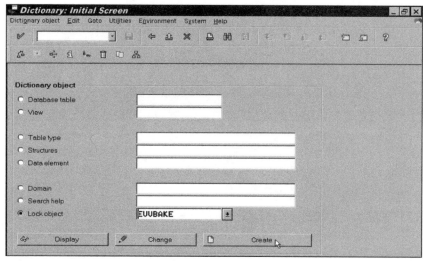

FIGURE 10-3

The Dictionary: Initial Screen when creating a lock object

Creating Lock Objects

Creating a lock object is a relatively simple task. This section will step you through the procedure of creating a lock object. Use these steps:

1. Navigate to the Data Dictionary through transaction SE11. The Data Dictionary: Initial Screen will appear, as shown in Figure 10-3.

2. Select the Lock Object option, then type your object name. A lock object must start with the letter E. Click the Create button to navigate to the ABAP Dictionary: Display Lock Object (Attributes) window shown in Figure 10-4.

3. Type a short description in the Short Text field and the name of the primary table in the Primary Table field. To link other tables, you must link them utilizing a foreign key.

4. Click the save button. You will be prompted to assign the lock object to a development class. Pick a development class applicable to your solution.

Now it is time to decide if you want to lock other tables along with your initial table. Continue defining your lock object with these steps:

1. From the Goto menu, choose Tables.

2. Click in a secondary table box, and then choose Edit | Choose Sec. Tab. A list of tables linked to your main table via foreign keys appears.

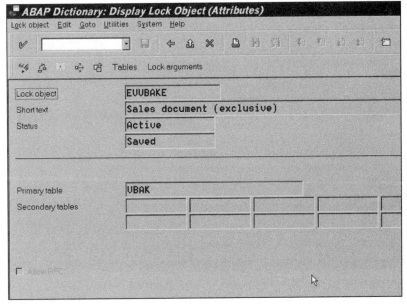

FIGURE 10-4

Maintenance Screen for Lock Object EVVBAKE

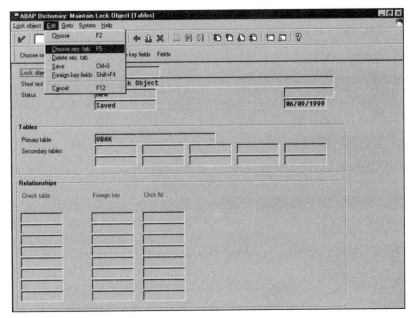

FIGURE 10-5

Menu path for navigation to include secondary tables

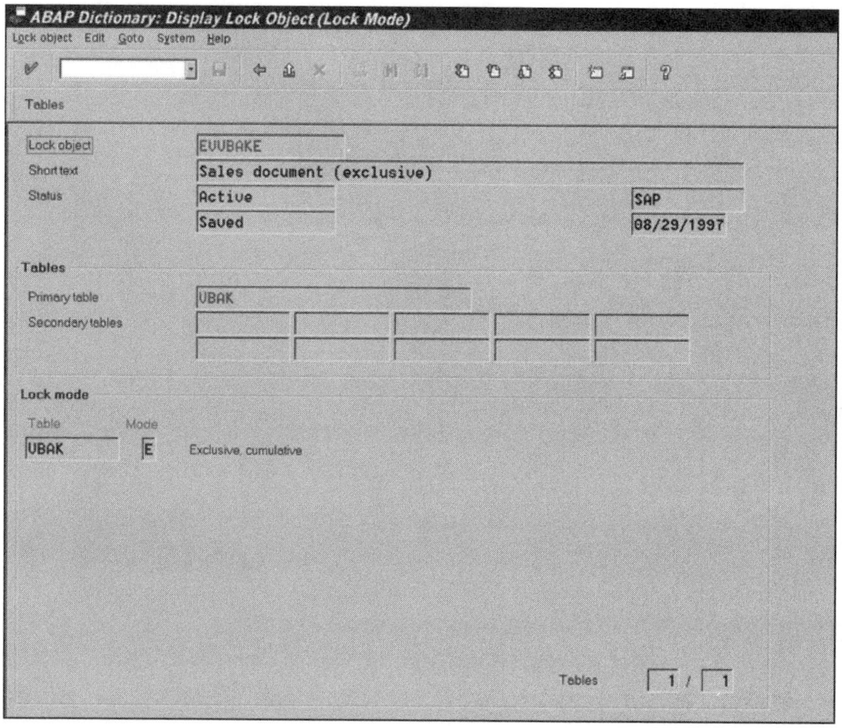

FIGURE 10-6

Definition of lock modes for selected tables

3. Select the first table you want to use, then click Choose. Repeat until all tables are selected.

4. When you've selected all of the tables you need, click the Copy button. A window will appear with all of the secondary tables already assigned (Figure 10-5).

5. From the Goto menu, choose Lock Mode. The ABAP Dictionary: Display Lock Object (Lock Mode) window appears listing the selected tables with the default value of E beside each table.

In the Goto menu, you can choose Lock Arguments. This menu command will take you to the window where lock arguments are defined. Remember that the lock arguments consist of the key fields of the primary table (Figure 10-6).

6. To return to the initial screen (ABAP Dictionary: Maintain Lock Object (Attributes), choose Goto | Attributes. You can set the Allow RFC flag to allow remote function calls (RFCs) when the lock object is activated.

7. Choose Lock Object | Activate to check the lock object and generate

the function modules. You should also check for the existence of the `ENQUEUE` and `DEQUEUE` function modules.

8. As a final step, you can also check the activation log to see if any errors were generated (choose Utilities | Activation Log).

Locking the Tables

When a lock object is defined in the ABAP dictionary, as shown above, two function modules are generated—`ENQUEUE_<object>` and `DEQUEUE_<object>`. To lock an object, use the `ENQUEUE` function module, and to unlock the object, use the `DEQUEUE` function module. To use either of these function modules, call them in your ABAP code as you would any other function module.

When calling either function module, you must provide a lock argument for the function module to determine which records it will lock in the lock object (primary and dependent tables). In addition to the lock argument, the lock mode must be specified. If another transaction or program now attempts to access those records (`ENQUEUE`ing them first), it will be informed that a lock has been placed on those specific records. The records you have locked are only protected if the other calling program utilizes the lock object and checks for a current lock on your records. If the program directly reads or writes to the database without checking the lock object, nothing will stop it from doing so.

Examine this example of locking a set of records:

```
REPORT ZTESTABAP .


TABLES: VBAK.


PARAMETERS: P_VBELN LIKE VBAK-VBELN.



SELECT SINGLE * FROM  VBAK
        WHERE  VBELN      = P_VBELN        .


CASE SY-SUBRC.
   WHEN 0.


     CALL FUNCTION 'ENQUEUE_EVVBAKE'
```

```
          EXPORTING

               MODE_VBAK      = 'E'      "Defines Mode

               MANDT          = SY-MANDT"Lock Argument

               VBELN          = P_VBELN "Lock Argument

               X_VBELN        = ' '

               _SCOPE         = '2'      "SCOPE

               _WAIT          = ' '      "WAIT

               _COLLECT       = ' '      "COLLECT

          EXCEPTIONS

               FOREIGN_LOCK   = 1

               SYSTEM_FAILURE = 2

               OTHERS         = 3.


   IF SY-SUBRC <> 0.

     MESSAGE ID SY-MSGID TYPE SY-MSGTY NUMBER SY-MSGNO

              WITH SY-MSGV1 SY-MSGV2 SY-MSGV3 SY-MSGV4.

   ENDIF.




   WHEN OTHERS.

      WRITE: / 'Invalid Sales Order number.  Please start over'.

   ENDCASE.
```

The MODE was previously defined, but the variable to be set is always named MODE_<table>. Set the mode to E, S, or X. The lock arguments are the values for the key of the primary table. SCOPE is a variable that determines how the lock is sent to the update program. If _SCOPE is equal to 1, the lock ends when the transaction ends. When equal to 2, the lock remains in place until an update program after the current transaction removes it. When it has the value of 3, the current program must remove the lock as well as the update program. _COLLECT determines if the lock request should occur immediately, or if it should be collected when a lock container is submitted to the database. A lock container is a collection of locks that are processed in one batch. Lock containers are explained in Chapter 20, which show more intricate ways to use lock objects.

Finally, the last variable, WAIT, determines the behavior of a lock if a conflict occurs. If _WAIT is set to , then the exception, FOREIGN_LOCK, is triggered. If _WAIT is set to X, then the locking mechanism waits a certain period of time and tries again to lock the object. If it fails this second time, then the exception FOREIGN_LOCK is triggered. The waiting times are defined by system time parameters.

There are two exceptions generated by this function module, and both are intuitive. The first, FOREIGN_LOCK, essentially means that someone has beaten you to the punch and has locked that record already. The user who set the lock is contained in the system variable SY-MSGV1, which is returned from the function module. SYSTEM_FAILURE is returned when a drastic problem has occurred when setting the lock. In that case, the lock has not been set.

Some minor differences occur for the DEQUEUE function module. Review the same example, now including the DEQUEUE function module:

```
REPORT ZTESTABAP .


TABLES: VBAK.


PARAMETERS: P_VBELN LIKE VBAK-VBELN.



SELECT SINGLE * FROM   VBAK
        WHERE   VBELN       = P_VBELN          .


CASE SY-SUBRC.
   WHEN 0.



        CALL FUNCTION 'ENQUEUE_EVVBAKE'
            EXPORTING
                MODE_VBAK      = 'E'      "Defines Mode
                MANDT          = SY-MANDT"Lock Argument
                VBELN          = P_VBELN "Lock Argument
                X_VBELN        = ' '
                _SCOPE         = '2'      "SCOPE
                _WAIT          = ' '      "WAIT
```

```
                       _COLLECT      = ' '       "COLLECT
              EXCEPTIONS
                       FOREIGN_LOCK   = 1
                       SYSTEM_FAILURE = 2
                       OTHERS         = 3.


      IF SY-SUBRC <> 0.
         MESSAGE ID SY-MSGID TYPE SY-MSGTY NUMBER SY-MSGNO
                   WITH SY-MSGV1 SY-MSGV2 SY-MSGV3 SY-MSGV4.
      ENDIF.
    WHEN OTHERS.
       WRITE: / 'Invalid Sales Order number.  Please start over'.
  ENDCASE.


  CASE SY-SUBRC.
     WHEN 0.


       < CODE TO PROCESS SALES ORDER ONCE LOCKED >



  CALL FUNCTION 'DEQUEUE_EVVBAKE'
         EXPORTING
                 MODE_VBAK = 'E'
                 MANDT     = SY-MANDT
                 VBELN     = P_VBELN
                 X_VBELN   = ' '
                 _SCOPE    = '3'
                 _SYNCHRON = ' '
                 _COLLECT  = ' '

                 .


  WHEN OTHERS.
  WRITE: / 'The sales order ', P_VBELN, ' is locked by ' SY-MSGV1.
  ENDCASE.
```

Here, the new variable, _SYNCHRON, determines how the lock is removed. If X is passed, then the function module waits for the lock to be removed. If a blank space is passed, then the lock is removed asynchronously—the program will not wait for the lock to be removed before continuing.

Summary

Lock objects are a very important part of the Data Dictionary. While they do not fit exactly in with tables, data elements, and domains, lock objects control how programs, transactions, and users interact with those elements of the Data Dictionary.

This chapter has covered the structure and definition of a lock object, how it works, and how to create and use it effectively. Be sure to utilize lock objects effectively, checking existing lock objects for access rights, and creating additional lock objects for custom tables in your solutions.

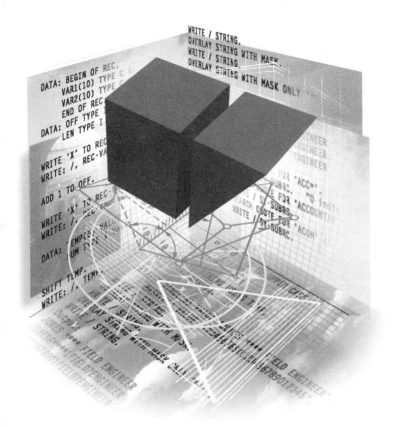

Chapter 11

**Creating
Search Helps
(Matchcodes)**

In This Chapter

♦ Defining a search help
♦ Creating a search help

A new type of dictionary object, called a search help, provides information as to what entries are available when the F4 key is pressed or an input field's down arrow is clicked. The display of the possible input values can be supplemented with descriptive information about the individual values. This is important when an input field requires the input of entries for which you are not yet familiar. Complex search help consists of several single search helps.

 NOTE

Prior to version 4.0, search help was referred to as matchcodes. Despite the new feature and name, the term "Matchcode" still appears on the hit list pop-up dialog screen.

Navigating around the Screen

Essentially, the search help is part of the Data Dictionary area of development. If you navigate to that environment, you will find that, rather than matchcodes, search helps are present in the list of dictionary objects. An example of a search help is displayed in Figure 11-1.

Creating a Search Help

To create your own search help, do the following:

1. Navigate to the development tool workbench (Tools | Development Workbench).

2. Click the ABAP Dictionary button to navigate to the initial screen of the ABAP Dictionary. From here, you can display current Search Helps. The initial screen of the ABAP Dictionary appears, as shown in Figure 11-2.

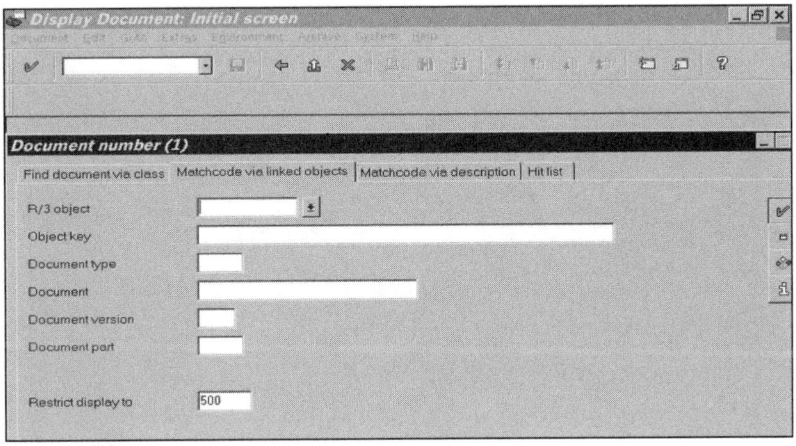

FIGURE 11-1

A search help initial screen

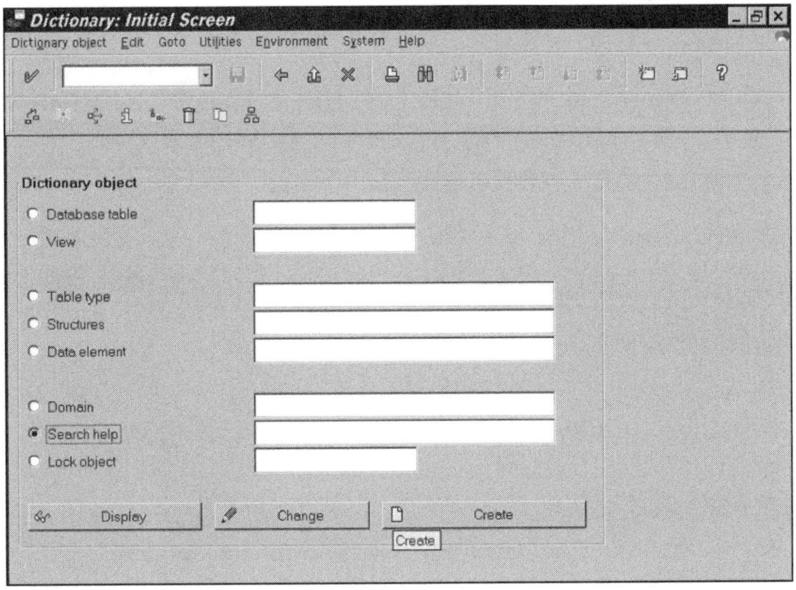

FIGURE 11-2

Initial screen of the ABAP Dictionary

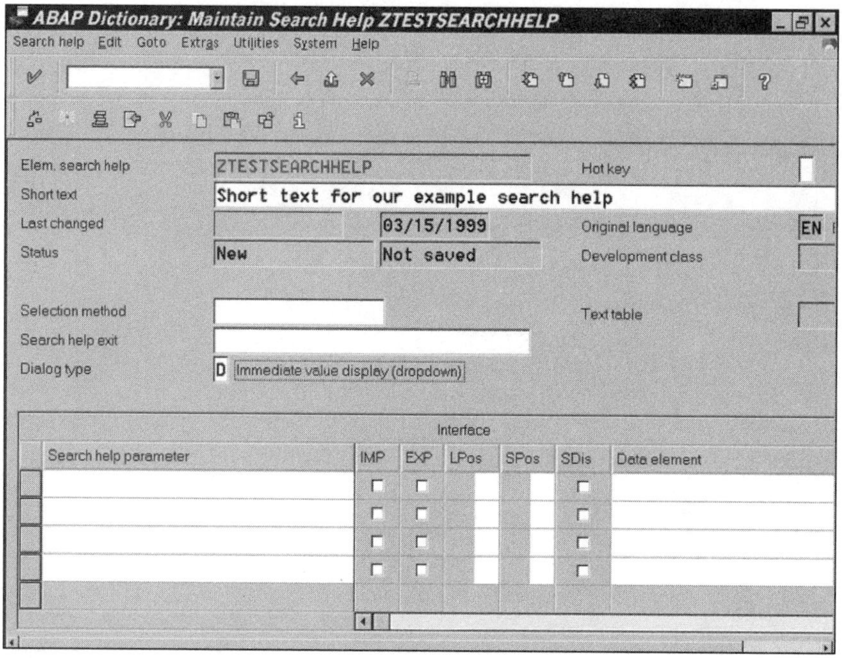

FIGURE 11-3

Elementary search help maintenance screen

3. Select the Search help option, enter the name of your new search help, and click Create.

4. Select Elementary Search Help, then click Continue. The maintenance screen for elementary search helps appears (see Figure 11-3).

Complete the maintenance screen using these steps:

1. Type a short description in the Short Text box. You should be sure that this description is a phrase that someone might intuitively search for when looking for this search help. You can search for this search help using the description of this object with the SAP R/3 Repository Information System (from the Utilities menu, choose Infosystem).

2. Select the selection method of the search help (a database table or a view).

3. In the Text Table box, type the name of the table or the view from which you want to show the possible entries shown in a search help.

4. In the Dialog Type box, specify the type of search help using one of the following codes:

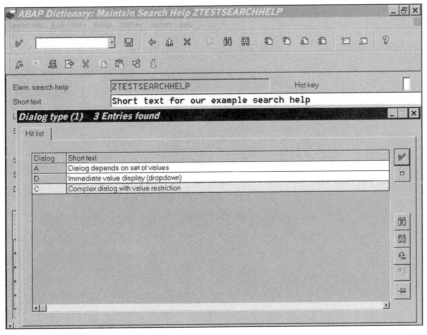

FIGURE 11-4

Choosing the dialog type

A	Dialog depends on set of values
D	Immediate Value Display
C	Complex dialog with value restriction

The dialog type defines how the hit list is displayed in the input help, as shown in Figure 11-4. Once you have assigned a dialog type to your screen help, you can define the parameters for the search help. These parameters will be the input parameters the user enters to search for the desired data. From your selection method, all of the fields will be shown. Define the search help parameters using these steps:

1. Choose the parameters you need from this displayed list by double-clicking on the choice. The Data Element field will be automatically copied from the Selection Method field.

2. Define the search help parameters as import or export parameters by checking either the IMP or EXP box. An import parameter is the text typed by the user to find the data; an export parameter is the field returned by the search.

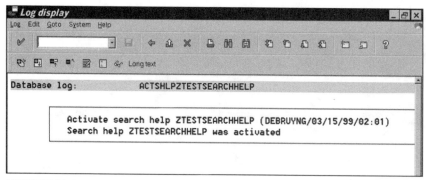

FIGURE 11-5

Activation log of a search help

Values for the fields Lpos, Spos, and SDis are required. Complete these values using these steps:

1. In the Lpos field, type the position in the hit list where the parameter should be displayed. Using no value or a value of zero causes the parameter to not display.

2. In the SDis field, setting the SDis flag will assign display-only characteristics.

3. In the Spos field, type the position where the parameter should appear in the dialog box for value selection. Similar to Lpos, typing a value of zero or leaving the field blank causes this parameter to not display in your search help.

4. Assign default values to parameters that are assigned if not specified by the user. These default values are assigned to the Default value field.

5. Finally, click the save button to save all your entries. Similar to the action that occurs when you develop a program and save it, a dialog box appears asking you to assign a development class. Once you specify this, you can activate the search help by clicking Activate.

To see if your search help has successfully been activated, check the activation log (from the initial screen, choose Utilities | Activation log). Figure 11-5 shows an example of a log.

Using Search Helps in Programs

There are three ways you can attach a search help to your program(s):

1. Assign the search help to a data element. The attachment of the search help to the data element is part of the definition of the data element. Refer to Chapter 7, "Working with Domains, Data Elements, and Fields," for information on how to do this when you create a data element.

2. Assign the search help to the definition of a table, or check table. The search help attachment is part of the definition of the table structure to which the search help is attached. Refer to Chapter 8, "Creating Tables."

3. Assign the search help to a screen field when you specify the attributes of that screen field. Refer to Chapter 15, "Using the Screen Painter," for information on how to accomplish this.

Summary

The 4.x environment search helps have replaced matchcodes from earlier versions. Before you create your own search helps, investigate existing ones already present in the Data Dictionary. A simple navigation via transaction SE11 or SE12 and some careful investigation will provide you with a good overview of what is already available. From there, if you still do not have the object you require, you can create and attach the desired search help.

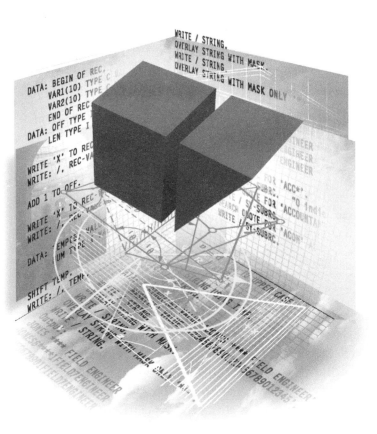

Chapter 12

Creating Logical Databases

In This Chapter

- ◆ Overview of logical databases
- ◆ Internal workings of logical databases
- ◆ When and when not to use logical databases

This chapter covers how to create and modify a logical database. In addition, it shows you how to search through existing logical databases, how to borrow from the system-defined databases, and when to rely on what is already available. There are times when creating a logical database is a good thing, but sometimes a more efficient method for retrieving data can be utilized.

Logical databases are special ABAP programs that read data from database tables. They are used by executable (type 1) programs (reports). At run time, you can regard the logical database and the executable program (report) as a single ABAP program that runs in a pre-defined order. Logical databases are advantageous when it comes to ensuring data is retrieved properly, since all of the select/check logic is pre-programmed, and the person writing the ABAP report does not have to worry about it.

Structure of a Logical Database

Figure 12-1 shows the structure of a logical database, which can be divided into three sections:

- ◆ Structure
- ◆ Selection part
- ◆ Actual database program

The structure of a logical database determines the database tables that it can access. It adopts the hierarchy of the database tables defined by their foreign key relationships and also controls the sequence in which the tables are accessed. For example, Figure 12-2 illustrates the structure of the SAP logical database VAV.

Selection Part

The selection part of the logical database defines input fields for selecting data. The run-time environment displays these on the selection screen when you run an executable program linked to the logical database. The corresponding fields are also available in the ABAP program, allowing you to do various tasks—for example, to change their values to insert default values on the selection screen. Figure 12-3 illustrates the selection screen of the logical database VAV.

Database Program

The final portion of the logical database is the database program. It is a container for special subroutines, in which the data is read from the database tables. These subroutines are called by the reporting processor in the run-time environment in a certain sequence.

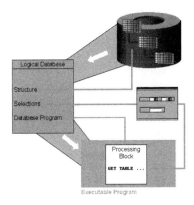

FIGURE 12-1

Structure of a logical database (Copyright SAP-AG)

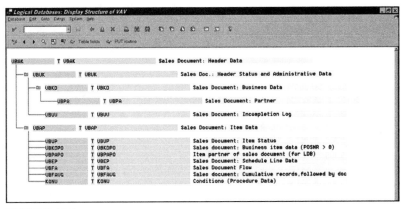

FIGURE 12-2

Structure of the logical database VAV, Sales Documents

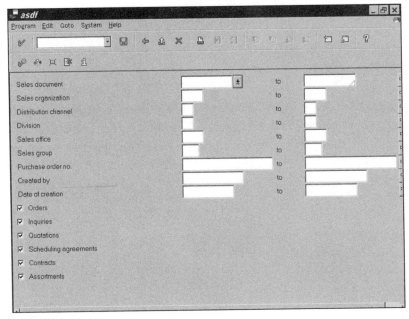

FIGURE 12-3

Selection screen of the logical database VAV, sales order documents

The subroutines of the database program, along with the code in the ABAP report, define how the logical database is accessed at run time. Apart from the structure and selections of the logical database, the GET statements in the report determine the behavior of the database at run time.

Figure 12-4 displays the initial screen of the VAV logical database. There are several places where the code is incorporated. First, there are the selections, a set of code that defines the selection screen and layout:

```
* INCLUDE DBVAVSEL

SELECT-OPTIONS: DD_VBELN    FOR   VBAK-VBELN MATCHCODE OBJECT VMVA.

SELECT-OPTIONS: DD_VKORG    FOR   VBAK-VKORG.

SELECT-OPTIONS: DD_VTWEG    FOR   VBAK-VTWEG.

SELECT-OPTIONS: DD_SPART    FOR   VBAK-SPART.

SELECT-OPTIONS: DD_VKBUR    FOR   VBAK-VKBUR.

SELECT-OPTIONS: DD_VKGRP    FOR   VBAK-VKGRP.

SELECT-OPTIONS: DD_BSTNK    FOR   VBAK-BSTNK.

SELECT-OPTIONS: DD_ERNAM    FOR   VBAK-ERNAM.
```

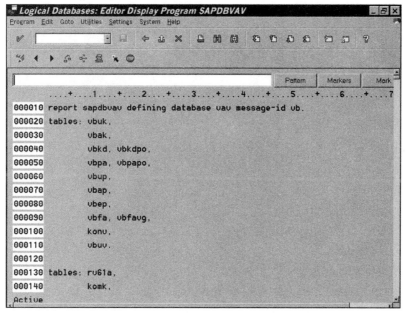

FIGURE 12-4

Initial ABAP code of the database program behind the logical database

```
SELECT-OPTIONS: DD_ERDAT     FOR   VBAK-ERDAT.


PARAMETERS: TRVOG_0 LIKE RVSEL-XFELD FOR TABLE VBAK DEFAULT 'X'.

PARAMETERS: TRVOG_1 LIKE RVSEL-XFELD FOR TABLE VBAK DEFAULT 'X'.

PARAMETERS: TRVOG_2 LIKE RVSEL-XFELD FOR TABLE VBAK DEFAULT 'X'.

PARAMETERS: TRVOG_3 LIKE RVSEL-XFELD FOR TABLE VBAK DEFAULT 'X'.

PARAMETERS: TRVOG_4 LIKE RVSEL-XFELD FOR TABLE VBAK DEFAULT 'X'.

PARAMETERS: TRVOG_5 LIKE RVSEL-XFELD FOR TABLE VBAK DEFAULT 'X'.



RANGES: ITAB_TRVOG FOR VBAK-TRVOG.


* Index Selektionen

* SELECTION-SCREEN BEGIN OF LINE.

* SELECTION-SCREEN COMMENT 1(30) TEXT-001 FOR FIELD INDEXNAM.

* PARAMETERS INDEXNAM LIKE RALDB-INDEXNAM FOR TABLE VBAK.

* SELECTION-SCREEN POSITION 74 FOR TABLE VBAK.
```

```
* PARAMETERS INDEXTYP LIKE RALDB-INDEXTYP FOR TABLE VBAK.
* SELECTION-SCREEN END OF LINE.

  SELECTION-SCREEN DYNAMIC SELECTIONS FOR TABLE:  VBAK,
                                                  VBAP,
                                                  VBUK,
                                                  VBUP,
                                                  VBUV,
                                                  VBKD,
                                                  VBPA,
                                                  VBEP,
                                                  VBFA,
                                                  KONV.


  SELECTION-SCREEN FIELD   SELECTION  FOR TABLE:  VBAK,
                                                  VBAP,
                                                  VBUK,
                                                  VBUP,
                                                  VBUV,
                                                  VBKD,
                                                  VBPA,
                                                  VBEP,
                                                  VBFA,
                                                  KONV.
```

This code declares parameters, select options, and ranges that define the initial selection screen of the program that uses this logical database (in this case, the VAV database).

The following portion of code defines the actual database program and illustrates how the logical database works when retrieving the code.

```
REPORT SAPDBVAV DEFINING DATABASE VAV MESSAGE-ID VB.
TABLES: VBUK,
        VBAK,
        VBKD, VBKDPO,
        VBPA, VBPAPO,
        VBUP,
```

```
        VBAP,

        VBEP,

        VBFA, VBFAVG,

        KONV,

        VBUV.


TABLES: RV61A,

        KOMK,

        KOMV,

        KOMP.



DATA: VBEP_TABIX LIKE SY-TABIX.

DATA: VBKD_TABIX LIKE SY-TABIX.

DATA: VBUP_TABIX LIKE SY-TABIX.

DATA: VBPA_TABIX LIKE SY-TABIX.

DATA: VBPAPO_TABIX LIKE SY-TABIX.

DATA: KONV_TABIX LIKE SY-TABIX.

DATA: VVBFA_TABIX LIKE SY-TABIX.

DATA: NVBFA_TABIX LIKE SY-TABIX.


DATA: BEGIN OF LVBAP OCCURS 10.

        INCLUDE STRUCTURE VBAP.

DATA: END OF LVBAP.

DATA: BEGIN OF ZVBAK OCCURS 10.

        INCLUDE STRUCTURE VBAK.

DATA: END OF ZVBAK.

DATA: BEGIN OF VVBFA OCCURS 10.

        INCLUDE STRUCTURE VBFA.

DATA: END OF VVBFA.

DATA: BEGIN OF NVBFA OCCURS 10.

        INCLUDE STRUCTURE VBFA.

DATA: END OF NVBFA.

DATA: BEGIN OF LVBEP OCCURS 10.

        INCLUDE STRUCTURE VBEP.

DATA: END OF LVBEP.
```

```
DATA: BEGIN OF LVBUP OCCURS 10.
          INCLUDE STRUCTURE VBUP.
DATA: END OF LVBUP.
DATA: BEGIN OF LVBPA OCCURS 10.
          INCLUDE STRUCTURE VBPA.
DATA: END OF LVBPA.
DATA: BEGIN OF LVBKD OCCURS 10.
          INCLUDE STRUCTURE VBKD.
DATA: END OF LVBKD.
DATA: BEGIN OF LKONV OCCURS 10.
          INCLUDE STRUCTURE KONV.
DATA: END OF LKONV.


DATA: SAVE_VBELN LIKE VBAK-VBELN.
DATA: SAVE_POSNR LIKE VBAP-POSNR.
DATA: SAVE_KNUMV LIKE VBAK-KNUMV.
DATA: SUBRC LIKE SY-SUBRC.
DATA: BERECHTIGUNGEN_FEHLEN(1) TYPE C.
DATA: OK(1) TYPE C.
DATA: L  LIKE SY-TABIX.
DATA: L_ZVBAK  LIKE SY-TABIX.


RANGES: ILAST FOR VBAK-VBELN.
DATA  : VBELNLAST LIKE VBAK-VBELN.


*     Aktivitäten für Berechtigungsprüfungen                      *
DATA:   ACTVT_03(2)  TYPE C VALUE '03'.        "Anzeigen


* schon geprüfte Berechtigungen
DATA:   BEGIN OF BER OCCURS 4,
          AUART LIKE VBAK-AUART,
          JA(1) TYPE C,
        END OF BER.
* schon geprüfte Berechtigungen
DATA:   BEGIN OF BER_VKO OCCURS 4,
          VKORG LIKE VBAK-VKORG,
```

```
            VTWEG LIKE VBAK-VTWEG,
            SPART LIKE VBAK-SPART,
            JA(1) TYPE C,
         END OF BER_VKO.


DATA:    BEGIN OF BER_VKO_KEY,
            VKORG LIKE VBAK-VKORG,
            VTWEG LIKE VBAK-VTWEG,
            SPART LIKE VBAK-SPART,
         END OF BER_VKO_KEY.


DATA: REPORT_SEL TYPE RSDS_WHERE.
DATA: L_TAB_FIELDS TYPE RSFS_TAB_FIELDS.


*_____*
*      FORM INIT                                          *
*_____*
* First Routine to be processed
*_____*
FORM INIT.

  REFRESH ITAB_TRVOG.
  ITAB_TRVOG-SIGN   = 'I'.
  ITAB_TRVOG-OPTION = 'EQ'.


  REFRESH ILAST.



ENDFORM.
*_____*
*      FORM PBO                                           *
*_____*
*      ........                                           *
*_____*
FORM PBO.
```

```
* Selection Screen: Process before output


ENDFORM.


*_____*
*        FORM PUT_VBUK                                    *
*_____*
*        Kopfstatus                                       *
*_____*
FORM PUT_VBUK..


  PERFORM REPORT_SEL_INITIALISIEREN USING 'VBUK'.

  SELECT SINGLE (L_TAB_FIELDS-FIELDS) INTO CORRESPONDING
        FIELDS OF VBUK FROM VBUK
        WHERE VBELN = SAVE_VBELN
        AND   (REPORT_SEL-WHERE_TAB).


  CHECK SY-SUBRC = 0.
  PUT VBUK.


ENDFORM.



*_____*
*        FORM PUT_VBUV                                    *
*_____*
*        Unvollständigkeitsprotokoll                      *
*_____*
FORM PUT_VBUV..


  PERFORM REPORT_SEL_INITIALISIEREN USING 'VBUV'.
  SELECT (L_TAB_FIELDS-FIELDS) INTO CORRESPONDING
        FIELDS OF VBUV FROM VBUV
        WHERE VBELN = SAVE_VBELN
        AND   (REPORT_SEL-WHERE_TAB)
```

```
      ORDER BY PRIMARY KEY.


    PUT VBUV.
  ENDSELECT.


ENDFORM.


*_ _ _ _ _ _ _ _ _ _ _ _ _ _ _ _ _ _ _ _ _ _ _ _ _ _ _ _ _ _ _ _ _ _ _ _.*
*        FORM PUT_VBAK                                                    *
*_ _ _ _ _ _ _ _ _ _ _ _ _ _ _ _ _ _ _ _ _ _ _ _ _ _ _ _ _ _ _ _ _ _ _ _.*
*        Verkaufsbelegkopf, Einstiegstabelle                             *
*_ _ _ _ _ _ _ _ _ _ _ _ _ _ _ _ _ _ _ _ _ _ _ _ _ _ _ _ _ _ _ _ _ _ _ _.*
FORM PUT_VBAK..

  IF TRVOG_0 = 'X'.
    ITAB_TRVOG-LOW    = '0'.
    APPEND ITAB_TRVOG.
  ENDIF.
  IF TRVOG_1 = 'X'.
    ITAB_TRVOG-LOW    = '1'.
    APPEND ITAB_TRVOG.
  ENDIF.
  IF TRVOG_2 = 'X'.
    ITAB_TRVOG-LOW    = '2'.
    APPEND ITAB_TRVOG.
  ENDIF.
  IF TRVOG_3 = 'X'.
    ITAB_TRVOG-LOW    = '3'.
    APPEND ITAB_TRVOG.
  ENDIF.
  IF TRVOG_4 = 'X'.
    ITAB_TRVOG-LOW    = '4'.
    APPEND ITAB_TRVOG.
  ENDIF.
  IF TRVOG_5 = 'X'.
    ITAB_TRVOG-LOW    = '5'.
```

```
        APPEND ITAB_TRVOG.
      ENDIF.


   L_ZVBAK = 0.



   DO.
    PERFORM REPORT_SEL_INITIALISIEREN USING 'VBAK'.
    SELECT (L_TAB_FIELDS-FIELDS) INTO CORRESPONDING
           FIELDS OF TABLE ZVBAK FROM VBAK
           UP TO 100 ROWS
                     WHERE VBELN IN DD_VBELN AND
                           VBELN IN ILAST    AND
                           VKORG IN DD_VKORG AND
                           VTWEG IN DD_VTWEG AND
                           SPART IN DD_SPART AND
                           VKGRP IN DD_VKGRP AND
                           VKBUR IN DD_VKBUR AND
                           ERNAM IN DD_ERNAM AND
                           ERDAT IN DD_ERDAT AND
                           BSTNK IN DD_BSTNK AND
                           TRVOG IN ITAB_TRVOG AND
                           (REPORT_SEL-WHERE_TAB)
                           ORDER BY PRIMARY KEY.
    IF SY-SUBRC NE 0. EXIT. ENDIF.
    LOOP AT ZVBAK.
       VBAK = ZVBAK.
       REFRESH ILAST.
       ILAST-SIGN = 'I'.
       ILAST-OPTION = 'GE'.
       ILAST-LOW = VBAK-VBELN.
       APPEND ILAST.
       IF VBELNLAST NE ' '.
         IF ZVBAK-VBELN = VBELNLAST.
           DESCRIBE TABLE ZVBAK LINES L_ZVBAK..
           IF L_ZVBAK = 1.
```

```
        EXIT.
      ELSE.
        CHECK 1 = 2.
      ENDIF.
    ENDIF.
  ENDIF.
  PERFORM BERECHTIGUNG_PRUEFEN          USING VBAK-AUART
                                              VBAK-VKORG
                                              VBAK-VTWEG
                                              VBAK-SPART.

  CHECK OK = 'X'.
  SAVE_VBELN  = VBAK-VBELN.
  SAVE_KNUMV  = VBAK-KNUMV.
  NVBFA_TABIX = 0.
  VVBFA_TABIX = 0.
  VBEP_TABIX  = 0.
  KONV_TABIX  = 0.
  VBKD_TABIX  = 0.
  VBUP_TABIX  = 0.
  VBPA_TABIX  = 0.
  VBPAPO_TABIX = 0.


  PUT VBAK.


ENDLOOP.
IF L_ZVBAK = 1. EXIT. ENDIF.
VBELNLAST = ZVBAK-VBELN.


ENDDO.


IF BERECHTIGUNGEN_FEHLEN = 'X'.
  MESSAGE S500.
ENDIF.


ENDFORM.
```

The database program consists of subroutine calls as well as some data declarations. SAP has precoded routines to VBUK, VBUV, and VBUK. If you navigate to the actual logical database screen, you see routines accessing all the tables in the structure you investigated before. To view the code, follow transaction SE36 to the logical database maintenance screen, select the code, and click Display (enter VAV as your logical database name).

Maintaining Logical Databases

The transaction for creating or maintaining logical databases is SE36 or SLDB. To proceed, choose Tools | ABAP Workbench | Development | Programming Environ. | Logical Databases (see Figure 12-5).

In the Logical Database field, type the name of a logical database. You can choose to look at or modify a logical database by selecting a logical database sub-object, then clicking Display or Change. Alternatively, you can create a logical database by clicking Create.

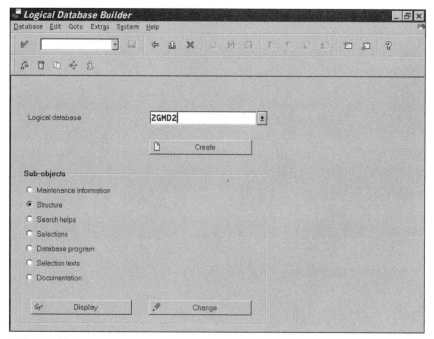

FIGURE 12-5

The Logical Database Creation/Maintenance screen

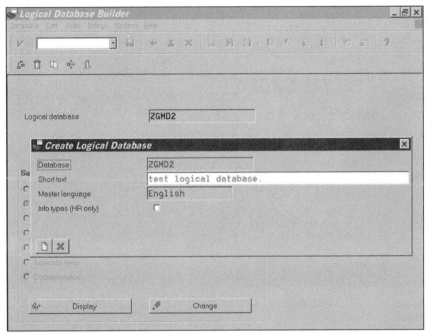

FIGURE 12-6

The creation of a logical database

When you create a logical database, the system does much of the work. You need to define the structure in the graphical editor and choose the selection options. The system offers choices for the selection options and, once those are chosen, self-generates the database program.

To create a logical database, type the new name of the logical database you want to create and click Create. A dialog box will appear, as shown in Figure 12-6. Type a short text description and then click Create. Specify a development class as well for the logical database.

Type the root node of the structure (the base table), the name of the base node, a short text description, and the database table you are referencing. Click Create, and the structure will have one node in its tree. You can add tables under your initial table by selecting your root node and choosing Edit | Node | Create (see Figure 12-7).

Once you are done defining your tree, save the structure. While the system will generate the access routines for your logical database, if you create a complex tree that has several "problem" tables referenced in it, the logical database will not

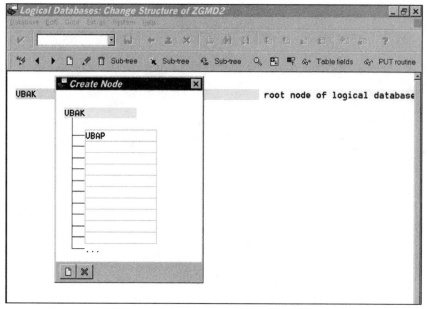

FIGURE 12-7

Adding nodes to your tree

perform well. Avoid large tables in your logical database such as AUSP or MSEG. Speak to your BASIS Administrator when you create this object to determine which tables to use. Just because you cannot write the JOIN statements yourself to put all of a certain group of SAP tables together doesn't mean that SAP can. If you connect several layers of very complex tables, do not expect your logical database to be successful.

A rule of thumb is that if you can write a program to access all of these tables, then this logical database is a doable object. Use the logical database object to allow multiple users to use the selection routines created by the system.

The system will automatically propose a selection include from your choices. Save the selection and then generate your database program by choosing Goto | Database Program. (You'll need to confirm your action in the dialog box that appears.) While the system automatically creates everything, it is up to you to increase the performance of the logical database.

From the initial screen of the SE36 transaction, select the database program of your new logical database and click Change. You will be navigated to the actual code of the program SAPDB<dba> where <dba> is the name of your logical database.

While you cannot change the names of the subroutines or the tables statements, you can rewrite the ABAP statements that access the database. Your skill as an ABAP programmer is required to review the code defined by SAP and to make it faster.

Declaring a Logical Database in Your Report

In the attributes of your ABAP report, be sure to specify the logical database you want to use. When you create your ABAP report, specify the logical database in the attributes screen. See Figure 12-8 to see where the logical database is specified. From this declaration, a selection screen is generated via the definition of the logical database.

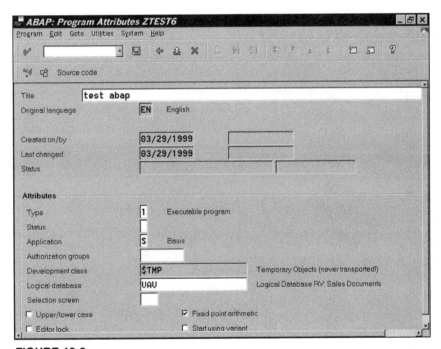

FIGURE 12-8

Logical database declaration in the attributes of an ABAP report

When to Use Logical Databases

SAP created logical databases so that access to certain tables and certain sequences of tables could be reused by many developers. While SAP maintains that they have been optimized to peak performance, these logical databases often have significant overhead and, if used incorrectly, can slow down a system drastically. A good time to use the logical database is if you are accessing the data only at a level below the root node. The data then returns quickly. However, if you access data at the bottom of the nodes, all of the data up the tree must be read. This causes a significant overload on the system and results in poor performance for your report.

The subnode structure can be used to determine the best method to access the different tables, thus giving you a good path to access the data. Code the exact data extraction routine you need based on the path provided by the logical database structure.

Database Examples

Generally, if you use the GET statement at the bottom node of the logical database and specify very few selection criteria, you will end up with one of the most performance-hogging programs of all time on your R/3 system. Even if you specify a very specific set of selection criteria at the bottom node of the logical database, you will not achieve very good performance results. For every record you GET at the level you are requesting, you are also GETting all of the corresponding information at every table level up the chain of the structure.

For example, if we GET VBPA in our VAV logical database, we also access tables VBKD, VBUK, and VBAK. While this example is possible, other logical databases might be nested several layers deeper. GETting VBPA is not a good example of a use of the logical database.

Instead, if we were to GET VBUP, we find that we access VBAP and then VBAK. All of these tables are related by key fields which makes access much faster, and the nesting level is only three deep. This is a good example of a use of the logical database.

Mapping Data Using Logical Databases

Knowing how to map efficiently the data you receive from the database is also useful. Look at the structure of the logical database, and rather than using the actual logical database, create your own select statements (as long as you are not nesting them) in a performance-preserving manner.

Summary

Logical databases are objects that come with the SAP system. They consist of predefined code that accesses certain predefined tables in a certain order. You can create your own logical database, but a significant investment in fine-tuning the performance is required. Be sure to visit the view option and perhaps define a view that can access the same table. Logical databases offer the advantage in that a selection screen is defined and becomes a part of the report you write, while a view is just a data source.

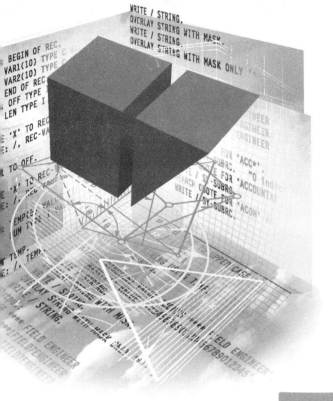

PART III

SAP TRANSACTION DEVELOPMENT

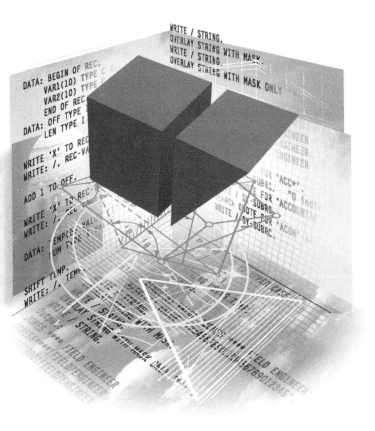

Chapter 13

Transaction Development

In This Chapter

- ◆ Transactions explained
- ◆ Components of a transaction
- ◆ Appropriate usage of transactions

Transactions Explained

An SAP transaction is an ABAP program which performs a group of operations within the R/3 system using input from a user or a batch program. These operations involve maintaining information in the database. A transaction might add a new vendor to the system, change the quantity of a product being ordered, or delete material no longer used. It is not important whether the transaction is being run online by a user or if information is being passed to it from a data file via an automated batch program.

Typically these operations must all be completed successfully or they will all fail–this safeguard is often referred to as transactional integrity. Another attribute of transactions is that they can be executed concurrently by multiple users without interference. For example, you might have a group of 50 people creating sales quotes with a single transaction. Developing transactions is sometimes referred to as dialog programming or module programming by SAP. All transactions should:

- ◆ Have a simple and consistent user interface
- ◆ Provide clear feedback of user errors and provide the capability to correct them
- ◆ Support concurrent users
- ◆ Ensure data consistency

Transactions in R/3 are represented by a group of one or more screens called dynpros. The user enters data in each screen and at the end can choose to save the data. Most transactions also allow the user to change existing data. SAP provides a set of tools to create transactions including Screen Painter, Menu Painter, and the ABAP editor. Each of these tools is discussed in detail in subsequent chapters of this book. Since SAP used these same tools to develop the standard transactions built into R/3, examine them for some great examples.

A user manually entering data into each screen may execute transactions. Also, a program can execute transactions through the use of a Batch Data Correction (BDC) session.

Components of a Transaction

Several components make up a transaction in R/3. They include the ABAP module pool, the GUI status, the flow logic, and the screen. This chapter introduces you to the terminology used by SAP to describe the different parts of a transaction. In the next chapter, a simple transaction will be presented in its entirety, and then in following chapters you will learn how to create each component in detail. A working transaction requires all four components to be completed.

 NOTE

To learn more about programming BDC sessions, see PRIMA TECH's *Introduction to ABAP/4 Programming for SAP.*

The ABAP Module Pool

The ABAP module pool is a set of functions providing the logic behind the transaction. Here is where the programmer will process the information provided by the user and perform the appropriate operations. A single module may be used with multiple transactions. For example, a transaction to display data and a second transaction that changes data might use the same module pool. Developing a module pool is covered in Chapter 18, "Using ABAP to Control Transaction Logic."

The Screen

A screen in R/3 may consist of data entry fields, text labels, buttons, and graphical elements such as boxes. The screen is the interface between the transaction and the user, so it's critical that it be well-constructed. SAP transactions are made up of one or more screens. When accessing SAP R/3 from a client PC using Microsoft Windows, an SAP screen will be displayed as a standard window. You should note that the terms screen and field have a specific meaning in SAP transaction development and are not generic terms. You will learn how to create SAP screens in Chapter 15, "Using Screen Painter to Develop Screens."

The GUI Status

The GUI status is made up of the screen title, menu bar, and push buttons. The GUI status provides a context for the users and helps them understand their options. Components such as these exist in all Windows programs, so you will be familiar with them already. SAP allows you to control these window components, as you will see in Chapter 16, "Using Menu Painter to Build a GUI Status."

The Flow Logic

The flow logic is an ABAP-like set of instructions controlling how user input and transaction output are handled by the screen. Flow logic is event-oriented; there are events for different types of input and output.

There is no clear-cut separation between a transaction and a standard ABAP program. A program can perform many of the operations that a transaction can. It can accept input from the user via its parameter screen, provide output to the user via list processing, perform database updates, and so on. Thus, it can sometimes be difficult to determine when it is appropriate to develop a transaction rather than a program. Usually the key factor is interactivity. Interactivity causes a solution to require a transaction. A transaction can respond to user input with a great deal more flexibility than can a program. If a solution requires the user to enter complex data, then often the feedback provided by a transaction is worth the added effort.

The downside to using a transaction is that they are much more complex to develop than a standard program. Each transaction requires all four components: screens, GUI statuses, flow logic, and a module pool. Even a simple transaction must have all four, so transactions are often overly intricate. If all you need is for a user to enter a few simple criteria such as material, company, or plant, you probably do not need a transaction.

Transaction Strengths:

- ◆ High interactivity
- ◆ Support for automation via BDC processing
- ◆ Support for complex database updates
- ◆ Support for advance error checking and correction

Transaction Weaknesses:

- ◆ Complexity
- ◆ High support costs
- ◆ Difficulty in debugging
- ◆ Difficulty in adding features

Summary

This chapter has defined transactions within the SAP concept. It covered the four components of an SAP transaction: the ABAP module pool, the GUI status, the flow logic, and the screen. Finally, the strengths and weaknesses of transactions were contrasted with standard SAP programs. In general, transactions offer greater flexibility and interaction than programs at a cost of much greater programming complexity.

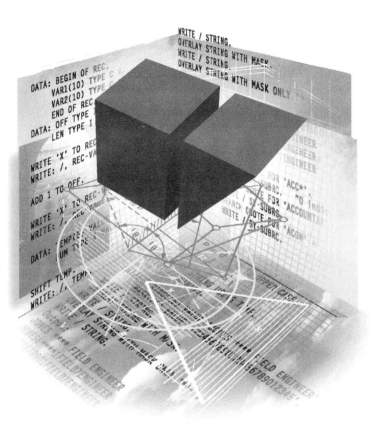

Chapter 14

Creating a
Transaction

In This Chapter

◆ Creating a module pool

◆ Creating a screen

◆ Creating a GUI status

◆ Adding flow logic and transaction logic

Because there are so many pieces to a transaction, the best way to learn how to create one is to build a simple transaction. This chapter will introduce you to the minimum steps required to create a transaction so you can see how to put one together. In the following chapters, each component of a transaction will be discussed in detail with a look at possible options.

As explained earlier, the components that comprise a transaction in R/3 include the ABAP module pool, the screen, the GUI status, and the flow logic. This chapter will create a simple calculator transaction that will accept two numbers as input from the user, then return their sum. Future chapters will build on this simple calculator transaction. Even if you are already comfortable with creating basic transactions, therefore, you may want to create the calculator to use as a foundation with other chapters.

Step One: Create a Module Pool

The first step in creating a transaction is to create a module pool. Creating a module pool is fairly simple—it's created in the same way a standard program is created, using the ABAP editor.

First, enter the ABAP editor by executing transaction SE38. In the Program field, you'll type the name of this transaction. Customer-created transactions should start with SAPMZXXX, where XXX is a three-character descriptor for your new transaction. In this case, name the transaction SAPMZTST, as shown in Figure 14-1. Click the Create button to reach the Program Attributes screen seen in Figure 14-2.

Type Calculator in the Title field, M (for "m"odule pool) in the Type field, and Z (indicating that the transaction is customer created) in the application field. Save the newly created module pool and you can move on to the next step.

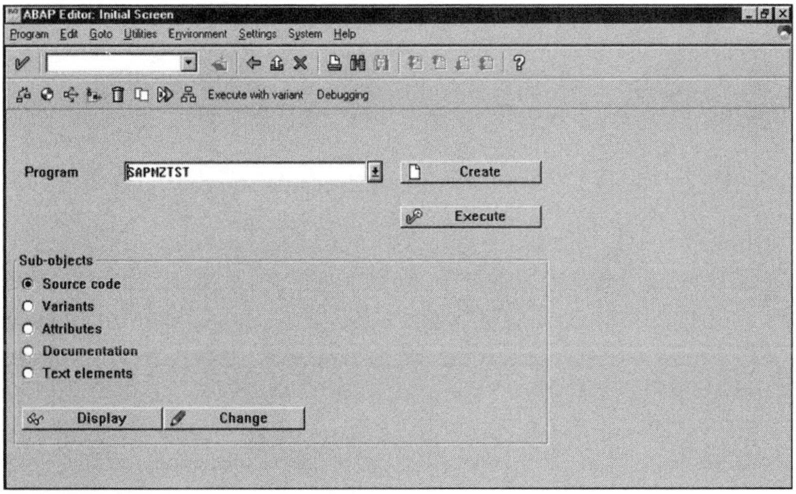

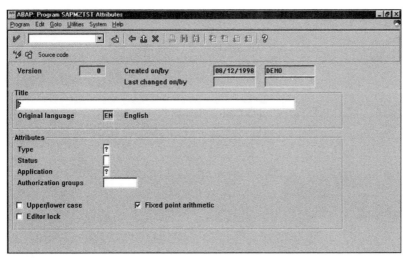

FIGURE 14-1

ABAP Editor: Initial Screen

FIGURE 14-2

ABAP Program Attributes

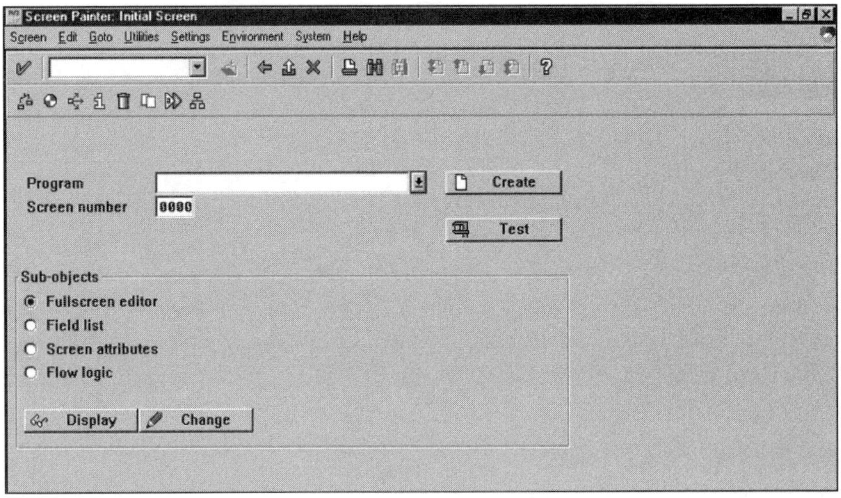

FIGURE 14-3

Screen Painter: Initial screen

Step Two: Create a Screen

Transaction screens are created with the Screen Painter, which is accessed by executing transaction SE51. The initial screen in the Screen Painter is shown in Figure 14-3.

In the Program field, type the name of your transaction, SAPMZTST. Next you must enter a screen number. Since a transaction can have multiple screens, each screen is assigned a four-digit number. A common practice for customer-created screens is to use the format 9XXX when numbering screens. Screens relating to one another should be numbered together; a transaction might have screens 9100, 9101, 9102, 9200, 9201, and 9300. In keeping with this practice, name the first screen 9100, then click the Create button. The Screen Attributes screen appears, as shown in Figure 14-4.

The next screen you will see is the screen attributes, as seen in Figure 14-4. All you need to do here is enter Main in the short description field and click the Save button. The short description field serves as a description of the usage this screen will have and should not be confused with a screen title because it is not visible to the user.

Next, click the Back button to return to the initial screen. You have now created a blank screen. To confirm your action, click the Test button. Your newly created blank screen will display. Click the Back button to return to the Screen Painter screen.

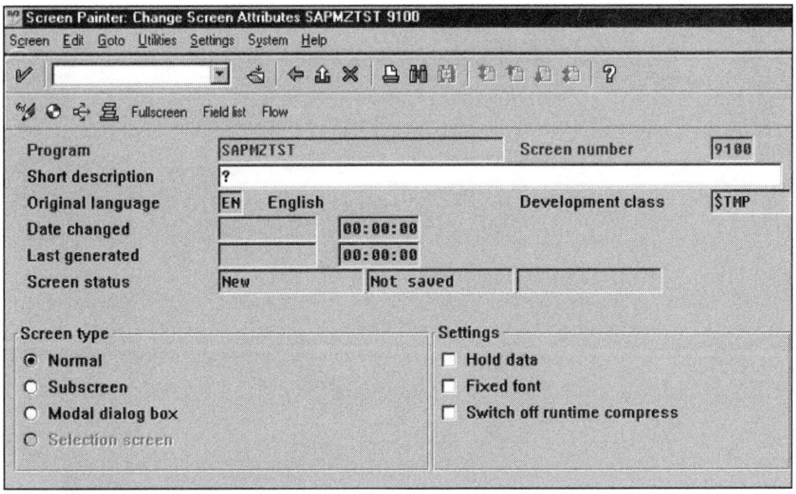

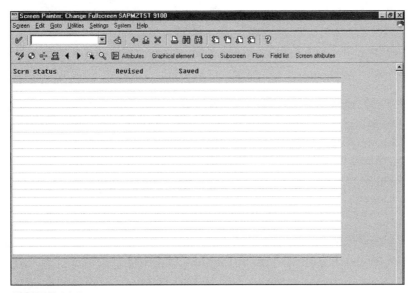

FIGURE 14-4

Screen Painter: Change Screen Attributes

FIGURE 14-5

Fullscreen editor

Now you must add pertinent fields to your blank screen to make it useful. From the Screen Painter screen, click the Fullscreen editor radio button, then click the Change button. The Fullscreen editor, shown in Figure 14-5, allows you to design your screen by adding various objects.

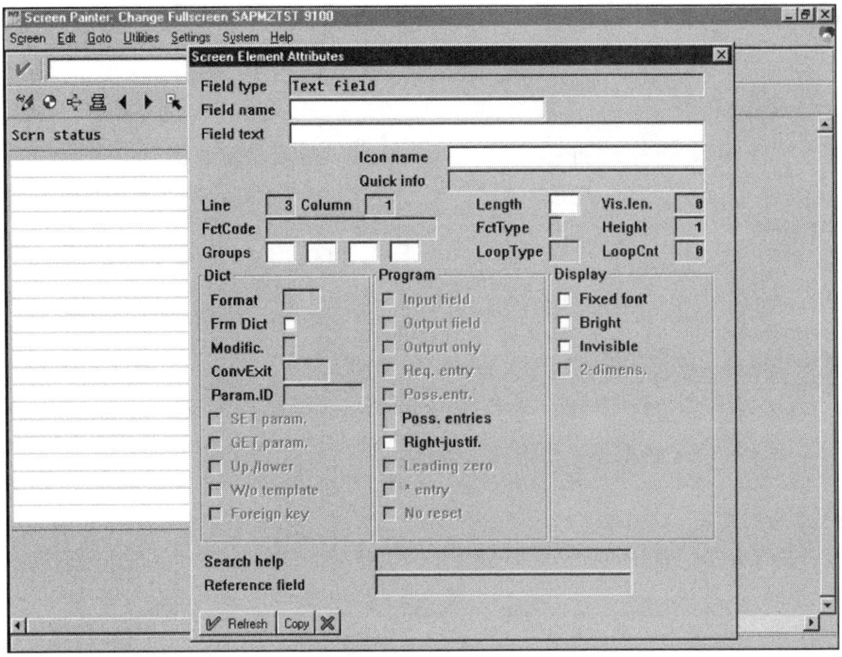

FIGURE 14-6

Screen Element Attributes

Screen 9100 starts out blank with no text boxes or descriptive texts. The Fullscreen editor is used to add any object to a screen. For this introduction we will add some simple text boxes and descriptions. Start by adding a simple text element, or text label, describing the purpose of your new screen. Click the fourth line down, then select Edit | Create element | Key word/text. This opens the Screen Element Attributes dialog box, shown in Figure 14-6.

Every object that appears on a screen has its own attributes. For now, name the text object by typing &MAINDESC as its field name and Enter two numbers to find the sum as its label. Click the Bright button to add a bold appearance to the object, then click the Refresh button to view your changes. As shown in Figure 14-7, fields, line, column, length, and vis. length are completed.

At this point we are ready to hit the copy button to create the text element. When complete, your screen will look similar to Figure 14-8. The location at which you originally clicked (before selecting Edit | Create element | Key word/text) is where the element will be placed.

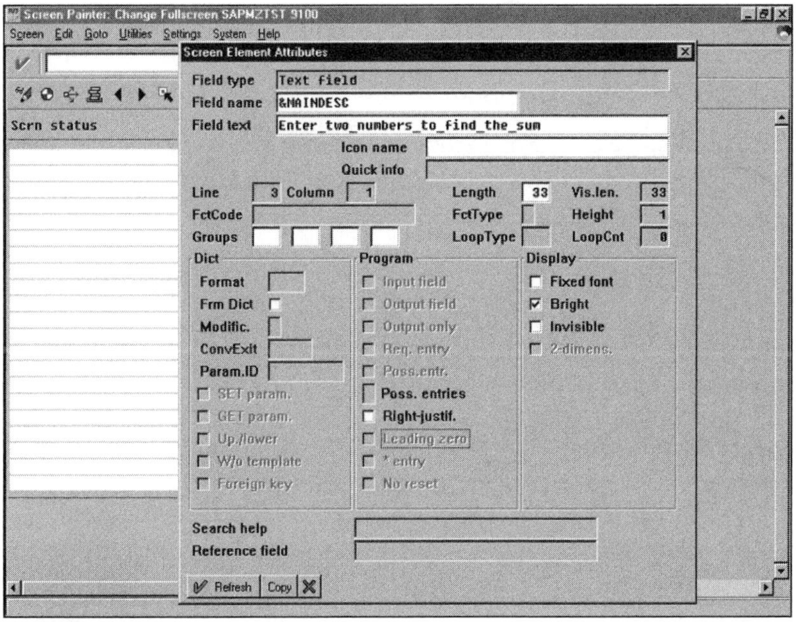

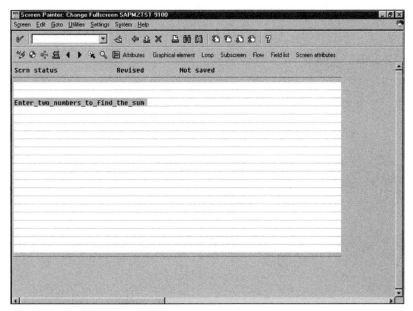

FIGURE 14-7

Attributes for &MAINDESC element

FIGURE 14-8

Calculator screen with text element added

Now that a text label is in place, you can add the input fields to your new screen. Remember that the calculator is designed so that the user can type two numbers. The calculator will then compute their sum.

To create the first field in which the user will type a number, click on the line below the label just added and select Edit | Create element | Input/Output from the window menu bar. The Attribute dialog box, shown in Figure 14-9, will open.

Complete the attributes for this input field by typing XNUM1 as the field name, and 8 as its length. Then press Enter (see Figure 14-10). This verifies that the input field allows entry of up to eight characters. To limit entry to four-byte integers, change the format field to INT4. Click the Copy button to add the element to your screen. Now add the second input field using the same procedure. Name this second field XNUM2. All remaining attributes are the same ones used for the first input field. Your screen will now look similar to Figure 14-11.

The calculator screen now contains the two input fields that will be used to enter the two numbers to be added. An output field is needed to display that sum. The same input fields we created earlier can act as output-only fields simply by setting the correct attributes. To add a third element to the screen, select Edit | Create

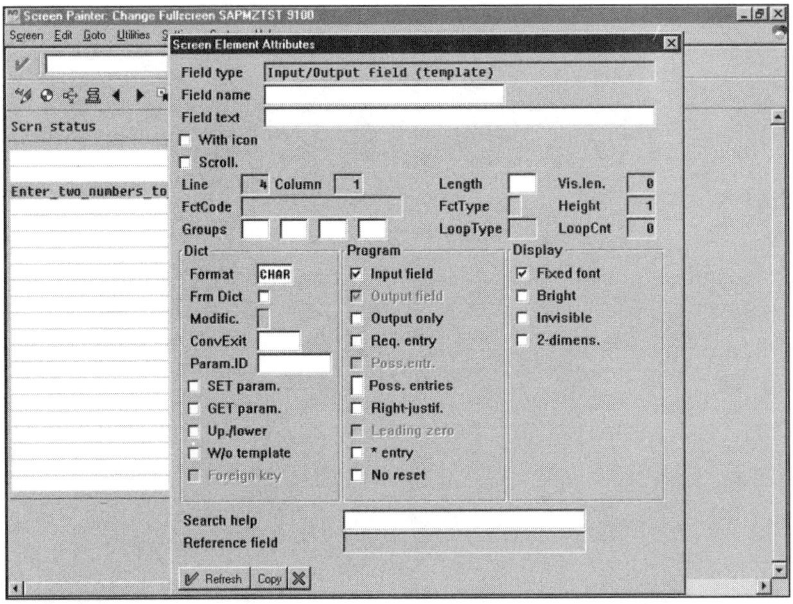

FIGURE 14-9

Input/Output element attributes

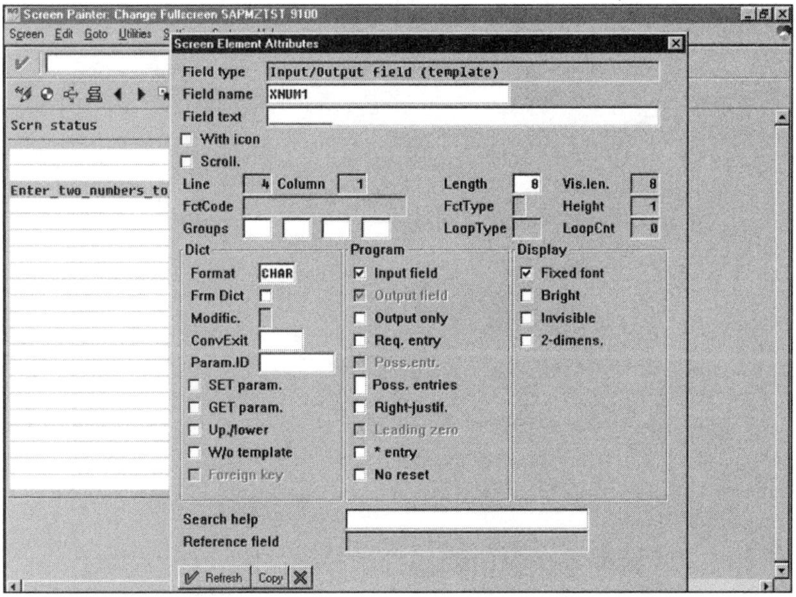

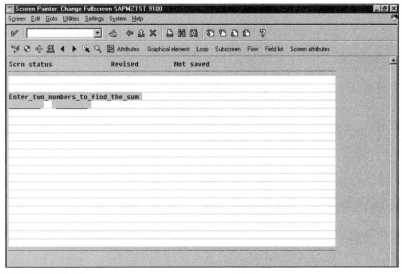

FIGURE 14-10

Attributes for XNUM1 Element

FIGURE 14-11

Calculator screen with input elements added

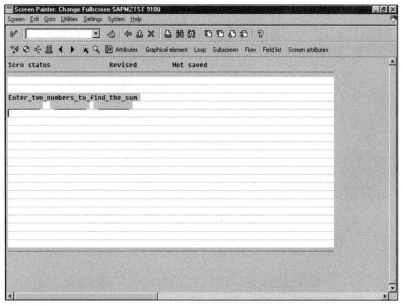

FIGURE 14-12

Calculator screen with output element added

element | Input/Output to open the Attributes dialog box. Complete the attributes by typing XRESULT as the field name, 8 as the length, and INT4 as the format. To force output only, clear the Input field check box, leaving the Output field check box checked. This will prevent the user from entering data into this field, allowing your transaction to display data in this field. Click the Copy button to view your screen. It should look something like Figure 14-12.

At this point, your screen is complete and you are ready to move onto the next step in transaction development. You might want to go back to the main menu and click the Test button to see what your screen looks like with your changes complete. It should look similar to Figure 14-13.

Step Three: Create a GUI Status

Creating the GUI status to be used with the Calculator transaction is the next step. In R/3, the GUI status can be thought of as the frame through which your screen is presented. The GUI status is made up of several components such as the menu bar and the toolbars that appear above your screen. For your simple example, only the most basic GUI status with only a few components needs to be created. A GUI status is maintained by the Menu Painter transaction. Open the main screen of the Menu Painter, shown in Figure 14-14, using the transaction code SE41.

The first step in building a GUI status is to type the name of your module pool, SAPMZTST, in the Program field. Next, give the GUI status a name. Type E100 in the Status field (see Figure 14-14). Click the Create button to open the Create Status dialog box shown in Figure 14-15. In the Short Text field, type Enter numbers to be calculated. Make sure the Online Status option button is selected, and then press Enter. The Maintain Status screen will appear next. From this screen you can maintain the components of your GUI status. See Figure 14-16.

FIGURE 14-13

Test of calculator screen

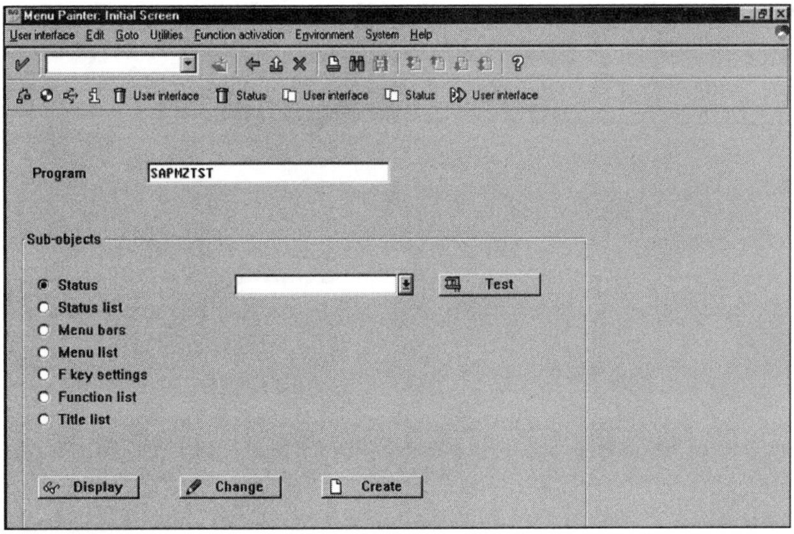

FIGURE 14-14

Main screen of Menu Painter transaction

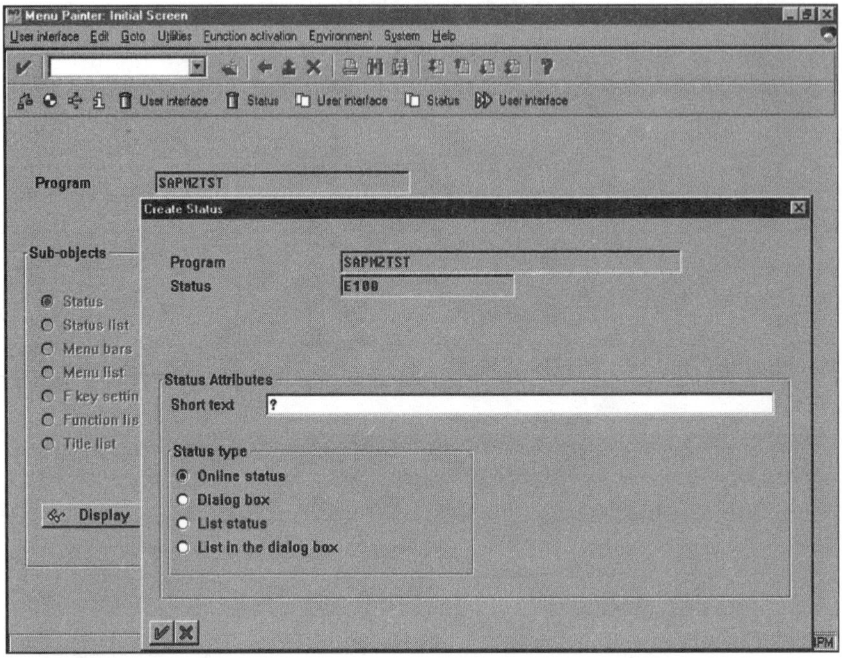

FIGURE 14-15

Create Status dialog box

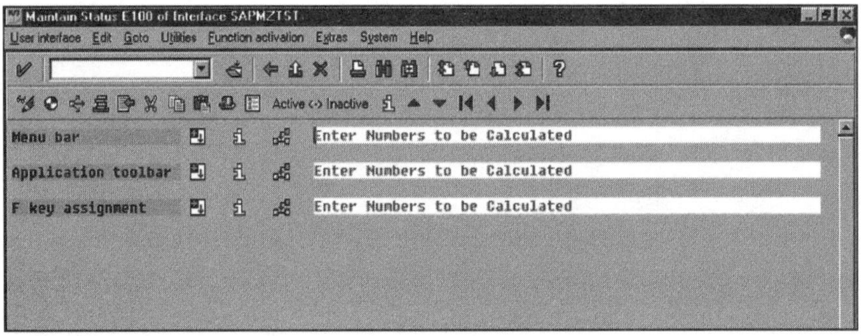

FIGURE 14-16

Maintain Status Screen

Next, add a menu bar to the GUI status. To do so, click the Menu Bar button; a new menu bar appears at the top of the screen displaying its default title and up to six standard menu names. The menu bar title defaults to the name of the screen. You can change each menu name to anything you want, but most SAP transactions follow a certain standard. The standard names of the menus are

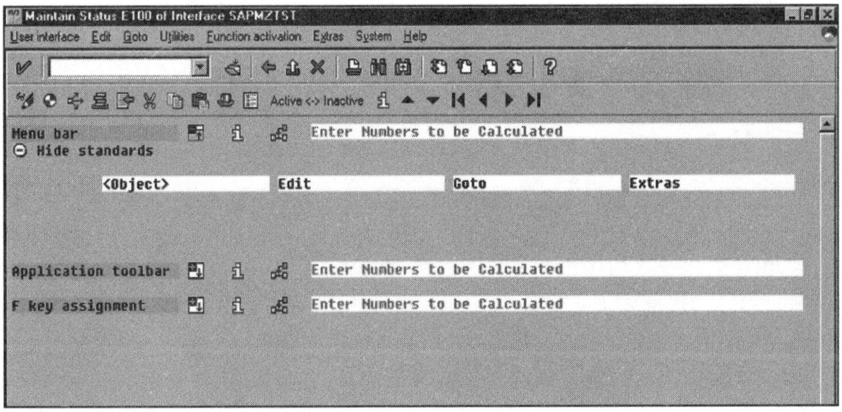

FIGURE 14-17

Status with standard menu names

Object, Edit, GoTo, Extras, and Environment, where object is the name of the object that the transaction affects. For example, a transaction that creates sales order would have "Sales Order" in place of object. You can have SAP suggest these standards for you by clicking on the text "Display Standards." After doing this, the screen should look like Figure 14-17.

To customize the standard menu names, click the menu name Object and simply type the replacement menu name, Calculate. A menu bar will not display an empty menu, so double-click on the menu name Calculate to display the menu's empty drop-down list. In the drop-down list are a number of suggestions for SAP standards. Replace the first command with ADD in the code column and Add Numbers in the text. Be aware that this new menu will not actually do anything at this point; but it will look good. For now, that is enough. Click the Save button to save your changes and return to the GUI status screen.

Once you have created a GUI status and added a menu bar, you must add its title. Every transaction screen has a title. In R/3, the title is a part of the GUI status; in fact, a GUI status can have multiple titles. In this example, one is sufficient. To create it, select Title List, then click the Create button. Type 100 in the number field and Calculator as the title and click the Save button. Finally, go back to the main screen.

Step Four: Add Flow Logic and Transaction Logic

Adding the flow logic and the transaction logic is the final step in creating an SAP transaction. Flow logic is a programming language similar to ABAP, which is used to control events during screen processing. There are two main events that occur during screen processing: Process Before Output (PBO) and Process After Input (PAI). It is these two events around which the flow logic is written. Transaction logic refers to the ABAP code that executes the database and other operations the transaction is to carry out.

The Process Before Output event is triggered before the screen is presented to the user. During this event, the programmer can control what data will be presented to the user. The Process After Input event is triggered when a user completes data entry and triggers a function. A function can be triggered by pressing the Enter key, clicking a button on the screen or on a toolbar, or by selecting a menu command. During this event, the programmer can process the data entered by the user and prepare for the PBO event, which will occur next.

The flow logic does not actually perform any operations; it simply controls processing of the screen. In order to do something, you must call ABAP code. This is done using the module command in flow logic. Add some simple flow logic to get your calculator up and running.

Flow logic is edited from Screen Painter, transaction SE51. From Screen Painter, identify the screen on which you want to work by typing the module pool name SAPMZTST in the Program field and 9100 in the Screen Number field. Click Flow Logic, and then click the Change button to access the editor where the default flow logic appears. The default flow logic simply consists of the keyword for each event and a commented module call. Figure 14-18 shows the editor and a screen's default flow logic.

In flow logic, the MODULE command calls a subroutine much like the PERFORM command in ABAP. Start by removing the commenting asterisk from the line of code 'module status_9100'. The first thing you must do in the PBO event is to instruct the module to set the GUI status. Double-click the module name to open the Create Object dialog box, as seen in Figure 14-19. Click the Yes button. You will be prompted to save the change to the flow logic. An include file is suggested in which to create the status_9100 module. Accept the suggestion to open the new include file in the ABAP editor so that the transaction logic can be added.

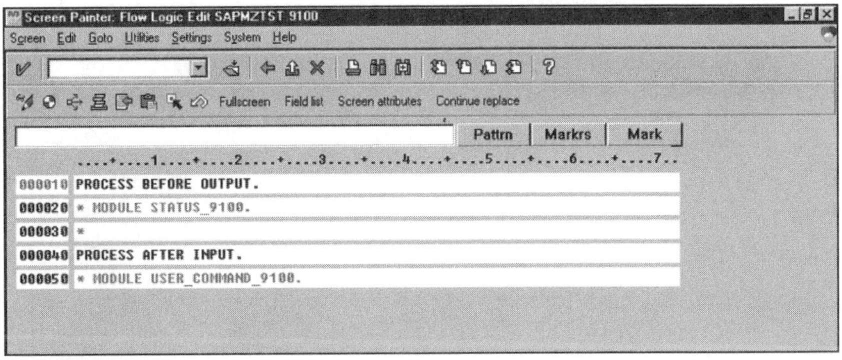

FIGURE 14-18

Flow logic editor and default flow logic

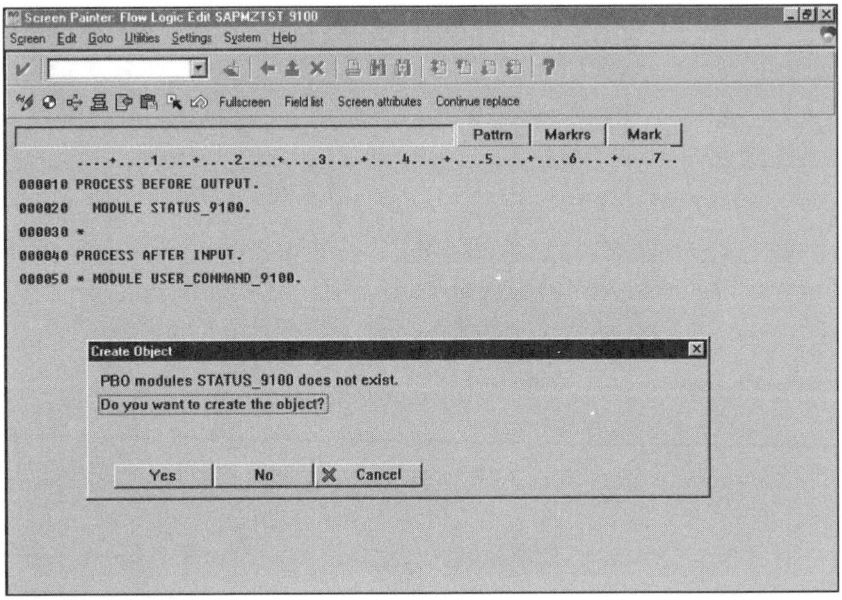

FIGURE 14-19

Create Object dialog box

As seen in Figure 14-20, SAP will suggest some commands for you. A module is defined by the MODULE ... ENDMODULE commands much like the FORM ... ENDFORM commands define a form. The SET command assigns a number of different transaction attributes. The calculator transaction requires that the GUI status and title bar be specified using the SET command.

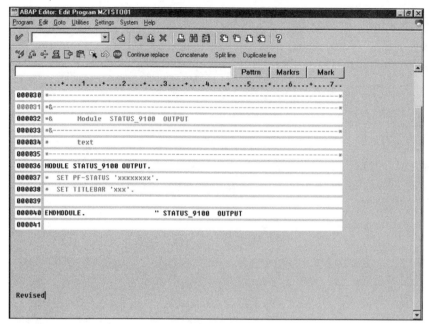

FIGURE 14-20

Default module commands

Remove the asterisks from each line, then type E100 as the name of the GUI status and 100 to identify the title bar. Your module should look like this:

```
*_____.
*&_____*
*&      Module   STATUS_9100   OUTPUT
*&_____*
*       text                                              *
*_____.*
module status_9100 output.
  SET PF-STATUS 'E100'.
  SET TITLEBAR '100'.

endmodule.                   " STATUS_9100   OUTPUT
```

Every time your screen reaches the PBO event, it will use the GUI status and title bar you created earlier due to the SET command. When you have completed your edits, save the changes and return to the flow logic editor.

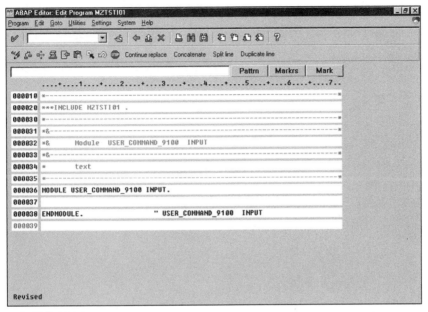

FIGURE 14-21

ABAP Editor and a new module

With the PBO logic complete, you can now complete the PAI logic. The PAI logic is where the heart of the transaction is found. When using the sample calculator, the user will enter two numbers, and press Enter. The PAI event will then provide the sum of those two numbers.

As before, remove the commenting asterisk from the user_command_9100 line, and then double-click to open. Follow the same set of instructions as before to create an include and reach the ABAP editor. You should see the ABAP editor, as shown in Figure 14-21. Now you can go ahead and write the ABAP code to sum the user's input and return the results.

The Calculator screen now contains three fields: XNUM1, XNUM2, and XRESULT. One of the great properties of SAP module programming is the way it handles screen fields. If you give a global variable in your module pool the same name as a screen field, then SAP matches the data held by the variable and displays it in the screen field having the same name. For example, if in your ABAP code you set the variable XRESULT equal to the value 7, then after the next PBO event the field XRESULT on your screen will display the number 7. On the other hand, if a user enters the value 100 in the XNUM1 screen field, then after the next PAI event the variable XNUM1 will also equal 100. It is a simple concept, but it makes module programming much easier because you do not need to worry about moving data back and forth between your code and the screen.

With the knowledge of how data is shared between variable and screen fields, it becomes pretty easy to write the ABAP code needed to sum the numbers entered by the user:

```
*_____*
***INCLUDE MZTSTI01 .
*_____*
*&_____*
*&      Module  USER_COMMAND_9100  INPUT
*&_____*
*       text                                    *
*_____*
module user_command_9100 input.


*XNUM1 and XNUM2 are entered by the user.
*XRESULT is the sum to be returned to the  user
xresult = xnum1 + xnum2.


endmodule.                  " USER_COMMAND_9100  INPUT
```

Use the syntax checker to verify that the code entered is correct by selecting Program | Check | Main Program. You should see an error message that says, "Field "XNUM1" is unknown." This error occurs because XNUM1 is in neither of the specified tables nor defined by a DATA statement. Even though a screen field was created for XRESULT, the associated global variable was not created in the module pool. The easiest way to create the global variables is to double-click the variable name XRESULT. This opens the Create Object dialog box. When prompted, answer yes to allow the global variable to be created in the default include program. The variable declaration should look like this:

```
data: xresult type i,
      xnum1 type i,
      xnum2 type i.
```

Save your changes, then run the syntax checker again. You should get no errors.

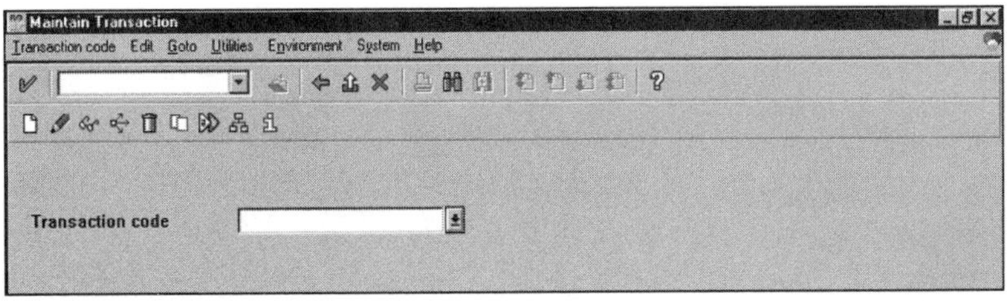

FIGURE 14-22

Create transaction code

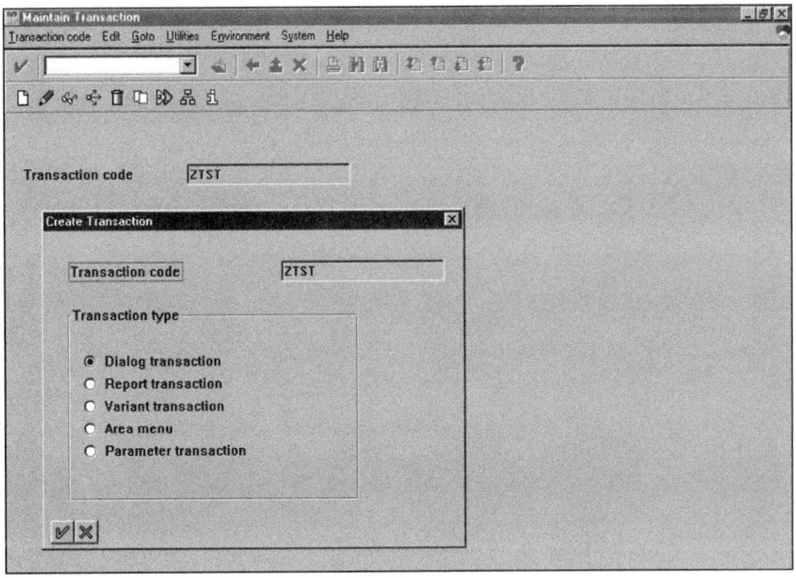

FIGURE 14-23

Create Transaction dialog box

This means your flow logic is now complete.

One last step is necessary before you can use your new transaction. As you know, every SAP transaction has executable transaction code. In the sample Calculator, that transaction code still needs to be created so that the SAPMZTST module pool can be run. Transaction codes are created using transaction SE93. The first screen you will see is shown in Figure 14-22.

Your transaction code name should match the last four characters of your module pool name. Type ZTST in the transaction code field and then select Transaction Code | Create. The next dialog box, shown in Figure 14-23, will ask what type of transaction code you want to create.

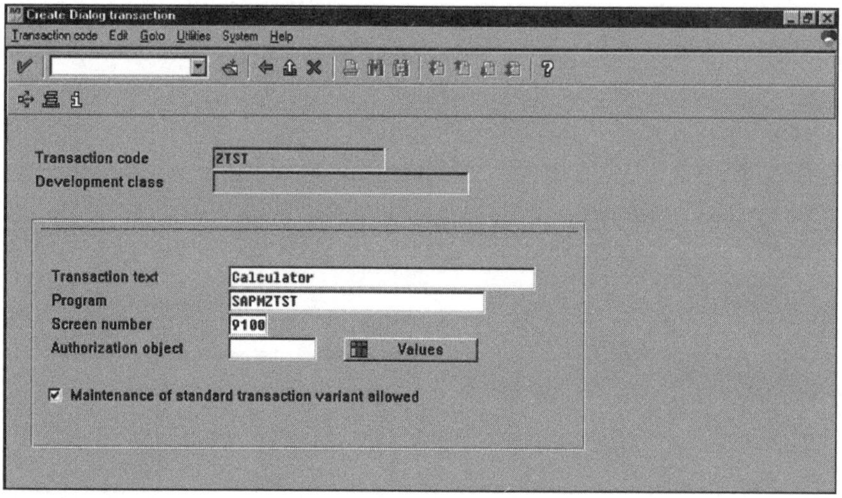

FIGURE 14-24

Transaction Code attributes

Select the Dialog Transaction radio button, then press Enter. Referring to Figure 14-24, complete the attributes for your transaction code. Save the transaction when you are done.

Now that the transaction code is complete, you can execute your calculator transaction for the first time. At the command line, type ZTST, then press Enter. Your completed screen, as shown in Figure 14-25, will appear.

Test your screen by typing numbers in the input fields and pressing Enter to calculate their sum. If you change the numbers and press Enter, you will see the sum change. Notice that the screen also displays a menu with menu names of Calculate, System, and Help. System and Help are always available; Calculate appears because it was added along with a function code. The other default menus (like Edit) do not appear because SAP will not display an empty menu.

When you are ready to move on, notice that the normal SAP navigation buttons, like the green back button and the yellow exit button, are disabled. There is no way to leave your new transaction. As you will see in future chapters, all of the normal SAP navigation functionality must be programmed into each transaction. Luckily, after you create your first transaction, you can use the various copy functions to reuse the navigation code you write. In this simple transaction, logic was not added to allow the user to exit the transaction. The command line is always available, however. Type /N, then press Enter to exit the transaction.

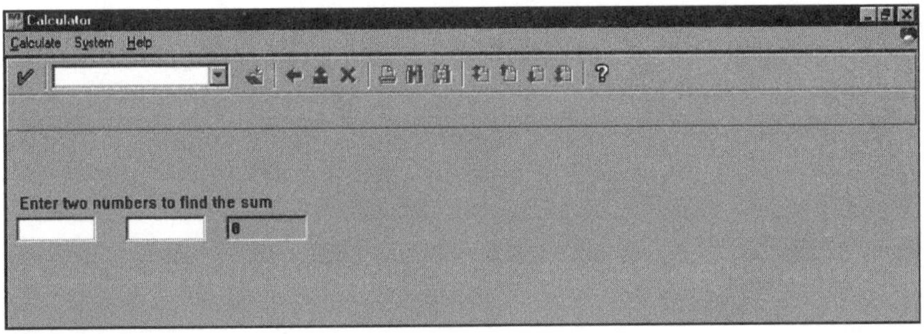

FIGURE 14-25

ZTST screen

Summary

Even the simplest transaction is far more complicated than an ABAP program. Every transaction is made up of several components, which are all interdependent. This is why it is always important to make sure that a solution really requires a transaction and cannot be done with an ABAP program. You can learn more about each step of transaction development in later chapters, while expanding the functionality of this calculator example.

In the following chapters you will learn in detail about the Screen Painter and Menu Painter transactions as well as how to write ABAP code to build transaction logic.

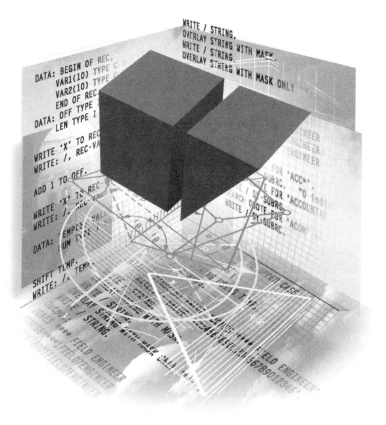

Chapter 15

**Using the
Screen Painter**

In This Chapter

◆ Setting screen attributes

◆ Editing screens in screen painter

◆ Adding text fields

◆ Adding graphical elements

◆ Adding input/output elements

◆ Adding buttons and boxes

In this chapter, the Screen Painter will be explored in detail. You will learn how to add different types of objects to a screen, format the screen with graphics, assign function codes to different types of buttons, and other screen-related activities.

Working with Screen Painter

As described earlier, the screen is the interface to the user executing the transaction. Unlike a standard ABAP report, you cannot use the WRITE statement to return information to the user. You can only return data using the fields you have predefined on the screen.

Setting Screen Attributes

Rather than completely creating a new transaction, a copy of the ZTST transaction created in Chapter 14 can be made so that we do not have to start from scratch. Once you have completed a few transactions, you can use the copy function to save time when creating new transactions.

To make a copy, go to the Object Browser, SE80. Select Program Objects, click Edit, then type SAPMZTST in the Program field. Verify that Program is selected, then choose Development object | Copy. When prompted for the source and target, type SAPMZTST and SAPMZTS2, respectively. Figure 15-1 shows the Program dialog box that appears, asking which parts of the program to copy. Check the boxes for GUI status, Screens, and Includes, then press Enter. When another dialog box opens displaying the default names for the include programs being copied, press Enter again.

You now have a complete copy of your first module pool including screens, statuses, and flow logic. The piece of the transaction that does not get copied is

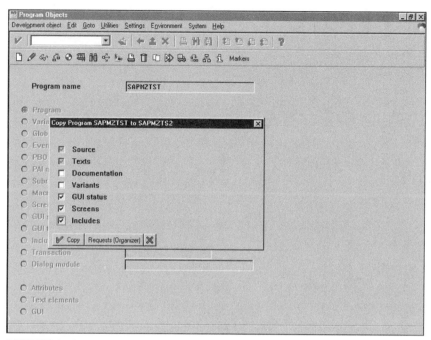

FIGURE 15-1

Copy Program dialog box

the transaction code, ZTST. Create a new transaction code, ZTS2, which refers to SAPMTS2, but this time use screen 9200 instead of 9100. We will use much of the code from ZTST, but we will create a new screen for this transaction and that is we want to use 9200 in the transaction code. Refer to Chapter 14 if you have problems creating the transaction code using transaction SE93, Maintain Transaction.

Now, open the Screen Painter with transaction code SE51 and type SAPMZTS2. In the Screen Number field, type 9200 and click the Create button to open the Screen Attributes, as seen in Figure 15-2.

The first piece of information to be entered here is the short description. Make sure you use a description that will identify its purpose for anyone who later looks at it. If you cannot come up with a short description, you may be trying to do too many things with a single screen. There is nothing wrong with creating multiple screens if it will simplify the interface for the user.

The next information you must provide is the screen type. Three screen types are available: normal, modal dialog box, and subscreen. A normal screen is what you

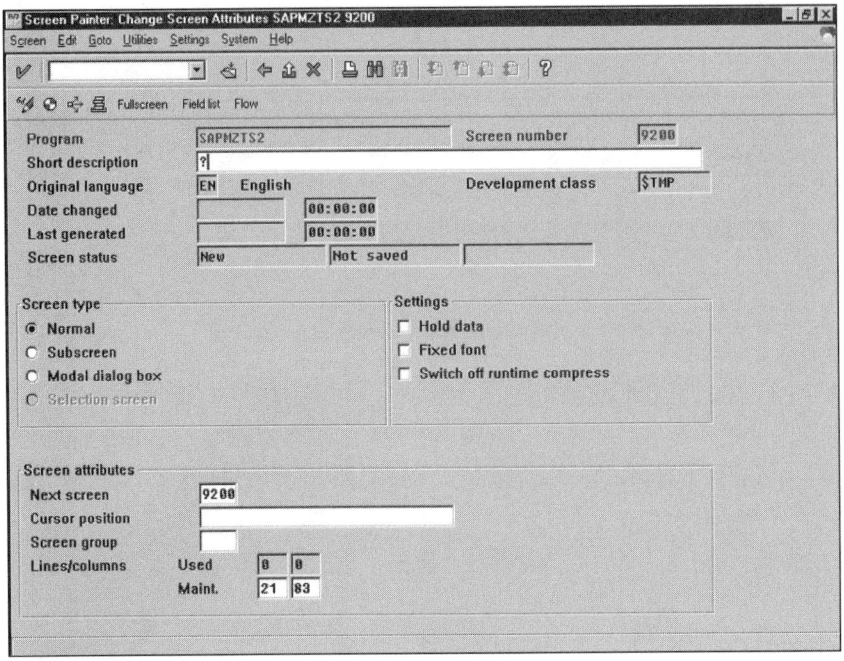

FIGURE 15-2

Screen Attributes dialog box

see when you start most transactions. It is a screen that occupies a full window, and the user is allowed to manipulate it in standard ways such as maximize, minimize, and resize. Use a normal screen when creating a screen to display a large amount of data or allow a user to enter a large amount of data. The next screen type is a modal dialog box. These are the standard dialog boxes you see when the system wants to ask a user a question such as whether or not to save data when exiting a screen. Here the main screen does not change, but a second, usually smaller screen, opens and the user cannot return to the main screen until this second dialog box is processed. Typically, modal dialog boxes are used for small amounts of important data. Sometimes they will inform the user of critical information such as an error. Other times they are used to pose a question such as confirming if the user really wants to exit a transaction. The strength of the modal dialog box comes from the fact that the user cannot return to the main screen until the user deals with the dialog box. In Figure 15-3, the dialog box with the title "Help - Screen Painter" is a modal dialog box.

The final screen type is a subscreen. A subscreen can be called by a normal screen and appear as part of that normal screen. You must define a block of space when

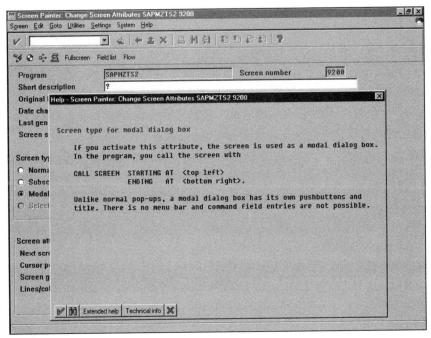

FIGURE 15-3

Example of a modal dialog box

creating the normal screen in which the subscreen will appear. The power of subscreens is that they are called dynamically. A single normal screen can call several different subscreens so the normal screen has the effect of changing based on user input. Many of the SAP written transactions you are familiar with use subscreens. The major benefit of using subscreens is to reduce the number of screens you need to create. If you create a single normal screen and several subscreens, you can display several different sets of data on a single screen. For example, if you create a transaction to display financial data, you can alter the fields that are displayed based on user input. By default, the screen might show data from a material perspective, but the user can click a button and the data will switch to a customer perspective without changing screens. Subscreens are covered in detail in Chapter 20.

The next information which may be provided to the editor is the attribute information. Several fields may be maintained:

Next Screen defines the screen that will be displayed by default after the current screen closes. This field by default assigns its own screen number; usually you can leave this default. In general, however, this field is not used because you should call screens dynamically in your transaction logic. The point of developing a custom transaction is to allow the user to interact with the program and decide when to move from one screen to another or when to exit. Obviously, the value in this field cannot anticipate what the user will want to do, thus you will want to control what screens are displayed dynamically in the program.

Cursor Position allows you to place the cursor in a specific field when your screen is first called. If not explicitly assigned through the cursor position attribute, the cursor will appear in the top, left field on your screen. Unlike many programming tools such as Visual Basic, SAP does not allow you to define a tab order for the fields of a screen. Also, you cannot set fields to be skipped from the tab order. The only thing you can control is where the cursor first appears on a screen. After that, when the user presses Tab, the cursor will simply jump through the controls from left to right, top to bottom. Thus it is critical to think ahead when laying out fields on your screen. Think about what fields are required and what the most logical order for the user to enter them would be. The goal is to minimize the amount of mouse usage the user will have to perform. If the critical fields are laid out right to left, top to bottom, the user can enter the data and use tab to quickly move to the next field. Otherwise, the user will have to take a hand off the keyboard and move the cursor with the mouse. If your transaction is being used to enter large amounts of data for minutes or even hours at a time, this added effort will cause even the best transaction to be disliked by its users.

Screen Group is a four-character code that you can assign to screens. By assigning the same code to several screens you can identify those screens at run time and perform actions on all of them. The group code for the current screen can be read from the system field SY-DYNGR during transaction execution. For example, you might want to perform a security check on several different screens in a transaction. By assigning them all a code of CHEK, you can check each screen as it is displayed using a single piece of code and trigger the check based on the group code instead of hard coding screen numbers, which might change at a later time.

The Lines/Columns fields show how many lines and columns are used by the objects, such as fields and buttons, on your screen. In the Maint fields you can define the total size of the screen by entering numbers for the lines and columns of the screen. The total size may be larger than the size used; this will simply make the window larger than needed to display all objects. In a normal screen, this has limited effect since the user can always control the size of the window they are using by resizing the window. In a dialog box, this is powerful since the user cannot change the size of a modal dialog box. So, even if you have one or two buttons on a dialog box, you can make it very large to attract attention from the user.

The Hold Data Box enables support for the hold data function when checked. If you allow hold data, then the user running the transaction can use the System | User Profile | Hold Data function to retain entries made in all fields appearing on the screen. When that user encounters the screen again, the previous entries will appear. This is very useful for people entering large amounts of data for which many fields do not change.

The Fixed Font box forces all text to be displayed on the screen in fixed font instead of the standard proportional font when checked.

The Switch Off Runtime Compression check box turns off runtime compression of the screen. By default, SAP will compress the screen if there are lines that hold no useful data. This box prevents that compression in most cases. Normally there is no need to check this box. Check the online help for this box for more details.

For this example (screen 9200), type Test as a short description and select normal as the screen type. Leave the remaining default values unless you want to experiment with anything; none of the other attributes will prevent you from continuing with this chapter. When you've completed your settings, save the screen, and then click the Fullscreen button to open the full screen editor.

Editing Screens in Screen Painter

Before discussing the different elements that can be added to a screen, it's important that you are comfortable with some of the basics of how to edit a screen. Many of the normal editing tools you would expect are available in Screen Painter. Functions such as copy, paste, delete, and move are available. To add a simple text field to the screen, choose Edit | Create element | Text field to open the Element Attributes dialog box shown in Figure 15-4.

Name the text field &DESC, with a label Some random text, then click the Copy button to add it to the screen. Now add a second text field below and to the right of the first. Use a name and label of your choice. Your screen should now look similar to Figure 15-5.

To insert a blank line between the two text fields, click on the lower field and choose Edit lines | Insert line from the Edit menu. This will result in a blank line being added above the current line. To practice deleting a line, click on a blank

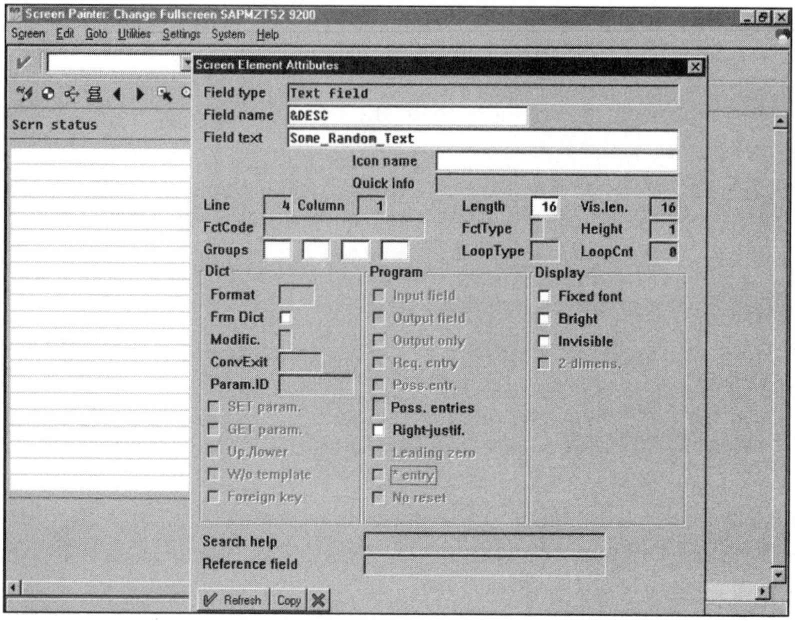

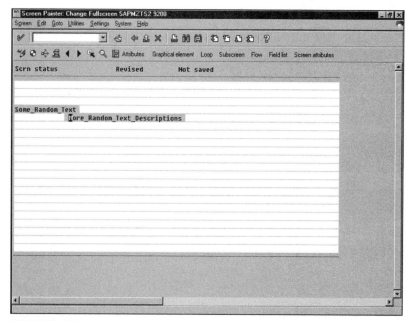

FIGURE 15-4

The Screen Element attributes dialog box

FIGURE 15-5

A screen with two text fields

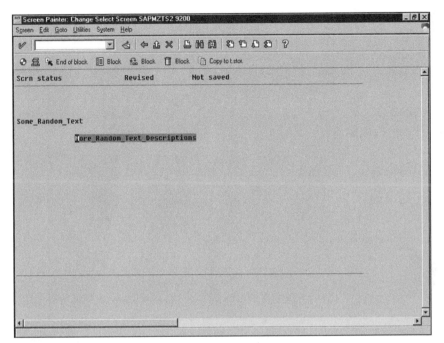

FIGURE 15-6

Example of selecting a text field

line and select | Edit lines | Delete line. This deletes the line on which your cursor was located. Be careful with the Delete Line command. It will also delete lines that contain fields. To do so on purpose, click on one of your fields, then choose Edit | Edit lines | Delete line. Before continuing through this chapter, re-create any deleted fields.

Elements can also be moved to new positions on the screen. To do so, select the field to be moved by double-clicking on it. With a selected field, the screen changes color and a new toolbar appears, indicating that you are now in block mode. See Figure 15-6 to view the screen appearance during block mode.

To move the element, click the location at which you want the element to appear, and then click Move button. The Move button is a little difficult to locate–it's labeled with three circles and an arrow and is located between the Delete Block button and the Block End button. Refer to Figure 15-6 for its screen location. After you click on the move button the element now appears in its new location and the screen returns to normal. Figure 15-7 shows the results of a field move.

You can move a group of fields together by double-clicking the first field to be included in the group. The screen changes color and you can expand the block

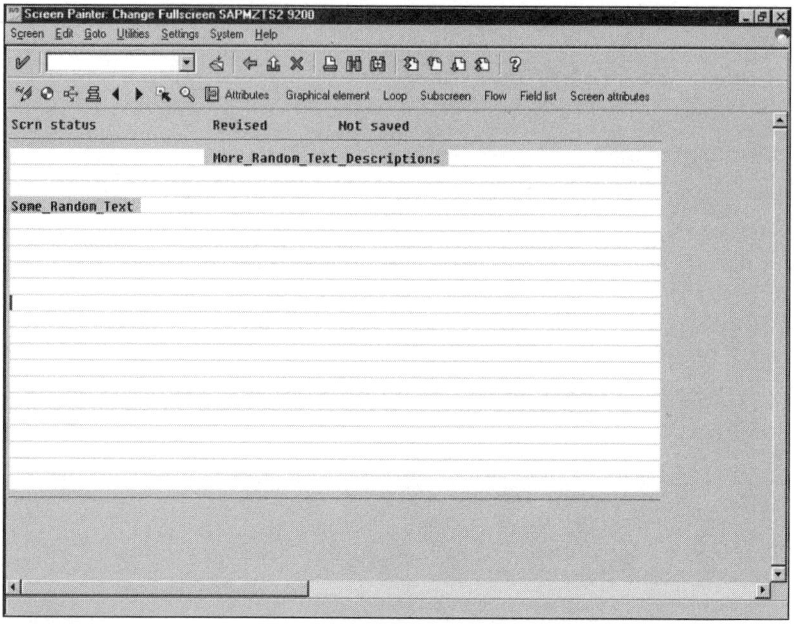

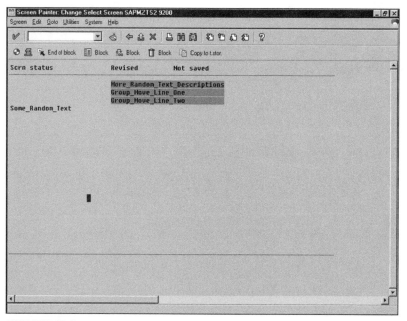

FIGURE 15-7

Screen after field move

FIGURE 15-8

Selecting a block of fields

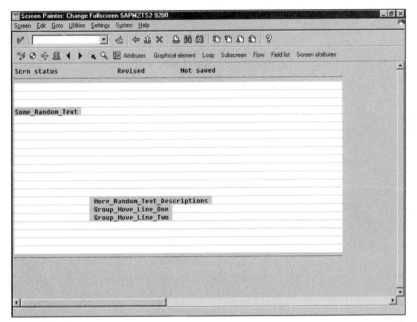

FIGURE 15-9

Screen after moving a block of fields

to include additional fields to be moved. The field you first selected becomes the start of the block. By clicking again somewhere on the screen, the block expands to include any field between the original field and where you clicked the second time.

With all fields selected, click the screen location you want to become the top, left corner of the block and click the Move button. Figures 15-8 and 15-9 illustrate an example of a group of fields before and after a move.

A few more options appear when you are in block mode. These options affect all elements in the selected block. The Delete button will delete all objects and the Copy to T. Stor. (copy to temporary storage) button will copy the objects to the clipboard. You can then use the Edit menu command Clipboard | Ins. frm. temp stor. to paste these objects to another screen. This is useful for transactions with multiple screens that have some objects in common.

Lastly, the ruler command comes in handy when editing a screen. Use the command Edit | Ruler on/off to toggle the screen ruler. See Figure 15-10 for an example of a screen with the ruler on.

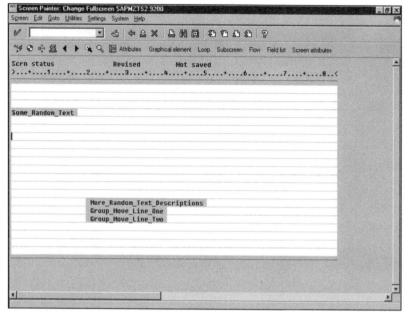

FIGURE 15-10

Screen Painter with ruler on

Adding Text Fields

Now that you have learned the basics of editing a screen, you can begin to create some objects for your screen. As you have seen before, the screen initially is blank. You add the fields and other objects needed to process the transaction. Use the block functionality to delete any fields on your screen so you can start fresh.

The most basic type of object is the text field. To add a text field, use the Edit menu command Create element | Text field to open the Element Attributes dialog box shown in Figure 15-11.

Initially the attribute fields, which can be changed, are Field name, Field text, Icon name, Group, From dict, Fixed font, Bright, Invisible, and Right-justified. You must complete the Field name, and either Field text or Icon name. Once you complete the required fields, the Length and Visible length fields are automatically completed, as seen in Figure 15-12. The next few paragraphs discuss the purpose of each of the attribute fields.

Field name is the label that identifies this field. In general it's standard practice to begin a field name with the "&" symbol if it is a text field that does not come from the Data Dictionary. This helps distinguish fields that are not tied to Data Dictionary objects or program variables.

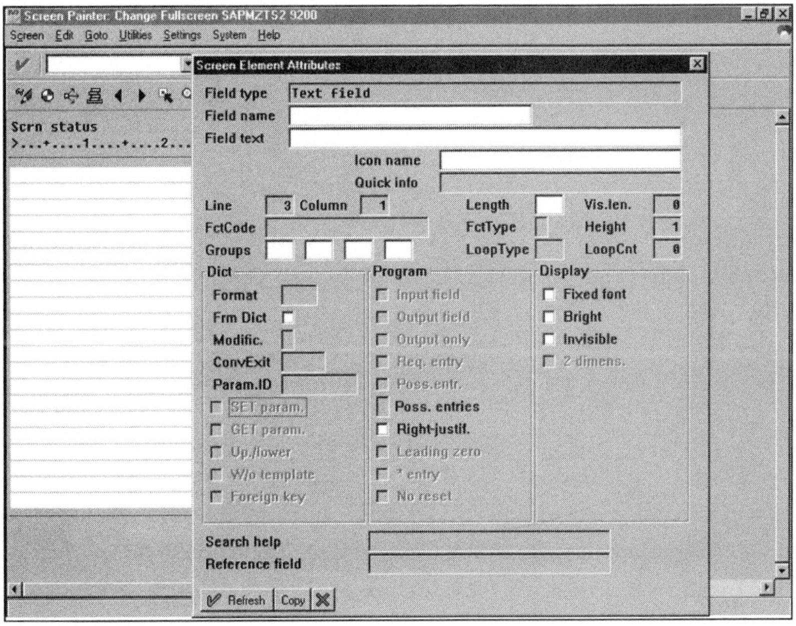

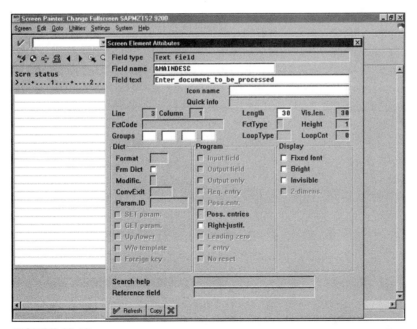

FIGURE 15-11

Text Field attributes

FIGURE 15-12

Text Field attributes after entering required fields

Field text is a phrase that appears on the screen. It can be used to tell the user what information should be typed in the field. Field text is case sensitive. Further, SAP will replace any spaces you use with underscores.

Icon name allows you to display an icon along with its description. Click the arrow to open a list of all icons and their default descriptions. It is not possible to add your own icons to the list.

The Quick info field, enabled only if an icon is selected, presents the description when the cursor is held over the icon.

Frm dict (from dictionary) indicates that this text field should be taken from the Data Dictionary. As you saw in earlier chapters, when a data element is defined you must supply a default text description. By checking this box, the system will get that default description and fill the text field with it. In order for this to work, your field name must match the name of a table field name active in the Data Dictionary (for example, VBAK-VBELN, the sales order document number creates a default description of "Sales order"). A full example of using Data Dictionary fields is presented next.

Fixed font indicates that the text for this field will be displayed in fixed font rather than the standard proportional font.

Bright indicates the text for this field will appear in bold.

Invisible hides the field from the user. This can be useful to conceal or reveal a field based on particular input. In later chapters you will learn how to modify screen fields at run time. So a field that starts out as invisible can have the invisible attribute turned off based on user actions.

Right-justif (right-justification) aligns text at the right edge of the field length.

Group fields allow you to assign four character codes to this field. If you assign several fields the same group ID, you can identify them at run time and modify them together. For example, you might assign several fields the code "INVS" and select the invisible field for them. Then, at run time, based on user input, the invisible attribute for all fields with the group id of "INVS" can be removed. This type of run-time modification of fields will be explained in detail in Chapter 18.

Give this new text field the name of &DESC1, text of Enter document to be processed, and icon name of ICON_LED_RED. Now, copy it to the screen and you should see something like Figure 15-13.

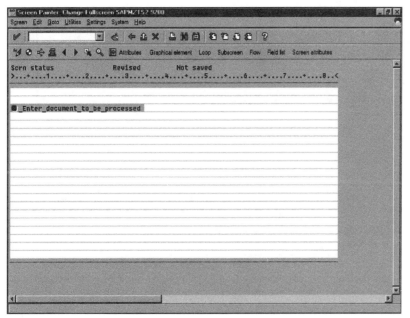

FIGURE 15-13

Screen with &DESC1 text field

Next, add a text field from the Data Dictionary. Choose Edit | Create element| Text field to create a new text field. In the Attributes dialog box, name the field VBAK-VBELN, click the Frm dict. box and press Enter. The ABAP dictionary will open (see Figure 15-14). From this dialog box, you can choose which of the descriptions from the Data Dictionary you want to use. You can use the suggested short, medium, long, or heading descriptions or you can choose Leave Modified to overwrite the dictionary default with your own description. For this example, select the medium keyword. SAP will complete the field with the text Sales_document_.

TIP

There is no automatic link between the Data Dictionary and the screens you will create. If someone changes the medium description for VBAK-VBELN in the dictionary, this dialog box will not be automatically updated. A person must manually edit the field, then use the Refresh button to refresh the values from the dictionary and change the field text if needed.

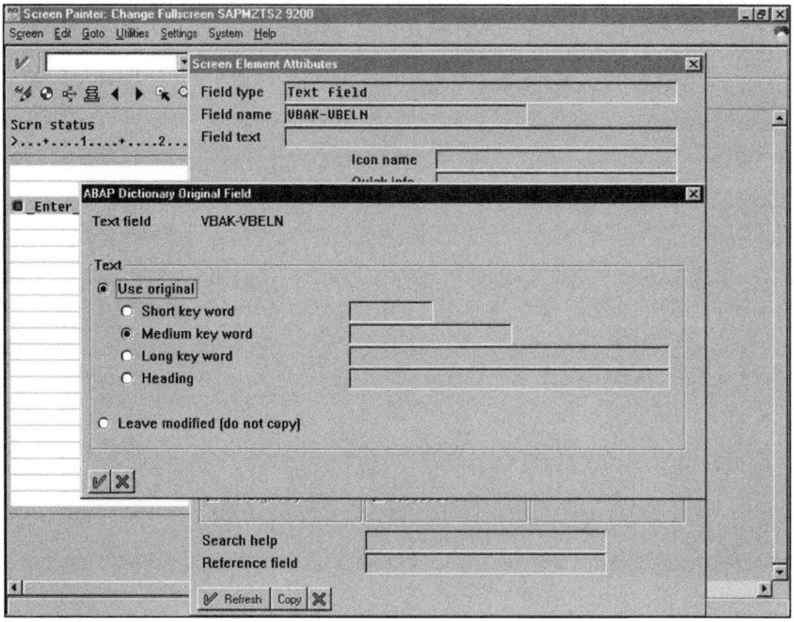

FIGURE 15-14

Dictionary Description dialog box

Whether you assign the field text manually or retrieve it from the Data Dictionary, when creating a text element the other attributes can be set in the same way.

Adding Graphical Elements

SAP supports a single type of graphical element for screens—a box. You can draw a box around any area on your screen and add a title for the box. In Figure 15-15, you can see a screen from the transaction Create Material (MM01) that uses several boxes to improve the readability of the screen. The boxes group related fields and have titles such as General Data, Material Authorizations, and Dimensions. This helps the user recognize the purpose of the field and assists the user in entering data. Boxes are a quick way to improve your user interface.

Creating a box works much like selecting a group of fields. In the original calculator transaction, open screen 9100 for SAPMZTST in the full screen editor. Currently, the ZTST transaction looks something like Figure 15-16.

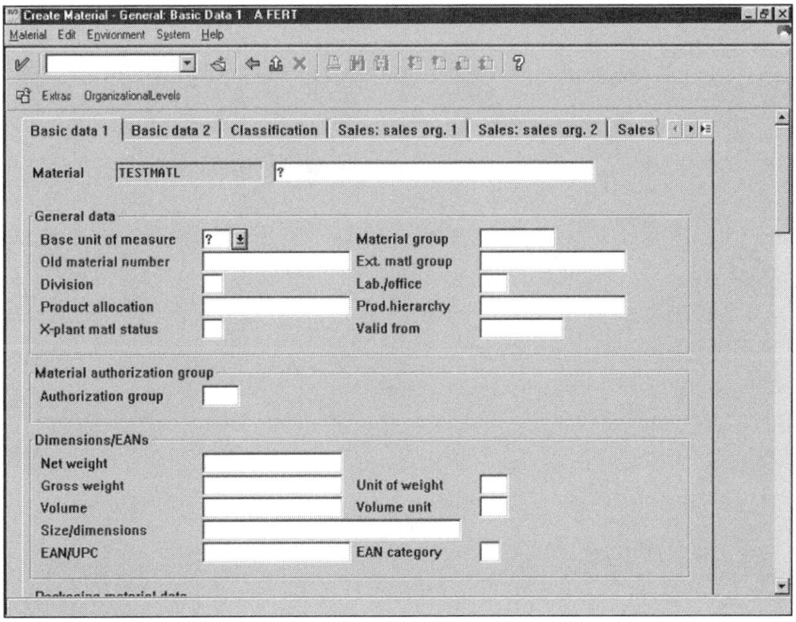

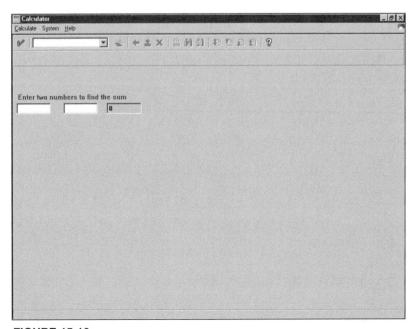

FIGURE 15-15

Screen with box graphic

FIGURE 15-16

Screen 9100 of SAPMZTST

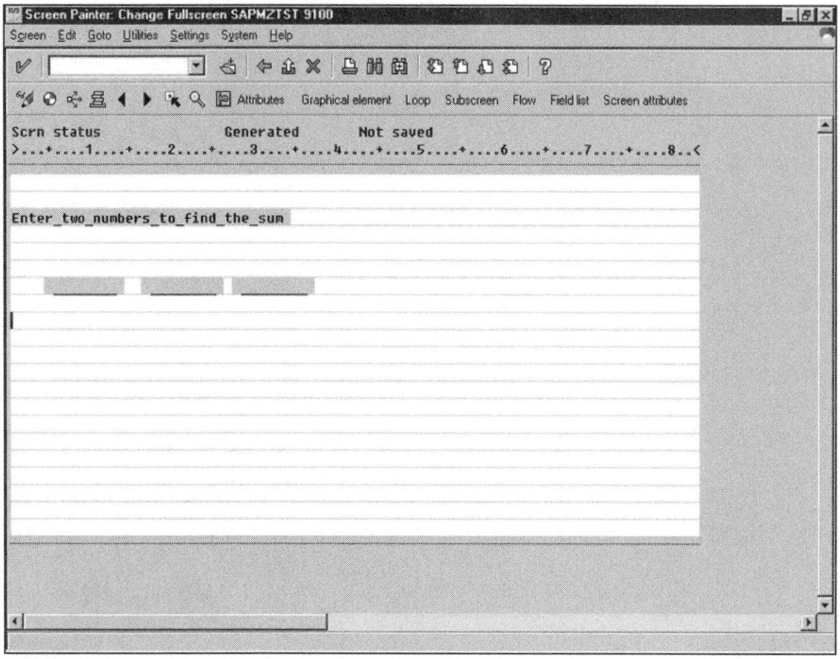

FIGURE 15-17

Modified screen 9100

To add a box around the input and output fields, first move the fields a few lines down and a few spaces to the left of the title on the screen so that it looks similar to Figure 15-17.

Place the cursor above and to the right of the fields you want to include in the box. The location of your cursor will become the upper-left corner of the box. Now choose Edit | Create element | Box to open the Box Attributes dialog box seen in Figure 15-18.

You must provide a name for the box and field text that becomes the box title. Once you've filled in those fields, click the Copy button to create the box. As with a text field, you have the option of setting the invisible attribute and the group codes. In this case, name the box &BOXINPUT and use a box title of Calculate.

TIP

If you name your box after an object in the Data Dictionary you can check the Frm dict. box and pull the text from the dictionary.

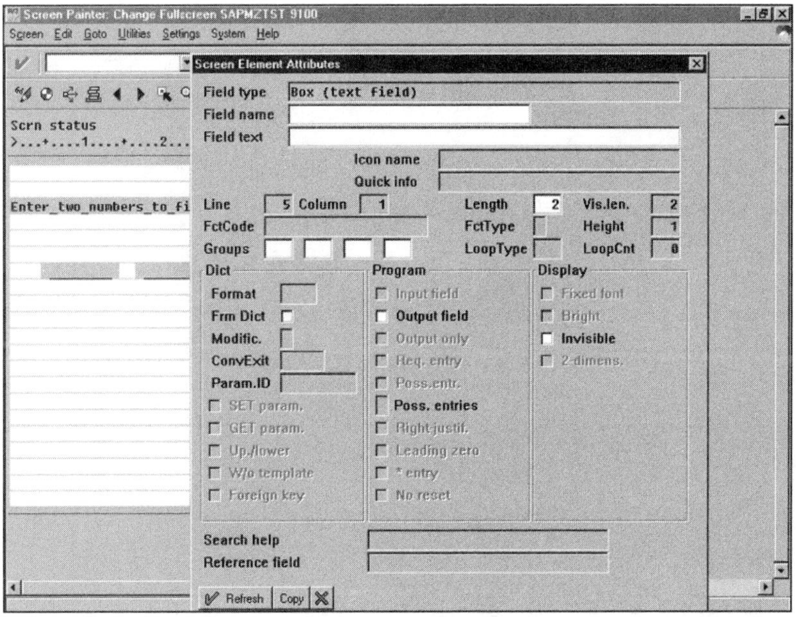

FIGURE 15-18

Screen Element Attributes dialog box

Once the box is initially created, the editor will change to graphic mode and any box title will appear as in Figure 15-19. You must then select the lower-right corner of the box and click Sel. box end to define the size of box you wish. The box must completely enclose any objects. You may not select a box end that would cause the box edge to divide any object. Now click the green arrow to return to the main editor screen. You will see the complete box, as in Figure 15-20.

If you want to modify the size of a graphic box after it is already created, simply click the title of the box, then the Graphic Element button. The screen will switch to graphic mode and you can resize the box by clicking on the screen where you want the new box edge and then clicking the Sel. box end button again. You can also delete a graphic box by clicking the Delete button while in this screen. Deleting a graphic box is done in two steps—first the box is deleted and the system converts the box title to a text element, then you double-click the text element and click the Delete button again.

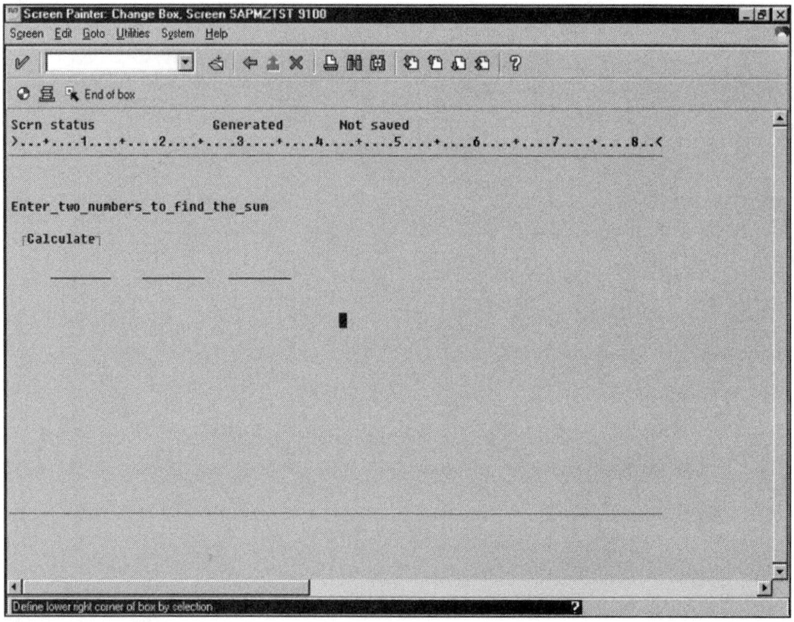

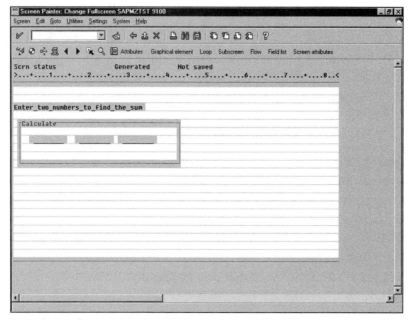

FIGURE 15-19

Graphic mode and a box title

FIGURE 15-20

Screen 9200 with box graphic

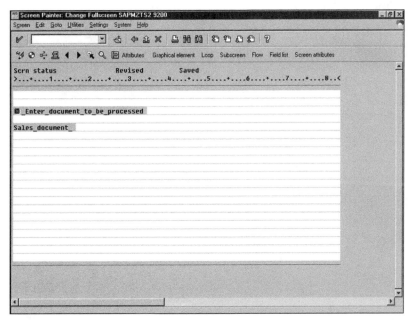

FIGURE 15-21

Screen SAPMZTS2 9200

Adding Input/Output Elements

When the calculator function was created, several input and output fields were added. This section will examine all the options in detail and discuss how to add input/output fields for Data Dictionary fields.

To follow along, go back to the new transaction created earlier, SAPMZTS2 9200, and open the full screen editor. A text field with the field description of VBAK-VBELN was created. Add an input field that allows the user to type the document number for a sales order. Figure 15-21 shows what screen 9200 should look like now. Use Edit | Create element | Input/Output field to see the attributes of the field, as shown in Figure 15-22.

You already know the purpose of the field name, field length, and field text boxes. Type XVBELN for the field name and 10 for the field length and press Enter. SAP will add underscores to the field text box showing that a maximum of ten characters can be entered. Since VBAK-VBELN is a character field, it's not necessary to change the format for this field. With the required entries made, turn to the option entries for an input/output field. Input/output fields have many attributes identical to those discussed earlier in the text element section. The following fields are new attributes, which have not been discussed before.

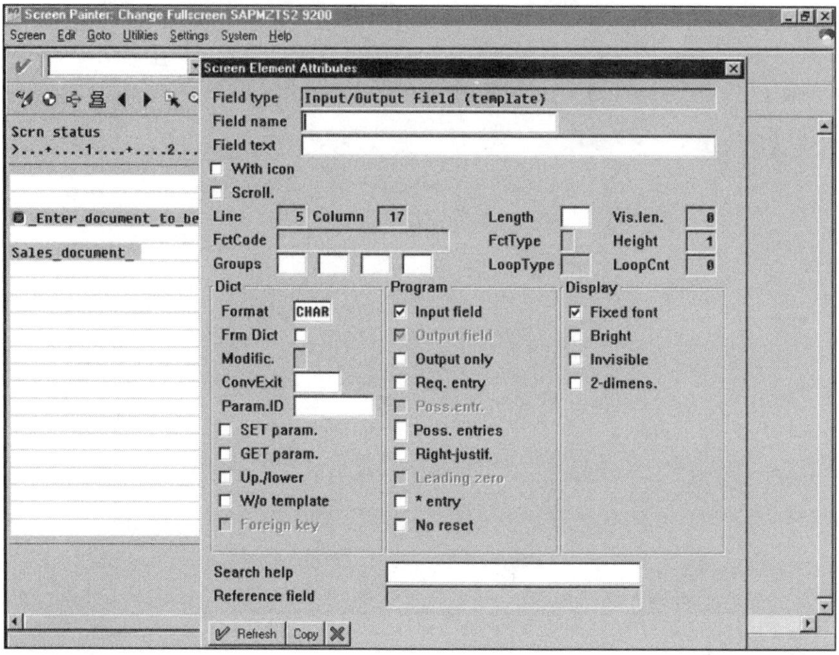

FIGURE 15-22

Input/output field attributes

Input indicates that the user can enter data into this field. If not selected, the field will be disabled so that only the transaction can assign data to the field and not the user.

Req. entry (required entry) indicates that this field must contain a valid value before the user can move forward in the transaction. This requires no additional coding from the programmer to make use of in a transaction. When the screen initially starts, this field contains a ?, indicating to the user that it is a required entry. If the user does not complete a required entry, an error message will appear saying, "XXXX field is required!" whenever any other button on the screen is clicked or Enter is pressed.

Poss. Entries (Possible Entries) determines whether or not the user is notified that the system can provide valid values for the input field. Four values can be made in this field. By default, SAP will show possible entries. Alternately, type a value of 0 to not display entries, 1 for temporary display, or 2 for a permanent display.

The *** entry** indicates that a special handling routine exists for this field that will execute if the user types * as the first character in the field. Field input is then transported starting from the second character, in accordance with the conversion specifications determined by the field format. The first * is not transported. By typing *, a module is started that is defined in the screen flow logic as FIELD ... MODULE ... ON *-INPUT. You can read more details in Chapter 17, "Using Flow Logic to Develop a Transaction."

No reset determines whether the user can cancel entries made in the field by typing the reset character !. Under normal circumstances users can type ! as the first character in a field where they have previously entered data and the system will clear the entire field. This saves users the effort of deleting data in the field manually. With this box checked, the reset character does not have any effect on this field.

Format allows you to choose what type of data this field will contain, given the following possible choices:

Frm Dict (from dictionary) indicates that the information about this field, such as its length and format, should be taken from the Data Dictionary. In order for this to work, the field name must match the name of a table field from the Data Dictionary exactly. Using dictionary fields will be discussed in detail later.

Param.ID (parameter identification) assigns a specific parameter ID, to be used to pass values in or out of this field. See Chapter 5, "Working with Global Memory," for more details on parameter IDs.

Set param (set parameter) indicates that this field should set the parameter ID specified above with the value the user enters into it. If this is not checked, an entry into this field does not change the value stored by the parameter ID specified.

Get param (get parameter) indicates that this field should get the value stored at the parameter ID specified earlier and place it in the input field the first time the screen is executed. Thus the value stored at the parameter ID serves as a default value.

Up/lower indicates that the user is allowed to enter uppercase or lowercase values in this field. If not selected, SAP will convert all user input to uppercase.

W/o template (without template) indicates that no template is used for a character field. This allows the user to enter special characters such as ! , ?, and _, which otherwise trigger special functions.

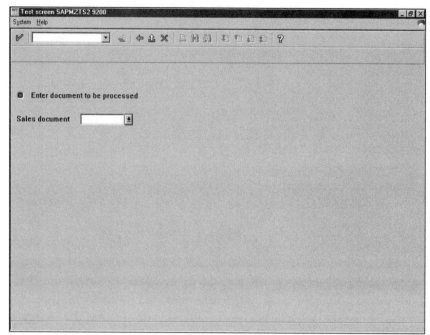

FIGURE 15-23

Screen with Sales Order entry field

The **matchcode** field allows the user to look up data from the Data Dictionary using a special search. This can help the user when completing this field. A matchcode is a program that allows the user to look up data with a special search. See Chapter 11, "Creating Search Codes," for more details.

It would be useful in the sales order entry form to remember the last sales order processed. To do so, set the parameter ID to AUN, the parameter for sales order, then check both Set param. and Get param. Next, to allow the user to search for a specific sales order through the use of a matchcode, type VMVA in the matchcode field. Once these settings are complete, click the Copy button to create the input field. Now save the changes to the screen. You will be returned to the Screen Painter main menu. Use the test button to display the screen, which should look like Figure 15-23. If you click on the XVBELN field, a drop-down arrow will appear; click the arrow to open the matchcode selection screen for sales orders, as seen in Figure 15-24.

Now return to the Full Screen editor to see the other option when creating input/output fields. This time, rather than manually creating a field for the sales

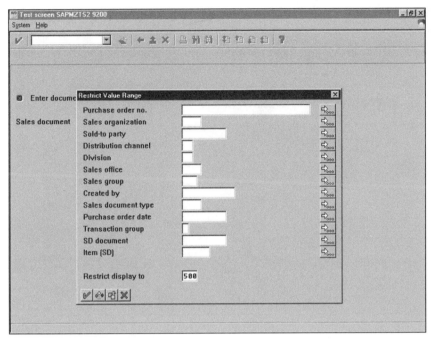

FIGURE 15-24

Matchcode Selection Screen

order number, use the Data Dictionary to create one. Create a new input field in the normal manner, Edit | Create element | Input/output field. As previously discussed, the key to using the Data Dictionary to create fields is to make the field name identical to the name of the table field in the Data Dictionary. Type VBAK-VBELN as the field name, then click Frm dict. and press Enter. A dialog box appears (see Figure 15-25), asking if you want to take the attributes from the Data Dictionary for this field. Answer yes. Now, many of the attributes such as Field length, Param. ID, and Foreign key are completed (see Figure 15-26). Do not check the Set param. and Get param. boxes because having two fields on the same screen both setting and getting the same parameter ID can cause some strange results. Finally, fill in the matchcode using VMVA.

The foreign key indicator is only available if the Frm dict. box is checked and the table field you picked has a foreign key. As explained in Chapters 7 and 8, a foreign key means that the values that can be entered into this field are limited to those in the value table of the field's domain. If checked, SAP will enforce the value check for entries made into this field. Users will not be able to enter invalid values into this field, much as they are forced to enter values into a field that has

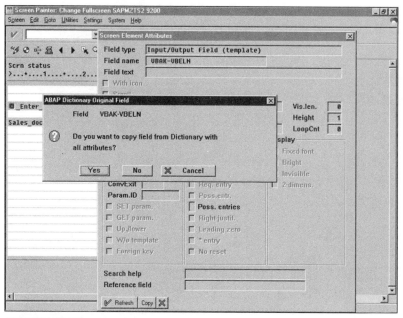

FIGURE 15-25

Data Dictionary dialog box

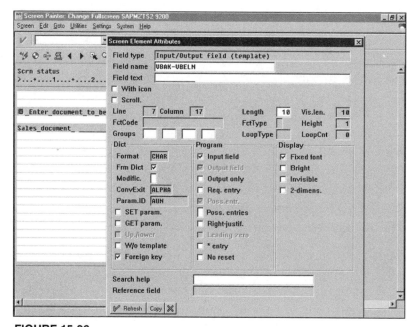

FIGURE 15-26

Input Field with Dictionary Link

the Req. entry attribute set. The nice thing about this value check is that it is completely invisible to the programmer and requires no additional logic. SAP ensures that the user enters a valid value and the programmer does not have to worry about it. This value checking is the best reason to create input fields with the Frm dict. attribute set if possible. Of course, there are many cases where the user must be allowed to enter any value into a field, but, when possible, it is always better to use the Data Dictionary to create fields.

Now select the Set param. and Get param. boxes, then type **VMVA** as the matchcode field. Click the Copy button to create the new field and then save your work and exit the full screen editor. To compare how these two input fields act during a real transaction, first click the Generate button to compile the changes to your screen. The next change required to compare the fields is to add both fields to the global data of SAPMZTS2. Use SE38 to edit SAPMZTS2, double-click the global data include MZTS2TOP, then add the following lines:

```
tables vbak.
data xvbeln like vbak-vbeln.
```

Notice a variable is not declared for VBAK-VBELN. Instead, use the tables statement to declare the entire table. You cannot create VBAK-VBELN by itself without the rest of the vbak table. Now that variables have been declared, the transaction knows about the two screen fields by the same name, and the screen can be tested. One last point: Notice that no new flow logic or transaction logic is added for these fields, so all the functionality in the transaction is automatically performed by SAP without the need for extra programming.

When ZTS2 is run, your screen should have two fields similar to Figure 15-27. The top field is XVBELN and the bottom is VBAK-VBELN, which is linked to the Data Dictionary. Click on either and the drop-down arrow that triggers the matchcode will appear. The difference between these two fields can be seen if you enter an invalid sales order number.

Figure 15-28 shows what happens when an invalid number is entered in the field XVBELN. Notice that no error is generated.

On the other hand, Figure 15-29 shows what happens when the same number is typed in the field VBAK-VBELN. The system displays an error message saying that 99999 is not a valid sales order. This shows the effect of the foreign key check on the VBAK-VBELN field. If you enter a valid sales order number, no error occurs.

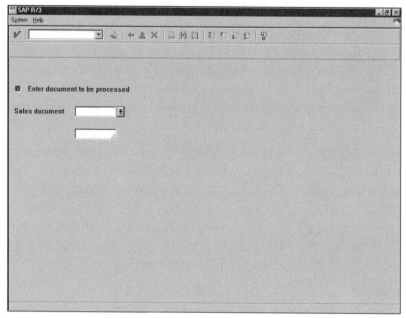

FIGURE15-27

ZTS2 with XVBELN and VBAK-VBELN

In conclusion, creating fields for input and output is a common activity during transaction programming. If possible, you should use fields that are linked to the Data Dictionary rather than create them manually.

Adding Buttons and Boxes

Buttons are used in two ways: to select an option (with a radio button or check box) and to trigger a function code (with push buttons).

First, a check box is actually a type of input field that is limited to two values. A check box holds the value of space if it is not checked and the value of X if it is checked. The user controls the value of the field by selecting or clearing the box. Like an input field, each check box should be tied to a global variable in the module pool. If you want the box to be selected by default when the screen is initially run, you can do this by creating a global variable with a default value of X.

Edit screen SAPMZTS2, 9200 in the full screen editor. Choose Edit | Create element | Check box to open the Attribute dialog box for a new check box as seen in Figure 15-30. Notice that most of the standard attributes are not available for

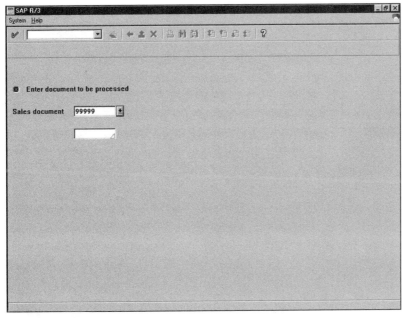

FIGURE 15-28

Entering an invalid order in XVBELN

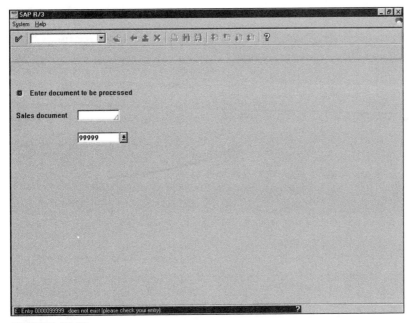

FIGURE 15-29

Entering an invalid order in VBAK-VBELN

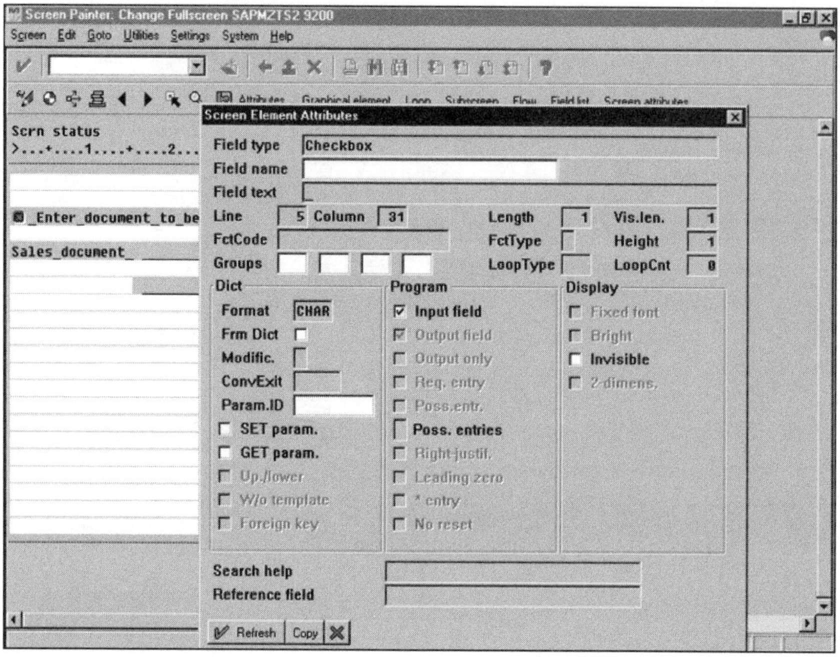

FIGURE 15-30

Check box attribute dialog box

check boxes—only Group, Input, Invisible, Frm dict., Set param., Get param., and Param. ID attributes can be set.

Type **XBOX_DETAIL_YN** as the field name, then click Copy to create the button. With the button created, your screen should look something like Figure 15-31. A check box by itself is not very explanatory, so go ahead and create a text field next to it, with the description **More Detail?** to tell the user what the check box controls. Save and generate the screen.

Like any other input field, a global variable must be created in the module pool to capture the check box value. Go to SE38 and add the following line to the global data include, MZTS2TOP, of SAPMZTS2:

```
data XBOX_DETAIL_YN value 'X'.
```

Save your changes to the module pool and run transaction ZTS2. The check box is checked due to the default value assigned to the global variable created for this screen field. To remove the default check, go back to the global data section of SAPMZTS2 and remove VALUE 'X' from the data statement and run ZTS2 again. This time the check box is cleared.

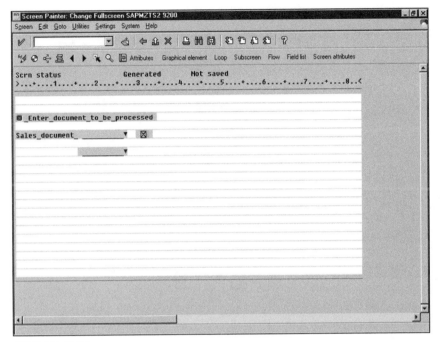

FIGURE 15-31

Screen with check box added

The next type of button to create is a group of radio buttons. Radio buttons differ from check boxes in that they are always found in a group of more than one in which only one button out of the group can be selected. Also, when creating a radio button, SAP forces you to create a text field to describe the button. An individual radio button behaves exactly like a check box.

Add a set of radio buttons to your sales order screen SAPMZTS2 9200. SAP supports several types of sales orders such as standard orders, returns, and credit memos. Suppose this screen will process different types of sales orders and the user will select which type. Since a sales order can be of only one type, it makes sense to use a group of radio buttons.

Open the transaction screen in the full screen editor and create a radio button by choosing Edit | Create element | Radio button. The first dialog box you see is the Radio Button attributes dialog box (see Figure 15-32). Similar to check boxes, many of the standard attributes are not available for radio buttons. Only the Group, Input, Invisible, Frm. dict., Set param., Get param., and Param.ID attributes can be set.

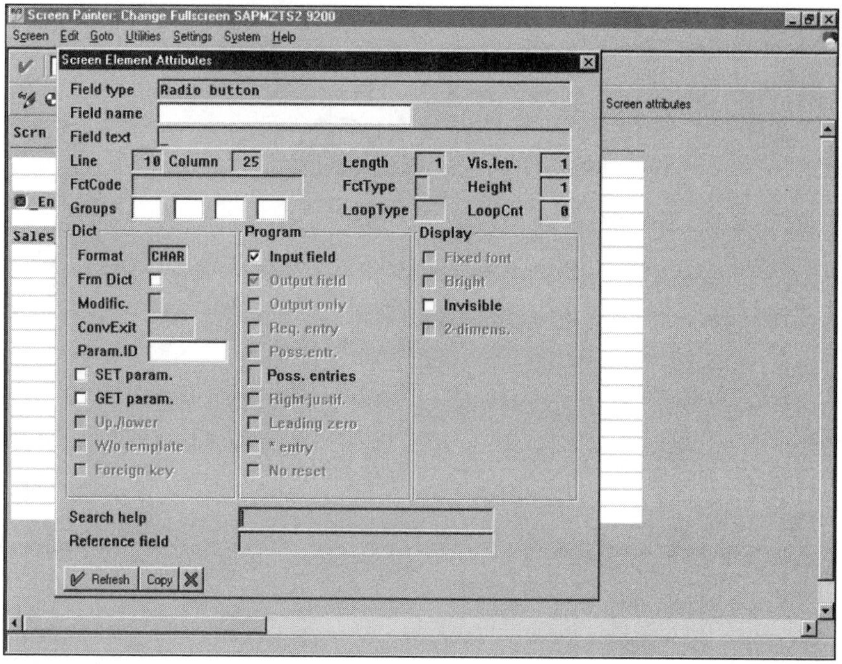

FIGURE 15-32

Radio button attributes dialog box

Name the radio button **RADTYPE1**, then click the Copy button. You immediately see the Radio Button Text Field dialog box, because it is required that you have a text field for your radio button. To describe the button, type **Standard** as the field text, then click the Copy button. This creates your first radio button on the screen, as seen in Figure 15-33. Next add two additional buttons—one for credit and one for return orders, with the names **RADTYPE2** and **RADTYPE3**.

After you have created all radio buttons, they must be grouped so that SAP knows they are linked. If you do not link them, then SAP thinks each one is a separate group and all of the buttons will default to being checked. Once you group them, only the first button will be checked. SAP will ensure that the user can select only one button in a group. If you wish to default on a button other than the first, you can do it by setting the global variable that is tied to the button to a default value of '**X**'. An important thing to remember is to never set more than one button in a group in this way because it will override the purpose of the radio button group.

In order to group the radio buttons, click on the first button. Then click the Graphical Element button. The screen should change color much like when working with block mode. Now click on the last button to be included in the

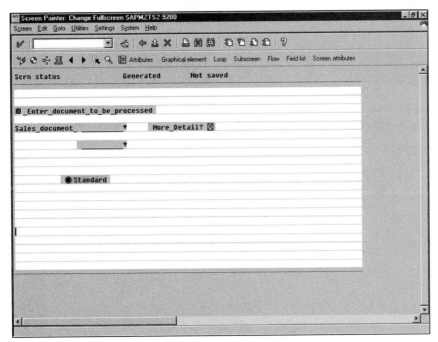

FIGURE 15-33

Screen with radio button

group and click the Define Graph Group button. If you have done this properly, you should see a message saying "Selection fields combined in a graphical group". The buttons are now grouped, and if you test the screen you should see that only one can be selected at a time. SAP supports multiple groups of radio buttons on a screen. Simply repeat this process for each group of buttons you need.

If you like, you can add a box around the radio buttons and give it a description of "Order Type." Often you will see that a box surrounds a group of radio buttons. Simply group your radio buttons, then follow the earlier instructions to create a box around them.

Once you are done, the screen should look something like Figure 15-34. The push button is important because it triggers a function code much like a menu item. A good screen will always give the user the choice of clicking a push button or selecting a menu item to trigger a function code. The next chapter, "Using the Menu Painter," explains how to trigger function codes from menu items.

A push button is different from a radio button or check box in several important ways. It is not tied to a program variable, but assigns a function code to the SY-UCOMM system variable, and triggers the Process After Input event. In the last

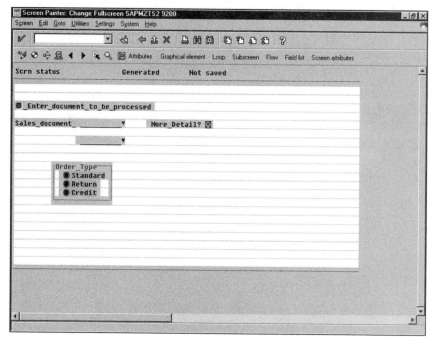

FIGURE 15-34

Screen with a group of Radio buttons

chapter we saw that the PAI event was triggered when the user pressed Enter; push buttons also trigger this event. Unlike pressing Enter, however, a push button triggers a function code. PAI processing and function codes will be explored in detail in Chapter 18, but for now it is enough to know that a function code is a way for the user to tell a transaction to perform an action.

In the calculator transaction SAPMZTST, the user types two numbers and then always adds them in the PAI event. The user triggers the PAI event by pressing Enter. Now suppose you want to enhance the calculator not only to add numbers but also subtract, multiply, and divide them. How could these multiple actions be accomplished? Earlier you learned how radio buttons force the user to select one button, so one option might be to add a set of radio buttons to the screen. One button would represent each operation and the user would select the desired button before pressing Enter. A better way might be to add push buttons for each operation—that way when the user clicks the push button for subtract, a particular function code is set and the PAI event is automatically triggered. Using this approach, the SY-UCOMM variable would be checked and then perform the operation the user specified.

Open SAPMZTST 9100 in the full screen editor. Below the fields for user input of the numbers to be calculated, create a push button using Edit | Create element | Push button. You will see the attribute dialog box for a push button shown in Figure 15-35.

Like other buttons, the field name and field text are required. In addition, there are two new attributes available to a push button: fctcode and fcttype.

Fctcode (function code) is the function code you want to set when this button is pushed. Prior to version 4.0 of SAP, the function code had a maximum length of four characters. In version 4.0, that length was increased to twenty characters; most transactions still stick to four unless absolutely necessary.

Fcttype (function code type) is the type of function code set for this button. There are three valid types. By default, a value of space that indicates normal application function is set. Alternately, type **E** to perform an EXIT command (MODULE xxx AT EXIT- COMMAND), or **T** to call a transaction.

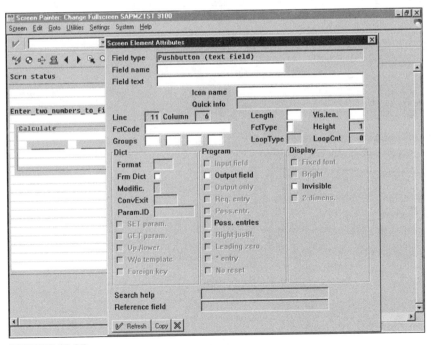

FIGURE 15-35

Push button attribute dialog box

Normally the Fcttype field is left blank, which indicates the function code act is used to set the SY-UCOMM variable in the PAI event as previously described. The value "E" indicates this is an exit function, which causes the transaction to end and the system to run the module specified by AT EXIT-COMMAND. The value "T" causes the current transaction to end and a new transaction to begin. Therefore, if you typed SE38 as the function code and T as the function type, this button would cause the current transaction to end and the ABAP editor (transaction SE38) to start.

To create a button that sums the user entries, type &BUTTONADD for the field name, Add for the field text, and ADD for the function code. Click Copy to create the button. You can control the size of your button by changing the length field but it must be long enough to display the field text. Making the button length 6 characters is sufficient since the word Add only contains three letters. Your screen should look something like Figure 15-36 after the button is created.

Create three more buttons for subtract, multiply, and divide. Name the function codes SUB, MULT, and DIV so that the associated code works. When you are all done, your screen should look like Figure 15-37. Make sure you save your work.

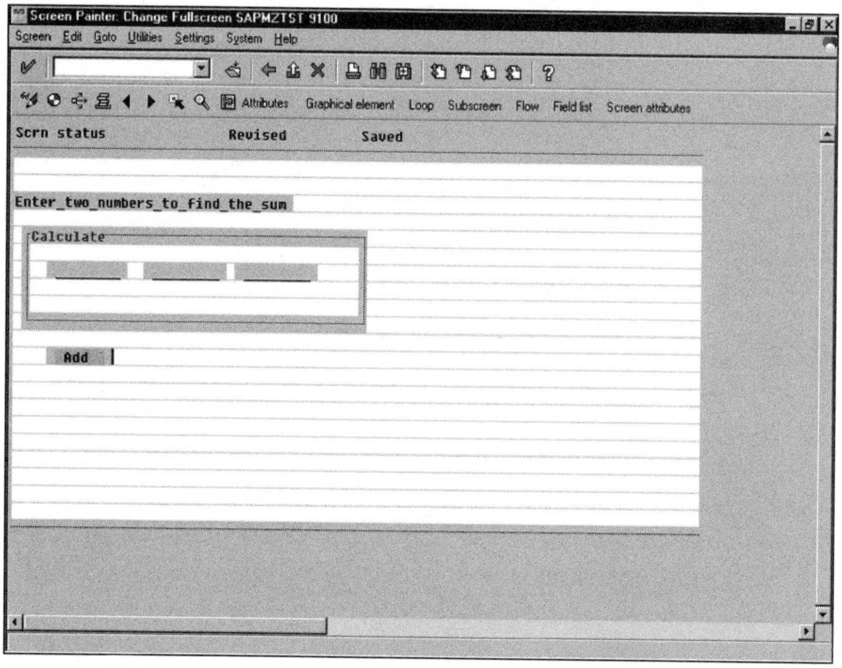

FIGURE 15-36

Screen with Add button

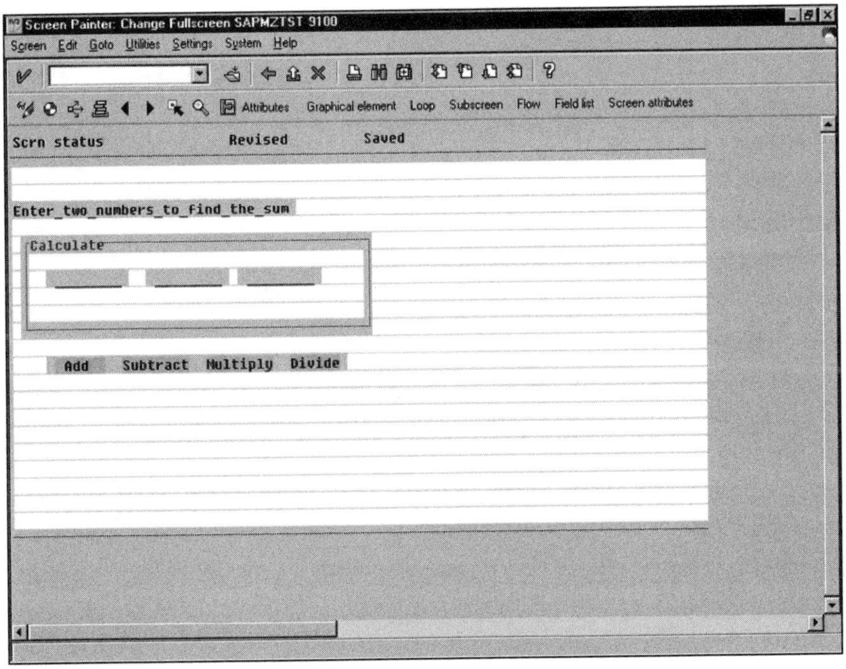

FIGURE 15-37

Screen with four buttons

Now that buttons have been created for the functions to be processed, you must write the ABAP code to do the work. In the last chapter the calculator was created with a single line of code, which added the two input fields and placed that sum in the output field. To make the additional functionality available, the function code must first be checked and then the appropriate operation must be performed. To react to the user's input, the code in the Process After Input event must be modified. First go to the main Screen Painter screen, select the button marked flow logic, and click the Change button. You will then see the flow logic for the calculator screen (see Figure 15-38).

To get to the ABAP code written for the PAI event, double-click user_command_9100. This opens the code for that module in the ABAP Editor. It should look like this:

```
*_____*

***INCLUDE MZTSTI01 .

*_____*

*&_____*
```

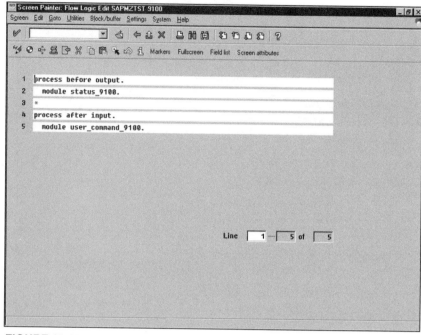

FIGURE 15-38

Flow logic editor

```
*&      Module  USER_COMMAND_9100  INPUT
*&— — — — — — — — — — — — — — — — — — — — — — — — — — — — —*
*      text
*— — — — — — — — — — — — — — — — — — — — — — — — — — — — —.*
module user_command_9100 input.
*XNUM1 and XNUM2 are enter by the user.
*XRESULT is the summation
xresult = xnum1 + xnum2.
endmodule.                    " USER_COMMAND_9100  INPUT
```

As you can see, every time the PAI event occurs, this code adds the values in the two input fields. What you want to do is add logic to look at the SY-UCOMM field and then perform the mathematical operation the user wants. A good way to do this is to use a case statement with the SY-UCOMM field like this:

```
case sy-ucomm.
  when 'ADD'.
```

```
    when 'SUB'.
    when 'MULT'.
    when 'DIV'.
endcase.
```

The CASE statement will decode the value in SY-UCOMM and trigger the code specified. All you need to do is add the code to perform the operation. Here is the code for addition:

```
case sy-ucomm.
  when 'ADD'.
*    XNUM1 and XNUM2 are entered by the user.
*    XRESULT is the summation
    xresult = xnum1 + xnum2.

  when 'SUB'.
  when 'MULT'.
  when 'DIV.
Endcase.
```

Now try to add the code for the rest, then run the syntax checker. If you get no errors, save your work and try running the transaction. Here is the complete code needed for all operations:

```
*_____.*
***INCLUDE MZTSTI01 .
*&_____.*
*&      Module  USER_COMMAND_9100   INPUT
*&_____.*
*        text
*_____.*
module user_command_9100 input.

case sy-ucomm.
    when 'ADD'.
*    XNUM1 and XNUM2 are entered by the user.
*    XRESULT is the summation
    xresult = xnum1 + xnum2.
```

```
      when 'SUB'.
*         XNUM1 and XNUM2 are entered by the user.
*         XRESULT is the difference
          xresult = xnum1 - xnum2.


      when 'MULT'.
*         XNUM1 and XNUM2 are entered by the user.
*         XRESULT is the product
          xresult = xnum1 * xnum2.


      when 'DIV'.
*         XNUM1 and XNUM2 are entered by the user.
*         XRESULT is the quotient
          xresult = xnum1 / xnum2.
    endcase.

    clear sy-ucomm.

endmodule.                        " USER_COMMAND_9100   INPUT
```

Notice the line toward the end that clears the SY-UCOMM field. This is required because the system will not automatically clear the contents of SY-UCOMM; if you click the Add button and then press Enter, for instance, the PAI event occurs twice with SY-UCOMM equal to "ADD" even though you did not click Add twice. In this case it is not critical, but in more complicated transactions you do not want functions to accidentally repeat each time the user presses Enter. Imagine if you had a function that deleted data—that could be cause for some real trouble.

Play around with your calculator now that you can add, subtract, multiply, and divide. Notice that nothing happens when you press Enter, only when you click one of the push buttons. Try subtracting a larger number from a smaller or dividing by zero. Your transaction will crash and give you a short dump, as seen in Figure 15-39. There is still a lot of work to do to make your calculator usable. In fact, you still cannot exit the calculator to start a new transaction. Work on the calculation will continue in the next chapter.

You've only scratched the surface of what can be done with functions and transaction logic. For now it is enough to be able to create a push button that sets a function code. More complicated examples will follow.

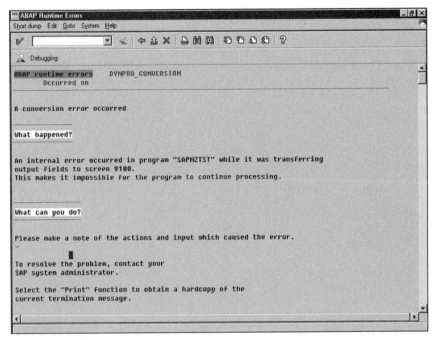

FIGURE 15-39

Short dump caused by divide by zero

Summary

In this chapter you learned how to add all of the basic screen objects such as text fields, input/output fields, graphics, and buttons. Adding objects to the screen is not enough. When you add an input field, check box, or radio button, you need to add a variable to your module pool with the same name. When you add a push button, you need to assign a function code and then write ABAP code to process that function code.

Screen objects are tightly integrated with the rest of your transaction. Eventually this integration and the steps needed to add new objects and logic to a transaction will become second nature to you. For now, try to make writing a transaction a step-by-step process. The process shown here is not the only right way to do it. Many people like to write the ABAP code first and then add the screen objects. The order is not important as long as everything gets done, so you should follow the process with which you are most comfortable.

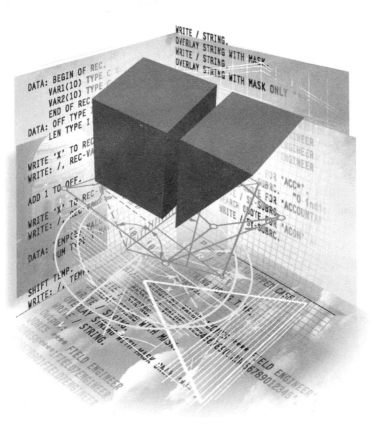

Chapter 16

Using the
Menu Painter

In This Chapter

◆ Creating GUI Titles

◆ Building the Components of a GUI Status

Transactions can perform a number of different functions. Each function is tied to a function code, which can be read in ABAP and used to determine which function should be executed. As you saw in the last chapter, function codes can be tied to screen buttons using Screen Painter. Function codes can also be tied to different parts of the GUI Status, which is maintained with the Menu Painter. Each GUI Status is made up of a menu bar, a standard toolbar, an application toolbar, and settings for function keys. The GUI Title is the title that appears at the top of each screen and is also maintained with the Menu Painter.

Creating GUI Titles

To access the Menu Painter, execute transaction SE41. Menu Painter opens, as shown in Figure 16-1. Type the name of the module pool for which you want to create, change, or display a GUI Status or GUI Title. If you want to create, change, display, or test a GUI Status, type the status name as well.

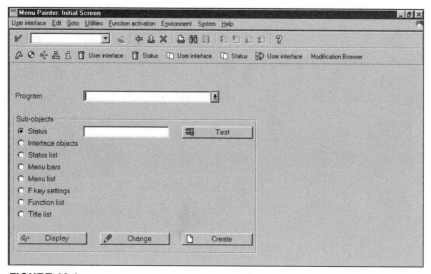

FIGURE 16-1

Menu Painter transaction

Next, select the option button that corresponds to the type of object that you want to work with. A list and description of option types follows:

Option Type	Description
Status	A single GUI Status
Status list	All GUI Statuses used in a transaction
Menu bars	All menu bars in the transaction
Menu list	All menus in the transaction
F key settings	Function keys and their function codes
Function list	Transaction function codes
Title list	All GUI titles used in the transaction

A good place to start when designing a transaction is to create any GUI Titles you will need. At the very least, you are required to create one title for each screen of your transaction. It is important to know before you start developing your transaction how it will be organized and how much work the transaction will require. The main purpose of a title is to identify each screen by helping the user understand where they are in the transaction; this is especially important in transactions with several screens.

For example, if you have a transaction that will allow the user to maintain a customer contact list, you could use two screens—an overview screen and a screen with a detailed information view. You might need five titles: Create Customer Contact, Edit Customer Contact, Delete Customer Contact, Edit Contact Details, and Display Contact Details. In this example you will create five titles even though only two screens exist in the transaction. Usually there is no need to create a completely different screen that is used to merely display data when you've already created one that allows the user to change data. You will learn later how to control fields on the screen to allow or disallow changes to the data they display.

Once you have created a list of titles, you can create them in the Menu Painter. To create a GUI Title:

1. Type the name of the module pool.
2. Select the Title List button.
3. Click Create. An empty screen appears, as shown in Figure 16-2.
4. Type an identifying number and the title you want to have appear at the top of your screen.
5. Click Save.

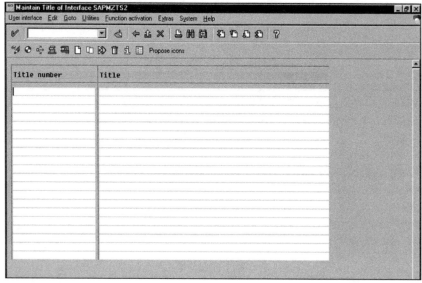

FIGURE 16-2

Create title screen

Remember, you can display a title bar using the ABAP command SET TITLEBAR. You will learn more about the SET command in Chapter 18, "Using ABAP to Control Transaction Logic."

Building the Components of a GUI Status

The steps used to create the components of a GUI Status are:

1. Create a menu bar.
2. Add entries to each menu.
3. Create a function key list.
4. Create a new GUI Status.
5. Assign a menu bar to the GUI Status.
6. Assign a function key list to the GUI Status.
7. Map function codes to the application toolbar.
8. Test the GUI Status.
9. Generate the GUI Status.

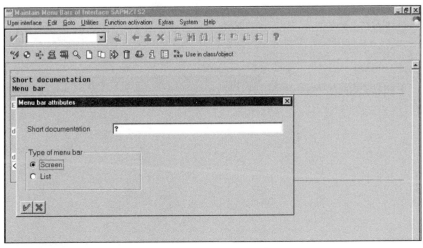

FIGURE 16-3

Create Menu dialog box

FIGURE 16-4

Menu Bar Edit Screen

Creating a Menu Bar

To create a menu bar, type the name of your module pool and then select the Menu option button. Click Create to open the Create Menu dialog box (see Figure 16-3).

Type a descriptive title in the short documentation field and make sure that the Screen button is selected. This indicates that your menu will be used in a transaction screen and not in list processing. Once complete, press Enter to move to the Menu Bar Edit Screen (see Figure 16-4).

Across the top of the menu bar edit screen are six blank menu fields. Each of these field titles contains a menu that can be activated by giving it a name. For example, if you want a menu named "File," you type the word File in the first blank field.

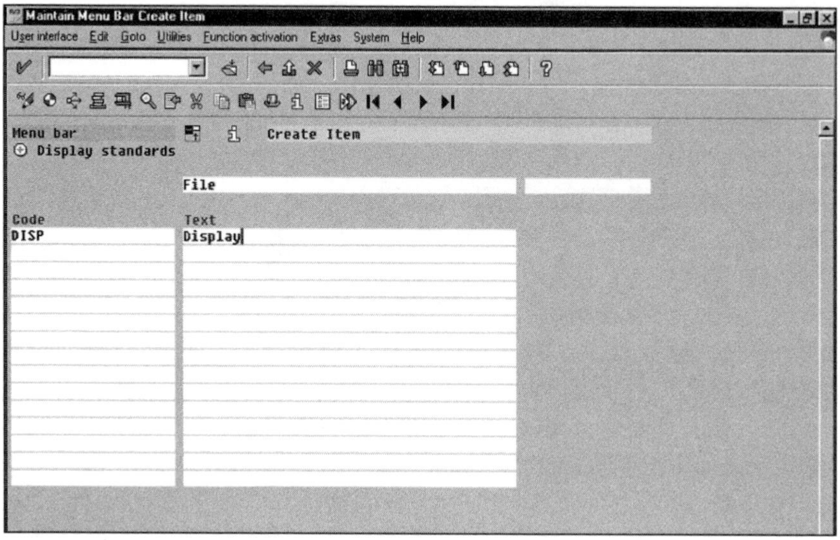

FIGURE 16-5

Sample menu command

You then double-click the word File and it will expand to allow you to add menu commands. It is these menu commands that the user selects to trigger a function code. Each menu command is made up of a function code, named in the first column, and function text, named in the second column. In Figure 16-5, you see a menu named File, which has a menu command named Display that triggers the function code DISP.

Recall that many SAP menu bars follow a standard of menus; the first menu is the object of the transaction. For example, in VA02, the change sales order transaction, the Sales Order menu has commands such as Display and Change. The next menu is usually named Edit and has commands such as Insert and Delete. The Menu Bar Editor can create these standard menus for you when you click the Display Standards button. The Menu Bar Editor containing the default menus opens (see Figure 16-6).

The default menu names are <Object>, Edit, Goto, Extras, and Environment. <Object> should be replaced with the name of the type of the object the transaction will process. Edit contains functions that change parts of the object. Goto controls screen processing such as moving back to the previous screen or canceling the transaction. Extras deal with miscellaneous commands that do not fit into any other menus. Environment contains commands that deal with data related to the object to be processed by the transaction, such as master data or a change log. Not every transaction requires every menu name contained in the default menu, so use only those that make sense to your transaction. If a menu name does not contain any valid menu commands, it will not be displayed to the user, even if you give it a title.

In addition to the default menu names, the system creates default menu commands for some menus. Note that the system only creates the function text. The function code is filled with <..> and the command will not be valid until you complete a proper function code. The following list contains the default menu names the system will generate.

Menu Name	Commands
<Object>	Text
	Other <object>
	Create
	Change
	Display
	Copy from
	Save
	Print
	Delete
	Exit
Edit	Text
	Select all
	Deselect all
	Select block
	Choose
	Cut
	Copy
	Paste
	Insert line
	Delete line
	Sort
	Cancel
Goto	Text
	Back
Extras	
Environment	

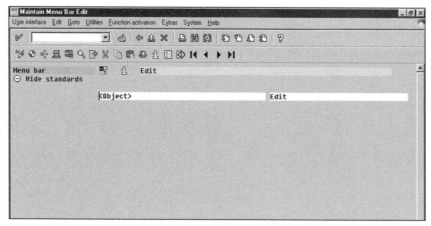

FIGURE 16-6

Menu Bar Editor with default menu names

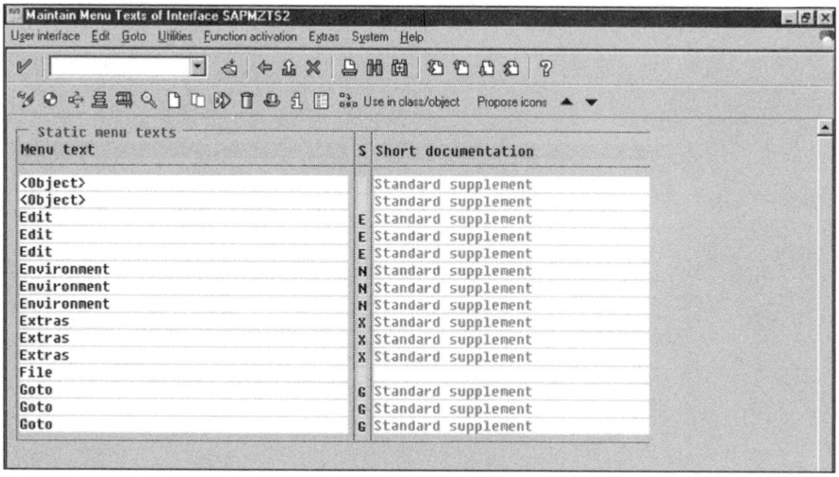

FIGURE 16-7

A Menu List

When you create your own transactions, you should decide how many menus you
require. Look at each activity you want your user to be able to carry out and decide
what menu bars will be required. For example, if your transaction allows the user
to create, change, and display data, you might require three menu bars. One menu
bar would be active in each mode, and each of the three menu bars might share
some common commands.

You can edit individual menus in Menu Painter by choosing the Menu List radio button rather than the Menu Bar radio button. Editing individual menus is not very efficient. When you choose the Menu List option, you will see all menus (see Figure 16-7). Menus appear more than once in the list. This program has two menu bars, both with a menu named Edit. Editing menus individually and not seeing the context of which menu bar they belong to can be confusing, so stay away from the Menu List option and stick with editing menu bars only.

In addition to menu commands, a menu can also have separators and additional cascading menus. A separator is simply a horizontal line that appears between two menu items. Often a menu will have groups of related menu items; using a separator between these groups can improve readability. Create a separator by placing the cursor on a blank command line and choosing Edit | Insert | Separator.

A cascading menu is a menu command that opens a submenu with a new list of menu commands. Cascading menus are great for keeping menus short and hiding complexity. If you find a menu has grown to more than eight items, you should consider creating a cascading menu. For example, you might have a menu command, Clipboard, that cascades into a new menu with the commands Insert, Append, and Clear.

To add a cascading menu:

1. Leave the function code column blank.
2. Type a name for the menu in the text column.
3. Double-click the menu name to open the cascading menu. The system will create a new menu to which you can add entries
4. Complete the submenu as you would any other menu. Figure 16-8 illustrates a cascading menu.

Creating a Function Key List

Once you create menu bars, assign function codes to function keys and the standard toolbar. A group of function key assignments is a function key list and each list can be assigned to GUI Status. The function keys are special keys on the keyboard that allow users easy access to function codes. In SAP, there are three types of function keys: reserved, recommended, and freely assigned. The following keys are reserved and cannot be assigned by the developer:

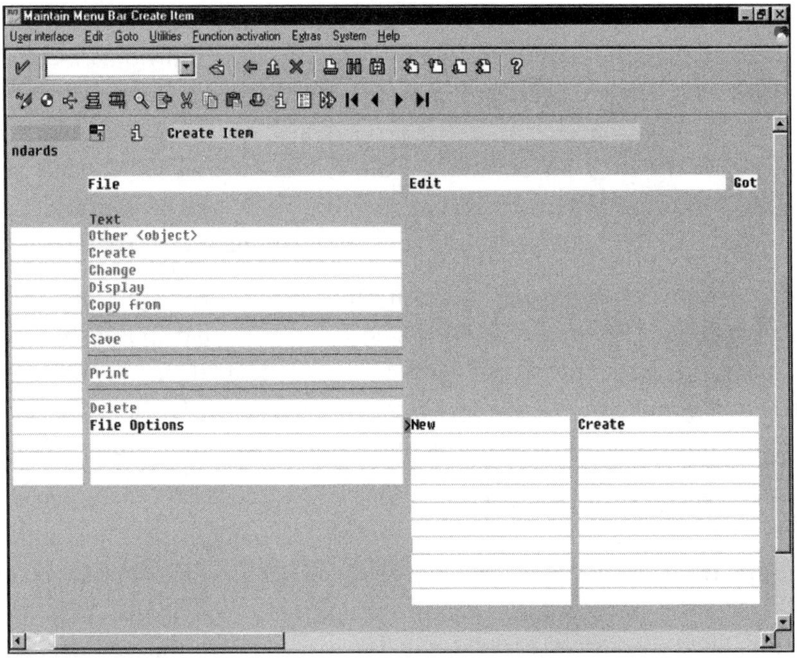

FIGURE 16-8

Adding a cascading menu

Reserved Key	Purpose
F1	Help
F3	Back
F4	Possible entries
F12	Cancel

In addition to the reserved keys, there are also recommended keys, which you will be familiar with from using SAP transactions. For example, F3 is the command for back, F8 is execute, and F11 is save in all SAP transactions. Your users will also be familiar with these standards, so you should stick with them. The recommended function keys can be displayed using the system's built-in help. For more information, see the SAP Style Guide by choosing Utilities | Help texts | Standards/Proposals.

Create a function key list by typing the name of the module pool, selecting the F key button, and then clicking Create. A dialog box will appear and you can type a short description for this group of function keys (see Figure 16-9). When complete, press Enter. You will go to the Function Key Editor (see Figure 16-10).

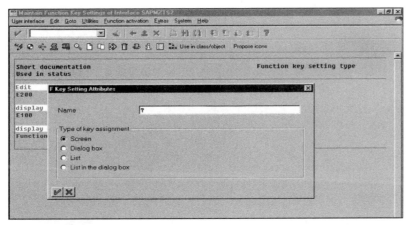

FIGURE 16-9

Create a Function Key List dialog box

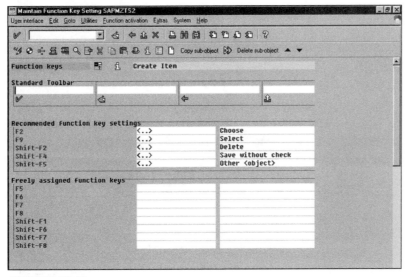

FIGURE 16-10

Function Key Editor

Along the top of the Function Key Editor is the standard toolbar. This toolbar is found on every SAP screen and should be kept consistent with other transactions. The icons in the standard toolbar from left to right are Enter, Save, Back, Start Over, Cancel, Print, Find, Find Again, Top of Page, Page Up, Page Down, Bottom of Page, and Help. You can assign your own function codes to these buttons or leave them blank (in which case the buttons are disabled).

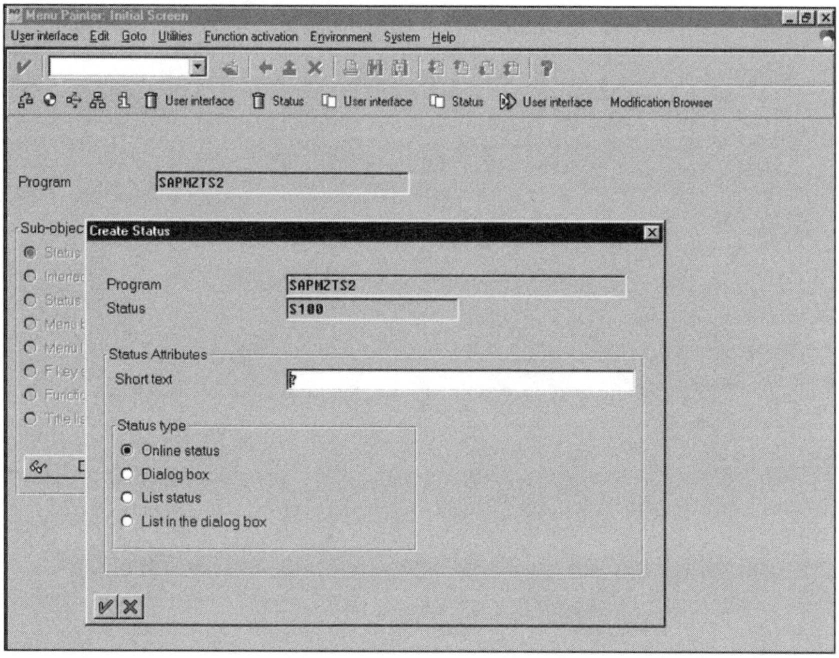

FIGURE 16-11

Create Status Dialog Box

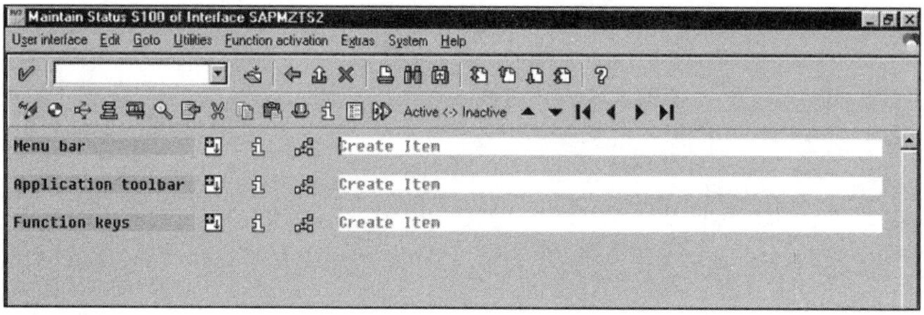

FIGURE 16-12

Status Editor

Below the toolbar are the function keys that can be assigned. To assign a function code to a function key, type the function code into the Key Name field. When all of the buttons and keys are assigned, click Save to complete the creation of the list.

Creating a New GUI Status

Now that a menu bar and function key list has been created, you are ready to create a GUI Status to which they will be assigned. To create a GUI Status, type the name of your module pool. Then select the Status option button and type a name for the Status of up to 20 alphanumeric characters. Click Create to open the Create Status dialog box (see Figure 16-11).

In the Create Status dialog box, type a short description for the GUI Status and select a status type. The status type determines what kind of status you want to create. For most transaction screens, you will select the first option. The following status types are available:

Status Type	Description
Screen	General transaction screen. Allows menu bars, standard toolbars, function keys, and application toolbars.
Dialog box	Allows function keys and application toolbars. Dialog boxes do not have menu bars or a standard toolbar.
List	Output list created with the WRITE command. Allows menu bars, standard toolbars, function keys, and application toolbars.
List in dialog box	Output list in a dialog box. Allows function keys and application toolbars. Dialog boxes do not have menu bars or a standard toolbar.

Once you have selected the type of GUI Status you are creating, press Enter to open the Status Editor (see Figure 16-12). You must first assign any menu bars you created to this Status. The assignment button is the third button to the left of the phrase "menu bar" and looks like three boxes with an arrow. Once you click this button, a list of all of your created menu bars appears. Simply select the menu bar you want to assign to this status. See Figure 16-13 for an example of assigning a menu bar.

Now you must assign the function key list you created to this GUI Status. To do so, click the assignment button that appears as the third button to the left of the phrase "function keys."

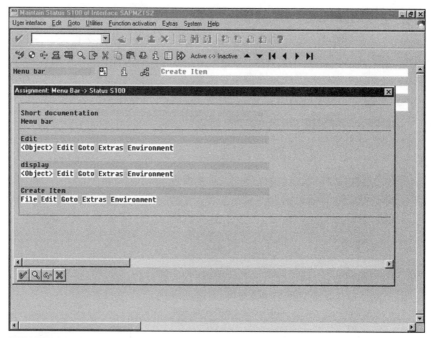

FIGURE 16-13

Assigning a menu bar to a GUI Status

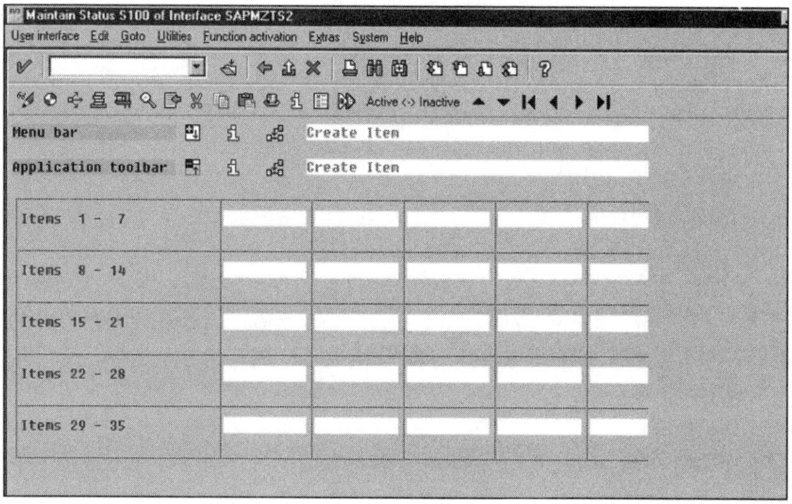

FIGURE 16-14

Status editor with expanded application section

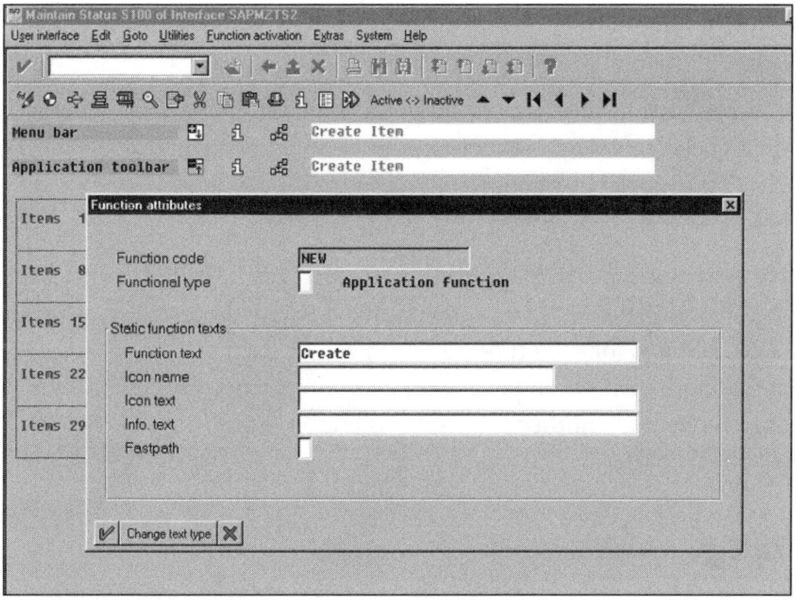

FIGURE 16-15

Dialog box to assign icons to application buttons

The final step is to assign any buttons you want to appear on the application toolbar. The application toolbar is used for functions that are specific to your transaction and do not appear on the standard toolbar. For example, if you have a screen that presents an overview of an object, you might have an application button named Details, which moves to a second screen and contains detailed information about the object.

To assign function codes to the application toolbar, press the first button, which looks like a plus symbol, to expand the application section. You should see a screen that looks like Figure 16-14.

In the expanded section, add the function code that the button will trigger and type the text that will appear on the button. In addition to a text label, you can also assign an icon to a button by double-clicking the function code name. A dialog box (see Figure 16-15) will open, from which you can choose an icon.

Both the menu bar and function key section of the Status Editor can be expanded. You can link a menu bar or function key list to a GUI Status at a later time by creating both of these objects directly in the Status Editor. Once you expand the menu bar and function key sections, you can follow the steps described earlier for both the menu bar editor and function key editor.

When all application buttons are assigned, your GUI Status is complete. Click Save, then click Generate. Generating the GUI Status is necessary before it can be used in a transaction. Whenever you revise a GUI Status, you must generate it again before the changes will be seen in a transaction.

You have now created a complete GUI Status that can be called from a transaction through the use of the SET PF-STATUS command. Remember that you will need to create a GUI Status for each mode a screen can be used in. Therefore, if you have a screen that both displays and changes data, you may need two GUI Statuses: one for change mode and another for display mode.

Summary

Every transaction screen requires at least one GUI Title and one GUI Status. The GUI Title is the title that appears at the top of a window, and the GUI Status is made up of four parts: the menu bar, the function key list, standard toolbar, and the application toolbar. Once you have created all titles and statuses required by your transaction, you can display them using the ABAP command SET.

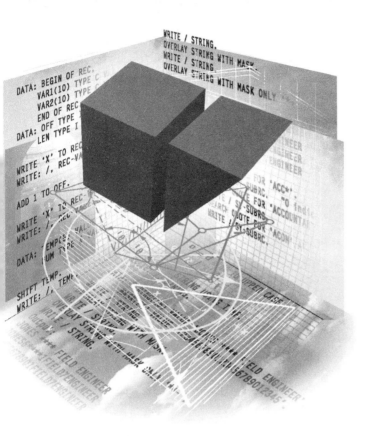

Chapter 17

Using Flow Logic to Develop a Transaction

In This Chapter

◆ PBO Event and PAI Event

◆ Using Modules to Execute ABAP Code (MODULE)

◆ Processing User Requests (FIELD and CHAIN)

◆ Advanced Flow Logic (LOOP and CALL)

In this chapter, you will learn how to use the flow control language to develop transactions to meet your requirements. As you learned in earlier chapters, flow logic is a specialized event-oriented language used to control actions during screen processing. It is not directly related to the ABAP programming language used to develop programs in SAP. Flow logic has the ability to call ABAP code through the use of the MODULE command. A module is a block of ABAP code, much like a form in a traditional ABAP program. These modules do the actual work, such as modifying data or providing feedback to a user, during a transaction. This is why a transaction is often referred to as a Module Pool. The flow control simply determines what actions should occur during screen processing. The actual code that implements each action is written in ABAP and placed in modules. Flow logic is edited within the Screen Painter and is tied to a single screen. Each screen has its own flow logic that is processed by the system when the screen is active.

Transaction flow control is broken up into two main events, PROCESS BEFORE OUTPUT (PBO) and PROCESS AFTER INPUT (PAI). Within each of these are subevents that can be detected. These sub-events are actions such as the user changing an input field, the user pressing a help key, or multiple items being placed in a screen loop. It is critical to understand the different events that trigger processing on a screen to understand the order of execution of your transaction. Event-oriented programming is very different from traditional serial program flow. In this chapter, you'll explore each of the flow control commands and how they behave during different events.

PBO Event and PAI Event

As discussed in Chapter 14, you should be concerned primarily with the PBO and PAI events during transaction processing. The PBO event is triggered before the screen is presented to the user. During this event, the programmer can control what data is presented to the user. The PAI event occurs when a user completes data entry and subsequently triggers an action. Actions such as pressing Enter, clicking a push button on the screen or toolbar, or choosing a menu command can trigger the PAI event. During the PAI event, the programmer can process the data entered by the user and prepare for the PBO event, which usually occurs next. This series of PBO, PAI, PBO, and so on will continue until the programmer interrupts it by leaving the current screen.

The flow logic does not actually perform any operations; it simply controls processing of the screen. In order to perform an operation, you must call ABAP code. This is done using the MODULE command in flow logic. Look at the following flow logic from the transaction ZTST, which you created in Chapter 14, to add two numbers:

```
process before output.
  module status_9100.


process after input.
  module user_command_9100.
```

When the ZTST transaction is run, the first action that occurs is the PBO event. The PBO event executes MODULE STATUS_9100. The ABAP code in the module executes, and since there are no other commands in the PBO section of the code, the transaction displays screen 9100 and turns control to the user. The user can then enter or change data, or click on any fields and no flow control will execute. It is not until the user presses Enter that control is returned to the flow control. The Enter key triggers a function, which is what tells the system that user input is complete and the PAI event should begin.

When the PAI event occurs, the program will execute MODULE USER_COMMAND_9100. The ABAP code in this module executes, and since there are no other commands in the PAI section of the flow control, the transaction then triggers the PBO event. This process of alternating between the PBO and PAI events continues until the user ends the transaction. You can end any transaction by typing /N in the command line of the SAP GUI. This is the only way you can end the ZTST transaction because no code was included to end the transaction.

The PROCESS BEFORE OUTPUT command indicates the start of the PBO section of the flow control; all statements below this command are executed before the screen is presented to the user. Since a PBO event always executes first when a transaction is executed, any initialization code that must execute when a transaction first begins should be placed here. The PBO event will execute each time a screen is displayed, not just the first time the transaction is run. Therefore, you can employ code that detects the first time the PBO event executes and does not execute each subsequent time (this technique is demonstrated in a future example).

The PROCESS AFTER INPUT command indicates the beginning of the PAI section. The PAI event occurs every time the user presses Enter—but you may not want to process data each time that occurs. A common habit is to press Enter to move from field to field, so it is important to ignore the PAI event in those instances. You will learn more in upcoming sections about how to detect exactly what the user is doing. Deciding whether or not to use the return key to process the PAI event really depends on the type of transaction you are developing. Simple screens can be triggered by the Enter key, but for more complex ones it is better to ignore it. Instead use screen buttons that tell the user exactly what will happen, such as buttons marked Copy, Delete, or Next.

Using Modules to Execute ABAP Code

The MODULE command is used to execute a block of ABAP code from within the flow logic. When an event occurs, you want to execute ABAP code to perform the logic of the transaction, which is contained in modules. Within a module, any ABAP statement can be used; in fact, a module can call ABAP forms.

A module name can contain a maximum of 20 characters and no blank spaces. The standard naming convention for a module is XXXXX_NNNN where XXXXX is a description of the purpose of the module and NNNN is the screen number from which the module is called. For example, GET_DESCRIPTION_9250 might be the name of a module that gathers descriptions from the database for entries made by the user in screen 9250.

The flow logic command MODULE has the following syntax:

```
MODULE <name> [at exit-command].
```

When the MODULE command is encountered, the named module is executed. The MODULE command can be used in either the PBO or PAI event.

The [AT EXIT-COMMAND] option can only be used in the PAI event. When this option is used, the module is only executed if the user triggers a function code that begins with E.

> **NOTE**
>
> The MODULE command can also be used as an option with the FIELD command, but only in the PAI event. This form of the MODULE command will be demonstrated later in this chapter.

In terms of program organization, module definition should be placed in include files based on their type. As you learned in Chapter 14, the naming convention for a single transaction is SAPMZXXX where ZXXX is the transaction code. If you are going to create multiple transactions in a single module pool, this will not be the case. Following this convention, all PBO modules should be placed in the include file named MZXXXBO. Similarly, all PAI modules should be placed in the include file named MZXXXAI.

A module definition in ABAP should follow this syntax:

```
module <modulename> output¦input.

…

endmodule.
```

When using this command, <modulename> is the name of the module you are defining and OUTPUT is used to indicate that this module is called from the PBO event or INPUT is used when the module is called from the process after the input event.

Here is a module example, called from the PAI event, that looks up the description of a material entered by the user:

```
module get_description_9300 input.


* pmatnr is an input field filled by the user
* pdesc is an output field
  select single maktx into pdesc from makt
                where matnr = pmatnr
                    and spras = sy-langu.


endmodule.
```

The flow logic utilizing that module might look something like this:

```
process before output.
```

```
   module status_9300.
process after input.
   module get_description_9300.
   module user_command_9300.
```

As stated earlier, the first time the PBO event occurs is before the first screen is presented to the user. Since program initialization is often performed in a PBO event module, the programmer must make sure that initialization occurs only once. In this example, several screen fields are initialized using parameter IDs. SAP automatically saves the last entry a user makes in some fields. This data is saved to specific parameter IDs; for example, the last sales order number entered is saved under the parameter ID AUN. The GET command can retrieve this data. In order to make sure this initialization occurs only once, a global variable called PINIT will be set to a value of 'X'. If the module is called again, an IF statement will prevent the initialization from occurring again. You can use this type of technique in your own transactions. Consider this module definition:

```
module initialize_screen_9100 output.


* Set screen fields the first time through only
   if pinit eq space.
      get parameter id "AUN" vbap-vbeln.   "Sales Order
      get parameter id "AUF" vbap-posnr.   "Sales Item
      pinit = 'X'.
   endif.
endmodule.
```

The flow logic would look something like this:

```
process before output.
   module initialize_screen_9100.
   module get_order_data_9100.


process after input.
   module user_command_9100.
```

The use of modules in flow logic is critical. Modules are the only way to access ABAP code from a screen. They also provide a good method of organizing your program since modules must be placed in the PAI and PBO events. Therefore, all of your chunks of code should be written either to process user input or to present output to the user.

Processing User Requests
(*FIELD* **and** *CHAIN*)

While the PAI and PBO are the main events in a transaction, there are subevents that can be detected as well. For example, it is possible to detect changes to screen fields by users. Two flow logic commands assist in detecting these events, FIELD and CHAIN.

The FIELD command allows you to process the data found in the screen field specified by ABAP code. Used by itself, the FIELD command would execute the specified ABAP code every time, but it is possible to limit the execution to certain events using options such as ON INPUT. The FIELD command supports several options so that the ABAP code is processed only when the data in the field changes or when the field is not blank. The syntax of the FIELD command is:

```
field <fname> values (<valuelist>).
```

Using the value form of the FIELD command, a domain of valid entries can be defined by the programmer. This form of the FIELD command can only be used in the PAI. In the value list, individual values and/or intervals of input values, which are allowed or forbidden, can be defined. The values must be entered between quotes and separated by commas. Here are the possible values that can be used in the list:

```
 [not] '<value>'
[not] between <value> and <value>
field <fname> select <select statement>.
```

Using the SELECT form of the FIELD command, user entry into a screen field can be checked against a database table. Once again, this form can only be used during the PAI. The SELECT statement must be in this form:

```
SELECT * FROM <dtab>
            WHERE table key <field1> = <entry field1>
                            and ....
            INTO <outfield>
```

```
WHENEVER FOUNDINOT FOUND
      SEND ERRORMESSAGEIWARNINGMESSAGE
           <number>
           WITH <field>.
```

Validating user input is one of the most common activities found in flow logic and using this command is a quick way to accomplish it.

```
field <fname> module <name> [on input]|[on request].
```

This form of the FIELD command calls a module to process a field. Only this field is processed in the module.

```
[on input]
```

This option, which can only be used in the PAI, specifies that the module only be processed if the field is not empty.

```
[on request]
```

This option, which can only be used in the PAI, specifies that the module only be processed if the user has changed the value in the field. The field command gives you a great deal flexibility to process user input. The most common options used are ON INPUT and ON REQUEST.

The CHAIN command is used in conjunction with the field command. The CHAIN command allows you to group several FIELD commands and process them together. For example, if you have two related fields such as a purchase order number and an item number, you might want to detect a change in either field and then process the fields together in a module. The FIELD command alone forces you to deal with each field individually, but with CHAIN they can be processed together. Here is an example:

```
process before output.
  module initialize_screen_9100.


process after input.
  chain.
    field p_po.
    field p_poitem module  get_po_data_9100
              on chain-request.
```

```
endchain.
module user_command_9100.
```

The syntax for the ON REQUEST option that is used with the FIELD command in this example changes to ON CHAIN REQUEST when used with the CHAIN command. The ON INPUT option likewise changes to ON CHAIN-INPUT. In the example above, the ON CHAIN REQUEST is triggered if either the p_po field or the p_poitem field changes. The syntax for the CHAIN command is simple:

```
chain.
<field statements>
endchain.
```

Among the most confusing aspects of flow logic are the FIELD and CHAIN commands. For most of the transactions you develop, complex usage of FIELD and CHAIN commands is not required, but many SAP-provided transactions do use these commands in complex ways. The FIELD command allows you to process the data found in the screen field specified with ABAP code. This is the typical usage of the module form of the FIELD command.

The FIELD command processes the value found on the screen, whereas the ABAP code processes data found in program variables. Essentially, if you give your screen field the same name as an ABAP variable, SAP keeps them in sync.

Suppose you have a screen with two input fields, a document number and a material number. At the start of the PAI event each FIELD...MODULE command is processed using the values captured from the screen. The first FIELD command is executed and the ABAP variable for document is again set to the value from the screen. Then the next FIELD command is executed and the ABAP variable for the material number is set to the screen value. Notice that the variable for a screen field is set only at the time of the FIELD command. So, if you change the ABAP variable for material number in the first module, that change will be lost when the second module is executed because the contents of the screen field are copied to the variable. If you want the values for multiple fields to be available in the same module, use a FIELD statement for each and attach the module to the last field in the list.

Another option is to not use a FIELD command for the screen fields that you want to process. Any screen fields that are not specified in a FIELD statement are transferred to the ABAP variable immediately at the start of the PAI event. These unspecified fields are available in any module and will not be overwritten. The way

SAP processes screen fields can lead to some very confusing behavior in screen processing. To make matters worse, there is an exception to this process. If the screen field is empty, when the module is executed, the value of the corresponding ABAP variable is not set to space if it was changed in previous FIELD commands.

Because of this potential for confusion, you should limit the use of the FIELD command and changes to screen input fields in modules. A better choice is to use the FIELD command to detect changes to input fields and then in ABAP make any changes to display only fields based on the new input. For example, you might look up the description of a material based on the material number entered by the user. In this case, the material description is an output field and cannot be changed by the user. Think of the FIELD command as an interrupt to SAP's normal screen processing. Normally, SAP will transfer the contents of screen fields to their associated ABAP variables with no intervention from you. By using a FIELD command in the flow logic, you tell SAP to stop the transfer process and turn control over to you when it reaches the specified field. This is very convenient, but you need to be careful or you can confuse SAP's screen processing.

When using options like ON REQUEST or ON INPUT, it is important to realize that these options refer to the screen field and not the ABAP variable. Therefore, if you assign a value to an ABAP variable in a module, the ON REQUEST or ON INPUT option will not be triggered. Both of these options require values in the screen fields. Of course, the values of all variables will be copied to the screen at the next PBO event. The key to understanding flow logic is to start simply and gradually increase the complexity of your code. Add statements one at a time, never adding more until you know that all of the existing statements work correctly. Try not to do too much with flow logic; instead place complexity in ABAP code.

Advanced Flow Logic (LOOP and CALL)

Often a screen will allow the user to type more than one value for a field. For example, the user might type a list of materials or a list of sales order and item numbers. To require the programmer to create a separate field for each possible entry would not make much sense. In that instance, instead of a single screen field called pmatnr, the programmer would add five fields named pmatnr1 ... pmatnr5. Creating separate fields, however, would not support the ability to scroll through a list. Screen Painter has the ability to create a group of one or more lines. These lines are referred to as a screen loop. This loop might have only a single field, such as a material number, or it might have several fields per line, such as PO number, quantity, and value.

In addition, a screen loop can be tied to an internal table of data. This allows the user to scroll through an internal table with a minimum of programming. If you use a loop on a screen, you must include a loop statement in both the PAI and PBO sections of your flow logic. The LOOP command acts much like a LOOP in ABAP—it executes once per entry on the screen loop. In the PBO event, LOOP

 NOTE

Only the basics of LOOP command syntax are presented here. The use of screen loops in a transaction are covered in detail in Chapter 19, "Screen Loops".

---

moves the data from ABAP variables to the screen, allowing the programmer to control what appears on the screen. In the PAI event, it moves the data from the screen into the ABAP variables, allowing the programmer to process the data entered by the user. Within the LOOP ... ENDLOOP block, the flow commands FIELD, MODULE, SELECT, VALUES, and CHAIN can be used.

Here is the syntax for the LOOP command:

```
loop [[at <itab>] [from <var1>] [to <var2>][cursor <var>] [with control <fctrl>]
[into <var>]]|[at <dtab>].

...

endloop.
```

The various options alter the effect of the command and can have different effects in the PAI and PBO events. These options are:

[at <itab>]

In this case, <itab> is an internal table defined in the global data of the module pool. Using this option ties the screen loop to an internal table. In the PBO event, each record in the internal table will be passed to the screen. In the PAI event, each line from the screen will be passed into the header line of the internal table.

[from <var1>] [to <var2>]

These options must be used with an internal table. They limit the data moved to and from the screen to only the range of line numbers specified with <var1> and <var2>. These variables must be defined in the global data of the module pool as LIKE SY-TABIX.

[cursor <var>]

During PBO, the internal table is displayed from line <var>. The field can be filled dynamically in the program. When scrolling with the scroll bar, <var> is filled with the correct index, and the index is increased by 1 on each loop pass. You can get the current index from the field SY_INDEX in the program.

During PAI, the internal table is also first read with the correct index in the relevant LOOP ... ENDLOOP processing. Only then is the field transport performed. When complete, the index is available in the field <var> so that the table entry of the internal table in the program can be modified.

[with control <fctrl>]

WITH CONTROL ties the screen loop to a table control. Table controls are discussed in Chapter 19 .

[into <rec>]

INTO moves the value from the screen loop into a record. The record must contain all fields found in the loop.

[at <dtab>].

AT ties the screen loop to a database table. In PBO, the table entries are read from the database in blocks and output to the loop fields. After a change on the screen, PAI writes them back to the database, if you specify MODIFY table in the structure LOOP ... ENDLOOP.

Here is an example of a loop in the flow logic:

```
process before output.
  module status_9100.
  LOOP AT TEMP CURSOR C.
  ENDLOOP.


process after input.
  LOOP AT TEMP.
    FIELD TEMP-FIELD1 MODULE READ_LOOP ON REQUEST.
  ENDLOOP.
```

```
module user_command_9100.
```

In this example the screen would have a screen loop called TEMP. A loop command is required in both the PBO and PAI events. In the PAI, the field command is used to process a field in the loop. Screen loops may contain one or more fields. The CALL command is used to call the flow logic from a subscreen. Subscreens are covered in detail in Chapter 20, "Advanced Techniques." The syntax of CALL is:

```
call subscreen <area> including <program> <screen>.
```

Subscreens are maintained in Screen Painter, like other screens. In the screen's attributes, specify the screen type as a subscreen. A subscreen cannot call another subscreen.

A normal screen can contain areas for several subscreens. CALL is not allowed between LOOP and ENDLOOP or between CHAIN and ENDCHAIN. This means that repetition of subscreens in a manner similar to repetition of fields is not possible.

Summary

Flow logic is used to control the interaction between a screen and the user. Flow logic is not used to implement the transaction logic that would read or modify data; it simply controls the screen actions and then calls ABAP code through the use of subroutines referred to as modules. Here is a summary of the flow logic commands:

Command	Use
PROCESS	Defines the start of a new processing event BEFORE OUTPUT / AFTER INPUT /ON HELP-REQUEST / ON VALUE-REQUEST
FIELD	Interrupts standard screen processing to allow user processing of a field
MODULE	Calls an ABAP subroutine to perform transaction logic
SELECT	Verifies user entry against a database table
VALUES	Defines a domain of valid field input used with FIELD command
CHAIN	Defines the start of a block of fields to be processed together
ENDCHAIN	End of a chain
LOOP	Defines the start of a block of code to process a screen loop
ENDLOOP	End of a screen loop

CALL SUBSCREEN	Calls a subscreen to process its flow logic

Flow logic is important and useful when developing a transaction. Flow logic can get very complicated and that many of its functions can be accomplished using ABAP as well. If you are comfortable writing ABAP code, it is often better to place complexity within the modules and leave the flow logic as simple as possible. If you look at SAP-provided transactions, you will find they often use very complex flow logic. You should not feel compelled to match their complexity in your transactions. Rather, you should stick with what you are comfortable and spend time testing your transactions to make sure that they interact with the user in a consistent fashion.

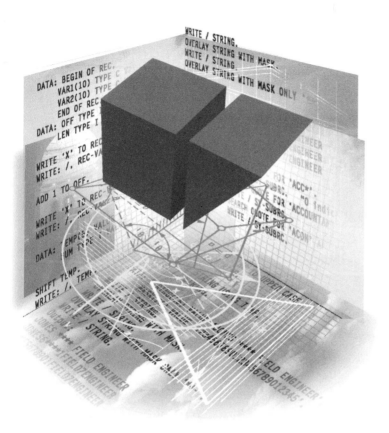

Chapter 18

Using ABAP to Control Transaction Logic

In This Chapter

- ◆ Processing user events
- ◆ Calling screens in ABAP
- ◆ Modifying screen fields with LOOP AT SCREEN
- ◆ Calling list processing within a transaction

In this chapter you will learn to use ABAP within your transaction to provide the required functionality. You will learn how to read the function codes triggered by users and execute ABAP code based on what the user requests.

Most transactions require multiple screens to present data in a logical and efficient manner. The first screen in a transaction is determined when you create the transaction code using SE93. If your transaction has any additional screens, however, you must write ABAP code to allow access to them. The different combinations of screens that appear in a transaction are often referred to as the screen flow. From your initial design, you will come up with the different screen flows. All screens do not have to be full screens; it is also possible to have small pop-up screens. For example, imagine that you have a screen where different information can be entered, such as document numbers or dates. Rather than placing all of these possible fields on a single screen, you might simply put a number of buttons on the screen so that when a user clicks a given button, a pop-up window appears with only the appropriate fields.

Sometimes you do not need a new screen to accommodate a new task. Perhaps you can simply expand a single screen to handle two tasks. For example, if you require one screen to display data and another screen that allows the user to change data, you can actually accomplish this with only one screen. Rather than changing the screen, you would change the fields from display fields to input fields. As you may remember from Chapter 15, "Screen Painter," when you create a field in Screen Painter you can control whether it is an input- or output-only field. But the attribute you set in Screen Painter is only an initial value that can be changed. Changing screen fields is accomplished through the use of the LOOP AT SCREEN and MODIFY SCREEN commands.

Finally, not every type of output from a transaction requires a screen. Sometimes it makes more sense to use a standard ABAP list output instead. List output is generated from the WRITE command in ABAP reports. Conversely, a screen is created explicitly by a programmer in Screen Painter and output is done only through screen fields. It is possible and often very useful to create standard lists in transactions. In order to display a list to the user, the current screen must be exited using the command LEAVE TO LIST_PROCESSING.

This chapter ties together everything you have learned about creating the separate pieces of a transaction. The screen, GUI status, and flow control are tied together and controlled by the ABAP code you will learn about here.

Processing User Events

As you learned earlier, the PAI event is triggered when the user presses the Enter key, clicks a button on the screen or toolbar, or chooses a menu command. During this event, the programmer can process the data entered by the user and prepare for the PBO event, which will occur next. When the PAI event occurs, a system variable called SY-UCOMM is set to the function code that triggers the PAI. In Chapter 15, you learned that when you create a screen button you specify what function code that button triggers and how you can read that function code by checking SY-UCOMM in the PAI event.

In flow control, you should always have a module that processes user input in the PAI event. The naming standard for this module is USER_COMMAND_XXXXX where xxxxx is the screen number. Typically this will be the last module in your PAI event. If you have any pre-processing of user input, it should be done in modules that appear before the USER_COMMAND_XXXXX module. For example, this flow logic shows how the PAI event should be structured:

```
process before output.
* Set GUI status and title
  module status_9100.
* Get default date
  module update_date.


process after input.
* When sales order/item changes update order description
  chain.
    field vbap-vbeln.
    field vbap-posnr
      module update_screen on chain-input.
  endchain.
```

```
* Display description for any codes entered
  module update_code_.
* Process function code entered
  module user_command_9100.
```

In this example, you see several modules and a chain—all of which occur before the module to process the user command is encountered. Typically, when the user enters information such as a material number or a document number, you will want to look up a description for that information. Once you have a description, it can be displayed in a screen field. Descriptions help the user visually verify an entry, thus helping to prevent errors. Once you update the screen as necessary, the last step in the PAI event is to process any function code entered by the user.

Not every instance of flow logic will be as complicated as the one presented above. Here's a simpler example:

```
process before output.
  module status_9200.


process after input.
  module user_command_9200.
```

This example is typical of a pop-up dialog box where the user enters a small amount of data. Here's another simple example:

```
process before output.
  module set_status_9300.
* Update screen before display
  module modify_screen_9300.


process after input.
  module okcode_9300.
```

In this case, OKCODE_9300 is called rather than USER_COMMAND_XXXXX. Occasionally you will see this naming convention. In SAP parlance, okcode is another word for function code. Be aware, therefore, that when you are looking at transactions created by other programmers that consistent standards are not always followed.

As stated earlier, when the user triggers a function code, the value is captured in the system variable SY-UCOMM. Typically a CASE statement is used to process this field in the user command module. Here is an example of a typical user command module:

```
*&———————————————————————————————*
*&      Module  USER_COMMAND_9100   INPUT
*&———————————————————————————————*
*       Controls GUI actions from screen            *
*—————————————————————————————.*
MODULE USER_COMMAND_9100 INPUT.

  CASE SY-UCOMM.
    WHEN 'BACK'.
*      Leave current screen
      LEAVE SCREEN.
    WHEN 'UEBE'.
*      Exit transaction.
      SET SCREEN 0.
      LEAVE SCREEN.
    WHEN 'EEOT'.
*      PF12 (Cancel) pressed.  Exit.
      SET SCREEN 0.
      LEAVE SCREEN.
    WHEN OTHERS.
      XFIELD1 = XFIELD2 + XFIELD3.
  ENDCASE.
  CLEAR SY-UCOMM.
ENDMODULE.                    " USER_COMMAND_9100   INPUT
```

As you can see in this example, the CASE statement allows you to list and process all possible function codes. When the user clicks the Back button, SY-UCOMM holds the function code BACK. The CASE statement evaluates SY-UCOMM and executes the matching code in the WHEN clause. Later in the chapter you will learn more about the SET SCREEN and LEAVE SCREEN commands; but for now it is enough to understand how to use CASE to evaluate the SY-UCOMM field.

After the CASE statement, a CLEAR command is used to clear the SY-UCOMM field. SAP does not clear SY-UCOMM automatically so you must make sure to clear it every time it is read. If you do not clear it, then the next time the PAI event is called, it is possible SY-UCOMM will hold the wrong function code. When the user presses a key that is not bound to a function code, the PAI event is still triggered. However, SY-UCOMM continues to hold the last function code if it is not cleared.

Here is another example of a more complicated user command module:

```
*&----------------------------------*
*&      Module   USER_COMMAND_9100   INPUT
*&----------------------------------*
*         Controls GUI actions from screen           *
*----------------------------------.*
MODULE USER_COMMAND_9100 INPUT.


  CASE SY-UCOMM.              "Holds function code
WHEN 'CLR'.
*      Clear Sales Order List
       CLEAR: INT_ORD[].
    WHEN 'FIND'.
*      Find planned orders based on sales order entered
       PERFORM FIND_ORDERS.
    WHEN 'TEST'.
*      Check input for errors
       PERFORM CHECK_ORDERS.
       PERFORM DISPLAY_RESULTS.
    WHEN 'EXAC'.
*      Process sales order
       PERFORM PROCESS_ORDERS.
       PERFORM DISPLAY_RESULTS.
       PERFORM CLEAR_PROCESSED_ORDERS.
    WHEN 'BACK'.
*      Move to previous screen.
       SET SCREEN 0.
       LEAVE SCREEN.
    WHEN 'UEBE'.
*      Exit transaction.
       SET SCREEN 0.
       LEAVE SCREEN.
```

```
      WHEN 'ENDE'.
*        PF12 (Cancel) pressed.  Exit.
         SET SCREEN 0.
         LEAVE SCREEN.
      WHEN OTHERS.
         CLEAR SY-UCOMM.
   ENDCASE.
   CLEAR SY-UCOMM.
ENDMODULE.                         " USER_COMMAND_9100   INPUT
```

In some cases you can process the command directly in the module or you can call a form to process the command in a subroutine. If you can process the function code in one or two commands, do it in the module. If the function code requires a large number of statements, call a form and process it in a subroutine.

In summary, a transaction processes user events when a screen is built with the required input and output fields. The developer decides what actions the user should be able to perform from the screen and maps those actions to function codes. For example, the user must be able to back out of the screen so a function code of BACK is defined. A user should also be able to save their work, so a function code of SAVE is defined, and so on.

Once you settle on the required function codes, you must give the user a way to trigger those codes. The function codes are mapped to screen buttons using the Screen Painter or to menu commands, toolbar buttons, and function keys in the GUI status using the Menu Painter.

Now that the user can trigger function codes, the last step is to write the USER_COMMAND_XXXXX module using a CASE statement to evaluate the SY-UCOMM field. Your transaction is then ready for use.

Calling Screens in ABAP

There are two techniques you can use to change the current screen of a transaction. The first method is to use the CALL SCREEN command to explicitly call a new screen. The second method is to use the SET SCREEN command to specify the next screen that should be shown and then leave the current screen using the LEAVE SCREEN command. The proper usage of these two techniques will be discussed next.

Using CALL SCREEN

If you want to move to another screen, the ABAP command CALL SCREEN can be used to transfer control. The CALL SCREEN command should be executed in a module in the PAI event. After the command is executed, the current processing ends and control is passed to the PBO event of the new screen. The syntax of the CALL SCREEN command is:

```
call screen <screen> [starting at x1 y1] [ending at x2 y2].
```

When the screen being called is a pop-up dialog, the addition of starting and ending options allow you to specify where the window will be located. In this example, control of the transaction is transferred to screen 9300 when the function code DETL is triggered.

```
*&——————————————————————————————*
*&      Module  USER_COMMAND_9200  INPUT
*&——————————————————————————————*
*       Controls GUI actions from screen              *
*————————————————————————————.*
MODULE USER_COMMAND_9200 INPUT.


  CASE SY-UCOMM.
    WHEN 'BACK'.
*      Leave current screen
      LEAVE SCREEN.
    WHEN 'DETL'.
*      Go to screen 9300
      CALL SCREEN 9300.
  ENDCASE.
  CLEAR SY-UCOMM.
ENDMODULE.                     " USER_COMMAND_9200  INPUT
```

SAP tracks what screens the user has visited and remembers them in a type of queue. Using the CALL SCREEN command adds the current screen to the queue and transfers control to the screen called. If the current screen is exited without specifying where to go next, SAP will return the user to the screen that called the current one. For example, if a user starts a transaction in screen 9100, calls screen 9150, then calls screen 9300, and exits screen 9300, control is transferred back to screen 9150.

In this next example, a pop-up dialog box is triggered when the user presses a button tied to the function code FIND. First view the user command module:

```
&———————————————————————————————.*
*&      Module   USER_COMMAND_9100   INPUT
*&———————————————————————————————*
*       Controls GUI actions from screen               *
*———————————————————————————————.*
MODULE USER_COMMAND_9100 INPUT.

  CASE SY-UCOMM.
    WHEN 'FIND'.
*      Call pop up find box
      PERFORM FIND_MATERIALS.
    WHEN 'TEST'.
*      Check input for errors
      PERFORM CHECK_MATERIALS.
    WHEN 'EXAC'.
*      Perform material_update.
      PERFORM PROCESS_MATERIALS.
    WHEN 'BACK'.
*      Return to previous screen
      SET SCREEN 0.
      LEAVE SCREEN.
    WHEN 'UEBE'.
*      Exit transaction.
      SET SCREEN 0.
      LEAVE SCREEN.
    WHEN 'ENDE'.
*      PF12 (Cancel) pressed.  Exit.
      SET SCREEN 0.
      LEAVE SCREEN.
    WHEN OTHERS.
      CLEAR SY-UCOMM.
  ENDCASE.
  CLEAR SY-UCOMM.
```

```
ENDMODULE.        " USER_COMMAND_9100   INPUT
```

When the find code is executed, a perform is executed to execute the ABAP code that makes the call to the new screen.

```
**************************************************************
*   Form Find_Materials
*_ _ _ _ _ _ _ _ _ _ _ _ _ _ _ _ _ _ _ _ _ _ _ _ _ _ _ _ _ _
*   This form ensures the user has entered a plant code and
*   if so calls screen 9300 which brings up a pop up box
*   where search criteria may be entered.
**************************************************************
form find_materials.

* Check for a valid plant and call 9300 if found
  if not ( marc-werks is initial ).
    select single werks into marc-werks from t100w
                       where werks = marc-werks.
    if sy-subrc eq 0.
      call screen 9300 starting at 30 10.
    else.
      message e999 with 'Invalid plant entered!'.
    endif.
  else.
    Message e999 with 'Please enter a valid plant!'.
  endif.
Endform.
```

Notice in the CALL SCREEN statement that only the starting position of the screen is specified. It is never required to specify the ending position. SAP will generate it automatically based on the starting position you give and the size of the screen.

Using SET SCREEN and LEAVE SCREEN

The other way to change the current screen is to use the SET SCREEN and LEAVE SCREEN commands. The LEAVE SCREEN command exits the current screen and turns control over to the screen that has been designated as "next." When you create a screen, one of the attributes that can be set is the default next screen. This default can be overridden at any time using the SET SCREEN command, explicitly setting the next screen. If you create a screen named 9300 and set the next screen default to 9100, you can override that default using the SET SCREEN command at any time.

Remember that the CALL SCREEN command explicitly turns control over to a new screen while adding the current screen to the queue. LEAVE SCREEN differs in that the current screen is not added to the queue; control is simply turned over to the next screen. Because leaving a screen does not add anything to the queue, you will more often use the LEAVE command than the CALL command. If you call any screens, the user must return to the original screen before the transaction ends because the transaction will not end until the queue is empty.

You can deliberately take advantage of the screen queue. If the next screen is set when you use the LEAVE command, control is transferred to that screen. But when the next screen is set to 0, the current screen is exited and control is passed to the last screen in the queue. If the queue is empty, the transaction ends. It is important to note that using the LEAVE SCREEN command does not automatically turn control over to the last screen in the queue. The programmer must set the next screen to 0.

Here is the syntax for both commands:

```
SET SCREEN <screen>.
LEAVE SCREEN.
```

The optional form LEAVE TO SCREEN is the functional equivalent of using both SET and LEAVE, combined in a single command as follows:

```
LEAVE TO SCREEN <screen>.
```

Several examples follow to demonstrate the use of SET and LEAVE, and CALL commands.

Suppose you have three screens, 9100, 9200, and 9300. The default next screen for each is 0, 9100, and 9300, respectively. Often a screen will have a default next screen of itself so the transaction does not leave the current screen without the programmer explicitly directing it to a new screen. If the following commands are issued starting from screen 9100, what screen will end up with control?

```
* From screen 9100
call screen 9200.

...

* From screen 9200
call screen 9300.
```

```
...
* From screen 9300
leave to screen 0.
```

In this case the screen that will end up with control is 9200. The first command adds 9100 to the queue and transfers control to 9200. The second command adds 9200 to the queue and transfers control to 9300. The final command exits screen 9300 and turns control to the last screen added to the queue—in this case, 9200.

Here is another example:

```
* From screen 9100
leave to screen 9200.
...
* From screen 9200
leave screen.
```

In this case, the screen that ends up with control is 9100. The first command transfers control to screen 9200. The next command turns control over to the default next screen for 9200, which is 9100.

Here is a final example:

```
* From screen 9100
leave to screen 9300.
...
* From screen 9300
leave to screen 9100.
...
* From screen 9100
leave to screen 9200.
...
* From screen 9200
leave to screen 0.
```

In this case, the transaction ends when the last command is executed. This last example is actually the most typical. Because the CALL SCREEN command forces the user to return to the calling screen before the transaction may be ended, most developers never use the CALL SCREEN command and the screen queue, but instead choose to explicitly control processing with LEAVE SCREEN or LEAVE TO SCREEN.

Modifying Screen Fields with LOOP AT SCREEN

Often you do not need multiple screens to accomplish different tasks. Instead you can modify the fields on the screen to achieve much of the same effect. Many of the field attributes described in Chapter 15, "Using the Screen Painter," can be modified with ABAP. Modification of fields is done in the PBO event—you modify the field and after the PBO ends the updated field is displayed.

In order to support modification of screen fields in ABAP, a special internal table is maintained by SAP. This system table is referred to as the Screen table and contains all fields of the current screen along with their attributes. The current screen is the screen from which the ABAP code is called. So, if in the flow control of screen 9200 a module named UPDATE_SCREEN is called, in that module the system table will contain all fields for screen 9200. Every time you change the current screen in your transaction, this system table is updated automatically with the fields from the new screen.

This system table can be looped through much like any other internal table, and information about the fields and attributes can be read and modified. This is accomplished through special versions of the LOOP and MODIFY commands. The syntax for these commands is simple. Here is the Loop syntax:

```
loop at screen.
...
endloop.
```

Here is the MODIFY syntax:

```
modify screen.
```

Table 18-1

SCREEN Table Field List

Field	Length	Type	Meaning
SCREEN-NAME	30	C	Field name
SCREEN-GROUP1	3	C	1st Group Setting
SCREEN-GROUP2	3	C	2nd Group Setting

Table 18-1 (continued)

Field	Length	Type	Meaning
SCREEN-GROUP3	3	C	3rd Group Setting
SCREEN-GROUP4	3	C	4th Group Setting
SCREEN-REQUIRED	1	C	Field input is mandatory
SCREEN-INPUT	1	C	Field accepts input
SCREEN-OUTPUT	1	C	Field is displayed
SCREEN-INTENSIFIED	1	C	Field font is bold
SCREEN-INVISIBLE	1	C	Field is invisible
SCREEN-LENGTH	1	X	Field length
SCREEN-ACTIVE	1	C	Field is active

When you loop through the system table, these fields are accessed as any field in an internal table. Attribute fields such as SCREEN-INVISIBLE and SCREEN-REQUIRED are stored as a '1' (attribute is set) or '0' (attribute is not set). An example of looping at the screen table would be the following, which loops through all fields on the current screen looking for a field named XVALUE1:

```
loop at screen.
  if screen-name = 'XVALUE1'.
    message i999 with 'Found the Field!'.
  endif.
endloop.
```

Just as you can read fields from the Screen table, normally you can also change some values, as in this example:

```
loop at screen.
  if screen-name = 'XVALUE1'.
    screen-input = 0.
    modify screen.
  endif.
endloop.
```

Much like a standard internal table, when you change a field in the Screen table, the change is not saved unless you use the MODIFY SCREEN command. When you change a field by modifying the Screen table, the change is presented to the user at the end of the PBO event. Therefore, changes should be done in modules called from the PBO event. Also the MODIFY SCREEN command can only be used inside of the LOOP AT SCREEN ... ENDLOOP loop.

The GROUPn fields correspond to the values found in the four group boxes when you create a screen field. They allow you to use a single identifier to make changes to a set of fields rather than hard coding the names of several fields in your loop. For example, look at these two code samples:

```
loop at screen.
  if screen-name = 'MARA-MATNR'
    or screen-name = 'MARA-WERKS'
    or screen-name = 'XDATE'.
    screen-required = 1.
    modify screen.
  endif.
endloop.


loop at screen.
  if screen-group1 = 'INS'.
    screen-required = 1.
    modify screen.
  endif.
endloop.
```

These two code samples would have an identical effect if the three fields, mara-matnr, mara-werks, and xdate were the only ones with a value of 'INS' set in the first group attribute. The value of using groups becomes readily apparent if you look at the two code samples. By using the group ID, you can add new fields to the screen without modifying the ABAP code in the second case. You would simply make sure to set the first group attribute to 'INS' for any new fields.

The next example demonstrates how a single screen could be used for display, edit, and creating data. Imagine a screen with a number of fields. When the screen is in display mode, none of the fields should allow input. When it is in edit mode, only non-key fields should allow input. Finally, when it is in create mode, all fields should allow input. In order to support this, all fields should have the group 1 attribute set to 'INS' and all non-key fields should have the group 2 attribute set to 'UPD'. By setting these attributes, you can control the two types of fields without hard coding any field names.

This first part of the example is the global data section of the transaction. Here, two variables will be created to keep track of when the transaction is in display, create, or edit mode.

```
*Global Data
* Indicates Display mode when transaction starts
data ws_display value 'X',
* When not in display (I)nsert or (U)pdate Mode
ws_ins_upd value ' '.
```

Next is the screen flow from the editing screen, which controls screen processing.

```
* Screen 9200 Flow Logic
process before output.
  module set_pf_status_9200.
  module modify_screen_9200.


process after input.
  module okcode_9200.
```

Here is the ABAP code for module okcode_9200, which controls the event processing in the PAI:

```
*&— — — — — — — — — — — — — — — — — — — — — — — — — — — — — — —.
*&      Module  OKCODE_9200 INPUT
*&  This module handles processing of function codes
*&— — — — — — — — — — — — — — — — — — — — — — — — — — — — — — —.
module okcode_9200 input.


*   Process depending on which key was pressed
  case sy-ucomm.
    when 'NEWL'.
*     Prepare for new entry
      ws_ins_upd = 'I'.
      ws_display = ' '.
    when 'AEND'.
*     Prepare for change/display mode
      if ws_display = 'X'.
        ws_display = ' '.    "Go to change
        ws_ins_upd = 'U'.
      else.
```

```
            ws_display = 'X'.    "Go to display
        endif.
    endcase.
    clear sy-ucomm.
endmodule.
```

Finally, the module modify_screen_9200 modifies the screen based on the display/change flags and sets the correct screen attributes:

```
*&- - - - - - - - - - - - - - - - - - - - - - - - - - - -·
*&      Module  MODIFY_SCREEN_9200  OUTPUT
*&- - - - - - - - - - - - - - - - - - - - - - - - - - - -·
*       Unlock fields on screen 9200 for edit or new entry
*       based on ws_ins_upd flag.
*- - - - - - - - - - - - - - - - - - - - - - - - - - - -
module modify_screen_9200 output.

  if ws_display = 'X'.
    loop at screen.
      check screen-group1 = 'INS'.
      screen-input = '0'.              "Zero locks field
      modify screen.
    endloop.
  else.
    loop at screen.
      check screen-group2 = 'UPD'.
      screen-input = '1'.              "One allows editing
      modify screen.
    endloop.
  endif.
  if ws_ins_upd = 'I'.
    loop at screen.
      check screen-group1 = 'INS'.
      screen-input = '1'.
      modify screen.
    endloop.
  endif.
```

```
endmodule.                " MODIFY_SCREEN_9200  OUTPUT
```

When the transaction begins, the display flag is set so all fields will be set to no input by the module modify_screen_9200 in the PBO event. After the screen is presented to the user, the update button can be pressed, which triggers the function code 'AEND'. Next, the PAI event occurs and the module okcode_9200 is executed. As you can see from the CASE statement, when 'AEND' occurs, ws_display will be set to 'X' and ws_ins_upd is set to 'U' indicating update mode. After the module completes, the PBO event is triggered and the module modify_screen_9200 executes again. Because the display and update flags are set, all fields with a group2 value of 'UPD' are set to allow input, and then control is again turned over to the user.

If, rather than pressing the update button, the user were to press the insert button, much the same would occur except that those fields with a group1 value of 'INS' would be set to allow insert. Because a field can belong to more than one group, it is easy to support both insert and update operations. It is typical that creating a new record requires more fields to be set to input than an update operation.

Calling List Processing within a Transaction

As you have seen, creating a screen can be a great deal of work. Many times, when you need to display a large amount of data to a user, you can accomplish it through the use of a list instead of a transaction screen. A list has a number of advantages over a screen. Since a list is dynamically re-created each time using write statements, it is much more flexible than a screen that can only present data in pre-defined fields. Also, a list can display any number of rows of data and can automatically handle many common user requests such as scrolling and printing. In the next chapter you will learn how to display a list of fields in a screen loop on a transaction screen. This task is not nearly as easy to accomplish as it was with a list.

SAP allows you to present a list to the user through the use of the LEAVE TO LIST-PROCESSING command. When this command is issued, the current screen ends and control is turned over to the list. A list has no screen number and is not created in Screen Painter in any way. But a list does require a GUI status and title to support standard list actions such as printing, scrolling, and downloading to a file. The

GUI status must be created like any other status in your transaction. Here is the syntax for the LEAVE TO LIST-PROCESSING command:

```
leave to list-processing [and return to screen <screen>].
```

The option [and return to screen <screen>] allows you to specify to which screen control is passed when the user exits the list processing screen. If you do not use this option, then control is passed to the last screen placed in the queue. The transaction ends if no screen is pending in the queue.

SAP refers to the execution of a transaction such as PAI and PBO events as dialog processing as opposed to the list processing as presented here. After you switch to list processing, you can use all of the standard commands that are used in ABAP reports, such as WRITE, SKIP, or HIDE.

In order to use list processing in a transaction, you must create a list-type GUI status. This is easy to do. With one exception, follow the instructions presented in Chapter 16, "Using the Menu Painter," to create a GUI status. However, when asked what type of GUI status you are creating, select the List Status option. This will create a GUI status that supports all normal list processing options. Unlike a standard GUI status, you do not need to make any changes or set any function codes. Then save and activate your status. The normal convention is to use the name, "LIST," for any list statuses. Also, a GUI title should be created to describe the screen that is presented to the user. Once the status and title are created, you are ready to use list processing in your transaction.

The following is an example of using list processing in a transaction. First, the flow logic is presented:

```
* Screen 9100 Flow Logic
process before output.
  module set_pf_status_9100.
process after input.
  module okcode_9100.
```

Next, the module okcode_9100 processes the function code. In this case, the module exits the current screen and switches to list processing:

```
*&----------------------------------------------
*&      Module  OKCODE_9100 INPUT
*& This module handles processing of function codes
```

```
*&- - - - - - - - - - - - - - - - - - - - - - - - - - - - - - -.
module okcode_9100 input.


*   Process depending on which key was pressed
    case sy-ucomm.
      when 'XREF'.
*       Display where used list
        leave to list-processing and return to screen 9100.
        perform where_used.
      when others.
    endcase.
    clear sy-ucomm.
endmodule.
```

Finally, here is the form, where_used, which sets up the screen and displays data from a custom table. Notice how this module uses standard WRITE statements similar to many ABAP reports you have written:

```
*&- - - - - - - - - - - - - - - - - - - - - - - - - - - - -*
*&        Form   Where_Used
*&- - - - - - - - - - - - - - - - - - - - - - - - - - - - -*
* Display a list of all requests in ZMREQST which
* are linked the current reference material
*- - - - - - - - - - - - - - - - - - - - - - - - - - - - -.*
form where_used.
* Enable standard list functions
  set pf-status 'LIST'.
* Display title for where used report
  set titlebar '100' with mara-matnr.


  move mara-matnr to ws_matnr.   "Save current material


* Display column titles
  write: /, text-001 intensified off,
            text-002 intensified off,
            text-003 intensified off,
            text-004 intensified off,
```

```
           text-005 intensified off.
   select * from zmreqst where rmatnr = mara-matnr.
*    Write information from table
     write: / zmreqst-matnr,
               zmreqst-werks,
               zmreqst-desc,
               zmreqst-position,
               zmreqst-level.
   endselect.
endform.
```

As you can see, once you exit to list processing and set the GUI status and title, the actual printing of the report is done exactly as you would in a standard ABAP report. This is the real strength of list processing—you can use all of your experience with ABAP to display information. In fact, list processing even supports the standard interactive reporting functions such as AT LINE-SELECTION.

NOTE

Users can exit list processing and return to the screen you specify in the AND RETURN… option by using the green back-arrow. However, if for some reason you want to exit list processing programmatically, you can do so with the LEAVE SCREEN command. Just as LEAVE SCREEN exits the current screen, it can also exit list processing if used that way in your ABAP code.

Summary

To summarize, there are a number of ABAP commands and techniques that can be used in a transaction to control processing. ABAP is used to read the function code triggered by the user from the sy-ucomm field. Once the code is read, standard ABAP commands can be used to display, change, or create data as needed by the transaction. Also, through the use of the SET/LEAVE SCREEN and CALL SCREEN commands, the programmer can control the flow of screens in the transaction. Then the LOOP AT SCREEN command can be used to modify the attributes of fields on the current screen. Finally, list processing can be used within a transaction as a more flexible method of displaying data rather than using a fixed screen. You are now ready to create robust transactions.

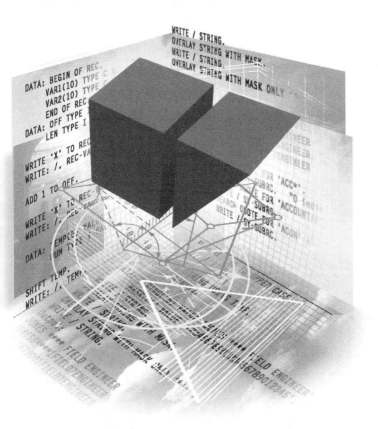

Chapter 19

Screen Loops

In This Chapter

♦ Using loops to process sets of data

♦ Updating data via screen loops

♦ A solution-tracking example

♦ Attributes of high quality table displays

Using Loops to Process Sets of Data

Step loops and table controls are the methods used to place tables of data on screens. The difference between the two is simply that table controls are enhanced step loops. Table controls were introduced in Release 3.0 of R/3 and replaced most of the step loops. With step loops and table controls, you define attributes of the table and each of its rows in the Screen Painter, and then control how the data and user commands are handled through the PBO and PAI flow control of the screen.

There are a few situations in which you still need to use a step loop instead of a table control: When you want to display two lines on the display for each row in the table, and when you want to build a transaction that will be used through the Internet Transaction Server, (ITS) which currently cannot handle the special attributes of the table control element.

Since the table control is basically derived from the step loop and the step loop is still required at times, the functionality of step loops will be described first and then expanded upon to discuss table controls.

Using the Loop Command

The basic syntax of the LOOP and ENDLOOP commands was covered along with the other flow control commands in Chapter 17, "Using Flow Logic to Develop a Transaction." The LOOP and ENDLOOP commands transfer data back and forth between the screen and the global memory area of the module pool. In the PBO event, this functionality is used to display a table on the screen for the user; in the PAI event it is used to retrieve any changes made to the table by the user and to update the associated data. An example of a simple table is shown in Figure 19-1.

If you want a table on your screen, you must have a corresponding LOOP statement in both the PBO and PAI—even if there are noprocessing steps in between the LOOP and ENDLOOP statements.

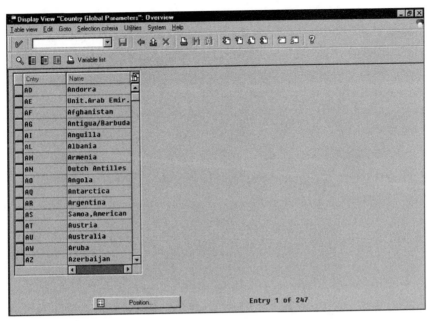

FIGURE 19-1

A simple table view

When you code a simple LOOP that has no additional parameters in the flow logic of your program, each row in a loop is comprised of fields, which are declared as global variables within your ABAP program (usually a module pool). During the PBO event, each pass of the LOOP statement will take the current contents of the ABAP variables and place them on the screen in the current row of the table that is indicated and controlled by the system variable SY-LOOPC.

During the PAI event, with each pass of the LOOP statement the contents of the current row in the table are transferred from the screen to these ABAP variables. You are then responsible for processing this data, including storing the data and handling the scrolling. You can use any flow logic control you want within a LOOP, including commands like FIELD, CHAIN, and MODULE, as discussed in Chapter 17.

Using the Loop Command with Internal Tables

The LOOP command is a bit more complicated when the "AT" parameter is added to associate an internal table with the loop.

```
LOOP AT INT_TAB.
... <processing logic>...
ENDLOOP.
```

During this processing, the loop processes the screen rows and the internal table in tandem while scroll bars are shown on the screen. The processing of the scroll bars is handled internally with no additional logic required. You can use the internal table option with both step loops and table controls. Variations of the LOOP with internal tables were discussed at the end of Chapter 17; these features allow you to control, for instance, which rows of the internal table you want processed in the loop.

Using the Loop Command with Table Controls

Using the LOOP command with table controls is the most popular method of creating tables on screens. Table controls have many advantages over step loops and will eventually totally replace the step loop. Some of the advantages of table controls are:

- ◆ The ability to allow the user to scroll both vertically and horizontally in a table and to scroll within a field if the field contents are longer than the field.
- ◆ The ability to allow the user to resize and/or interchange the columns and then save this configuration for future use.
- ◆ The improved table appearance through the use of features such as separators and column headers along with attributes that can resize the table if the user resizes the window.

The general syntax for a table control is as follows.

```
LOOP AT  INT_TAB WITH CONTROL <cnt1>.
... <processing logic>...
ENDLOOP.
```

Where <cnt1> is defined as a control with this CONTROL declaration:

```
CONTROL: <cnt1> TYPE TABLEVIEW USING SCREEN <nnnn>
```

Updating Data via Screen Loops

There are two key steps to update data through the LOOP command. The first is to put the table onto the screen and the second is to add in all of the associated logic.

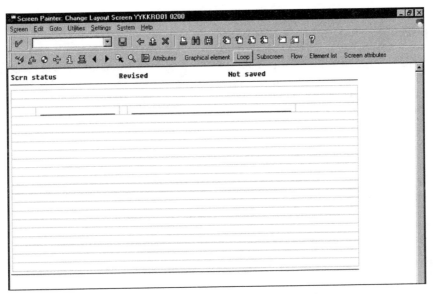

FIGURE 19-2

Building a simple table in Screen Painter

Creating the Screen Object for Step Loops

The first example table here is set up to contain rows with only two fields, which are then populated with a simple LOOP command. To set up this table, use these steps:

1. Create a new module pool and then go to the Screen Painter and create screen 0100.

2. When complete, go to the layout view in Screen Painter and place two fields on the screen, one 18 characters long (give it the variable name WS_MATNR) and the other 40 characters long (WS_MAKTX), as shown in Figure 19-2.

3. Next, mark the beginning of the loop by clicking the left side of the first field, then click Loop.

4. Mark the end of the loop by clicking the end of the second field, and then click End Loop. This defines the end of the loop block, which can be more than one physical line for step loops. Define the size of your table by positioning your cursor about five lines from the top of the highlighted area and clicking on the End Loop button (see Figure 19-3). Save the screen.

NOTE

If you are working in an SAP release lower than 4.0a, some of the commands and input fields will vary slightly in the Screen Painter. For example, the fixed loop flag is part of the attributes screen in 3.X. Conversely, in version 4.0, the fixed loop flag is a button in the Screen Painter and cannot be set via the attributes screen.

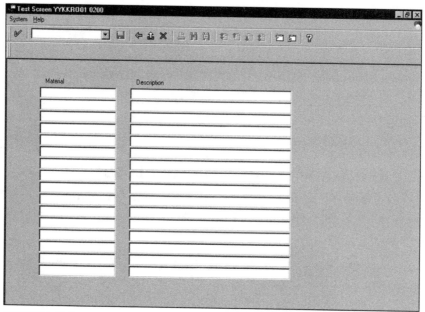

FIGURE 19-3

A simple table in Screen Painter with two input fields per row

TIP

You can define from within the Screen Painter if the loop is fixed or variable. A fixed loop will contain a specific number of rows that will not alter if the user changes the size of their screen. In a variable loop, the number of rows changes when the user changes the size of their screen or font.

Writing Flow Logic for Step Loops

The following is an example of how to set up a step loop through the LOOP command. While in the Screen Painter, you can apply this flow logic to the screen developed for Figure 19-3.

```
* Global Data Definition (can be placed in the "top" of the
* module pool
  DATA:             WS_MATNR LIKE MAKT-MATNR,
                    WS_MAKTX LIKE MAKT-MAKTX,
                    WS_INIT TYPE C.


DATA: BEGIN OF INT_DATAOCCURS 10,
                  MATNR LIKE MARA-MATNR,
                  MAKTX LIKE MAKT-MAKTX,
        END OF INT_DATA.


* PBO Flow Control
MODUEL INIT_0100.
LOOP.
    READ TABLEINT_DATA INDEX SY-LOOPC.
    WS_MATNR = INT_DATA-MATNR.   WS_MAKTX = INT_DATA-MAKTX.
ENDLOOP..


*PAI Flow Control
MODULEOKCODE_100.
LOOP..


  INT_DATA-MATNR = WS_MATNR.
  INT_DATA-MAKTX = WS_MAKTX.
  APPENDINT_DATA.
ENDLOOP.
```

The following modules are placed in the appropriate includes within your module pool (MYY00O10 and MYY00I10 for example):

```
MODULEINIT_0100 output.
  IF WS_INIT IS INITIAL.
```

```
        REFRESHINT_DATA.
          INT_DATA-MATNR = 'ABC123'.
  INT_DATA-MAKTX = 'TEST1'.
          APPEND INT_DATA.
  INT_DATA-MATNR = 'DEF456'.
  INT_DATA-MAKTX = 'TaEST2'.
          APPENDINT_DATA.
  WS_INIT = 'X'.
      END IF.
ENDMODULE.


MODULEOKCODE_0100 INPUT.
    REFRESHINT_DATA.
ENDMODULE.
```

Creating the Screen Object for Tables with Table Controls

The creation of the screen object for a table with table controls is fairly similar to that of a step loop:

1. Start with a new module pool and create screen 0100.

2. Click your cursor at the upper-left position where the table will begin. Now choose Edit | Create Eleament | Table Control.

3. Next, click the lower-right corner of the table display area.

TIP

Using Screen Painter, you can also create table controls by converting a step loop to a table control, and vice versa. To convert a loop from one type to another, select the loop and then choose the Edit menu to perform the desired conversion. Although this changes the Screen Painter object, you must still modify the flow logic portion to work properly.

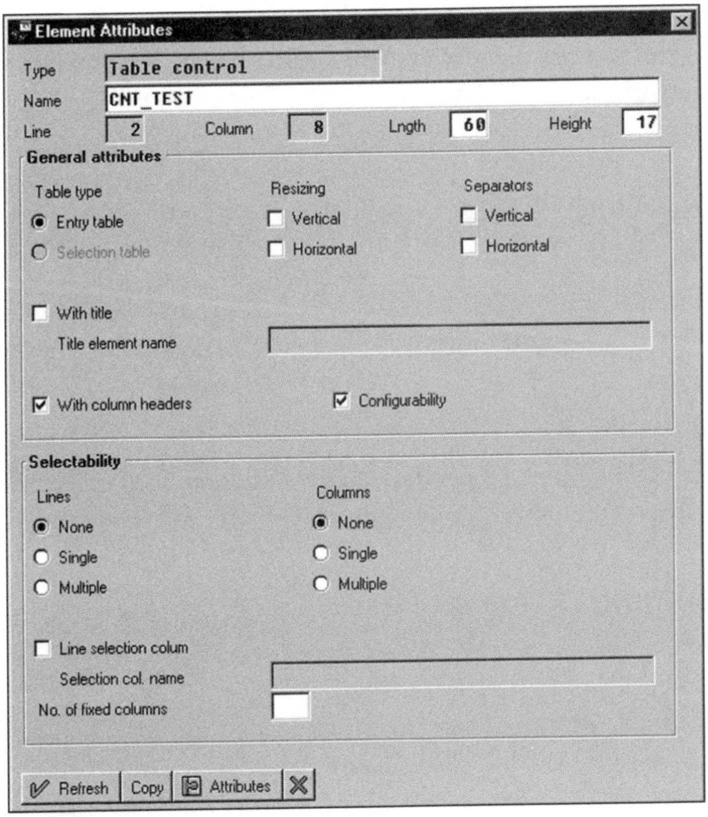

FIGURE 19-4

Table control element attributes

Once the block is defined, you can set up the general table and column attributes:

1. Click in the table area and then click the select button. This selects the entire area of your table.

2. Click the header attributes button to see a screen similar to Figure 19-4.

3. In the Name box, type the name for the table control. In this example, use the control CNT_TEST.

Table Type

A table type can be defined as either Entry or Selection. An Entry table should have at least one input field. All input fields are white by default, while all non-input fields are the same color as the screen's background. A Selection table is used to display data or to prompt the user to make a selection; all fields on a Selection table have a white (default) color.

Resizing

When selected, the resizing option maintains the distance between the bottom of the table and the bottom of the screen should the user resize the screen. You should set this attribute, because if you don't, the fields below the table may not be visible if the user shrinks the screen.

Separators

Selecting Horizontal or Vertical separators controls whether lines appear between the table cells, separating rows and columns.

Title and Column Headings

You can also select to have a title on your table by selecting the "With Title" checkbox. If this checkbox is selected you may also place a variable in the "Title Element Name" field, which will set the actual text in the title. You can turn column headings on or off via the "With Column Headers" checkbox. The header is then defined when you set up the configuration of the column itself.

Configurability

Selecting this option allows end users to configure the table to their preference and then save these settings for later use. This is a helpful feature for a user.

TIP

When using a screen where the Configurability option was incorporated, a user can save and load settings by clicking the button that appears at the top of the vertical scroll bar. A Table Settings dialog box (see Figure 19-5) appears from where the user can save and retrieve display configurations. However, you should be aware that these saved configurations are global—they affect all users.

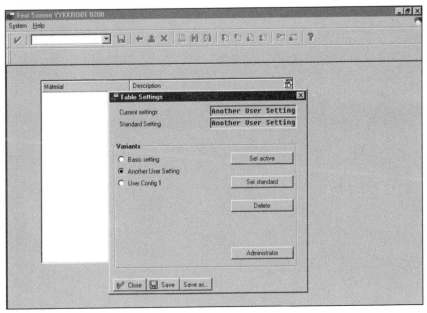

FIGURE 19-5

Saving/retrieving display configurations

Selectability

The options in the Selectability group controls how many rows or columns the user can select at one time. If you want a separate column on the table to indicate if it is selected or not (like a checkbox) you can select the "Line Selection Column" checkbox. If you do, you must also supply the name of the variable that will be used for this checkbox and place it in the "Selection col. name" field.

In this section you can also control how many of the leftmost columns will always be displayed, even if the user scrolls to the right. If you enter the value of '2' in the "No. of fixed columns," then the two leftmost columns will always be displayed regardless of how far the user scrolls to the right.

After you have defined the control table, you will build what each column will contain (see Figure 19-6) by clicking on the table and then pressing the Cntrl Element button. From the Column Elements screen, you can set the display and storage attributes for each column in the table.

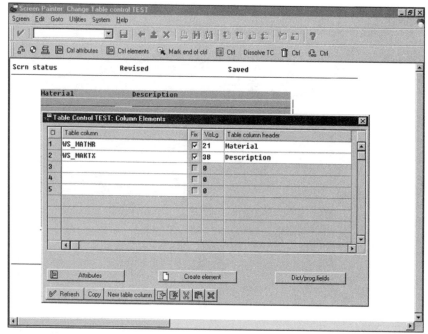

FIGURE 19-6

Column elements definition screen

Table Column

The Table Column field stores the name of the variable that will be used to display the data. The variable's Data Dictionary attributes (if they exist) will be inherited for this table column.

Fix

If Fix is selected for a column, then that column cannot be switched with other columns and cannot be resized. Only those columns that appear consecutively on the left side of the table can be set. For example, if you have ten columns in a table, you can fix the leftmost 5 columns (i.e. columns 1, 2, 3, 4, and 5) but you cannot fix columns 1 and 3 (you would have to fix column 2 as well).

Visible Length (VisLg)

This is the visible length for the field in columns. If you define this length to be larger than the field that is associated with the field, you will get an error. If you type in a value that is smaller than the length of the variable then you will only be able to see this many characters.

Table Column Headers

A table column header is the text string that appears above the columns. Here you are defining the field name for the column heading, not the column heading itself. Once you have entered a value in one of these fields, click Copy to go to a standard Screen Painter field attribute screen from where you can complete the field description. The description will be used for the column heading. In this way, dynamic column headings are created that you can control from within your program.

Writing Flow Logic for Table Controls

Now that you have seen how a simple table can work, you can try something a little bit more complicated such as creating the flow logic for the screen developed earlier (refer to Figure 19-3). The following flow logic example only discusses how the LOOP command is integrated. A full example later in this chapter will show some finer details such as database updates, paging, and search functions.

```
*Global Data Definition (for the module pool "top")
TABLES: MAKT. DATA:  BEGIN OF INT_DATA OCCURS 1,MATNR LIKE MAKT-MATNR,
MAKTX LIKE MAKT-MAKTX,      END OF INT_DATA.DATA: WS_COUNT TYPE I. CONTROLS
CNT_TEST TYPE TABLEVIEW USING SCREEN 0100.


* PBO Flow Control


MODULE INIT_0100.
LOOP AT INT_DATA WITH CONTROL
                        CNT_TEST CURSOR CNT_TEST-TOP_LINE.
           MODULE SHOW_DATA.
ENDLOOP.


*PAI Flow Control
MODULE OKCODE 100.
LOOP.
```

```
                  INT_DATA-MATNR = WS_MATNR.
                  INT_DATA-MAKTX = WS_MAKTX.
                  APPEND INT_DATA.
ENDLOOP.
* MODULES


MODULE INIT_0100 OUTPUT.
                  MAKT-MATNR = INT_DATA-MATNR.
                  MAKT-MAKTX = INT_DATA-MAKTX.
ENDMODULE.


MODULE OKCODE_0100 INPUT.
                  REFRESH INT_DATA.
ENDMODULE.
```

Nearly all of the attributes of the table control can be set at run time. Table 19-1 lists the field names of the control structure and a description of its purpose. Most of these values can be initially defined when you set up the table in Screen Painter. If you want to reset a table control to the settings originally defined in Screen Painter, you can perform this ABAP command:

```
REFRESH table control FROM SCREEN <screen number>.
```

Table 19-1

Table Control Attributes Usable by ABAP Commands at Run Time

Field Name	Description
FIXED_COLS	When selected, is used to set the column as fixed width. Only columns on the left side of the table can have this option selected.
LINES	The number of lines to be displayed in the table.
TOP_LINE	The row of the table that is displayed on the top row
CURRENT_LINE	The row that is currently processed in the loop.
LEFT_COL	The leftmost non-fixed column.
LINE_SEL_MODE	The method of line selection. 0 = None, 1 = Single Line, 2 = Multiple Lines
COL_SEL_MODE	The method of column selection. 0 = None, 1 = Single Column, 2 = Multiple Columns
LINE_SELECTOR	Controls whether the Line Selection check boxes are displayed.
H_GRID	Controls whether horizontal grids are displayed.

Table 19-1 continued

V_GRID	Controls whether vertical grids are displayed.
COLS	An internal table containing information about the columns. The structure is as follows:
COLS-SCREEN	Screen is the same structure you are used to with normal screen fields; it has fields such as input, active, and invisible. Do a show on the structure "screen" for a complete list.
COLS-INDEX	Index number of the column, starting with 0, on leftmost side.
COL-SELECTED	Indicates whether the column is selected.

Solution Tracking Example

In this section, you will create a simple table transaction used to keep track of customer-based solutions.

The Scenario

In this example there is a multinational business with many instances of SAP installed worldwide. They have some customer-developed bolt-ons that are developed in a central location and then distributed to all of their various SAP installations. They would like to have a simple transaction to track the transports for all of their customer solutions.

Solution Analysis

Keeping solutions synchronized across many SAP platforms is a common problem and an elaborate solution resolving it could be developed. A simple table and a transaction to maintain it will be illustrated here.

For this example, assume that the customer requests a transaction where they can maintain the table entries (add, delete, and change). This simple request could be done with the table maintenance generator, which really just uses table controls, but one will be built from scratch so that all aspects of its operation can be controlled.

Table Layout

The table in this example will be called YTRACK and will have the layout shown in Table 19-2.

Table 19-2

Table layout for YTRACK

Field Name	Key	Length	Description
BRANCH	X	10	Location of SAP system
SOLUTION	X	10	Name of solution
TRANSPORT	X	10	Transport number sent to system
TRANDATE		8	Date transport sent
INSTALL		1	Transport actually imported into destination system
COMMENTS		30	Brief comment with problem identifier

Building the Screen

The screen for this example will be a singular screen (0100) in the customer module pool SAPMYY00. The only contents will be a table display along with fields displaying the current record and the total number of records. The table control element will look like Figure 19-7. The individual column entries are shown in Figure 19-8.

Once the table has been set up, two additional fields—WS_CURREC and WS_TOTREC—are added to the screen near the bottom, as shown in Figure 19-9, to display the current record number and the total records. These two variables are defined as three-byte character strings. A simple GUI status was added in Menu Painter with the functions listed in Table 19-3.

Flow Logic for the Example

The flow logic for this program is fairly simple. The data must be displayed to the user while allowing the user to switch between display and change mode, and the user must be able to save the data. To keep this listing fairly short and to not confuse loops with other concepts, some functions will be left out that would normally be included in a transaction. For example, you'd want to include functions such as record locking, stricter exit control (such as checking to see if a change was made before letting the user exit the screen), and some other data checks.

Table 19-3

Example Functions of the GUI STATUS "MAIN"

Function Code	Description
BACK	Exit this screen
Exit	Exit this screen
SAVE	Save the data to the database
P—	Go to top of page
P-	Move backward one page
P+	Move forward one page
P++	Move forward to the last page
DIS	Display mode
CHG	Change mode
NEW	Create new entry

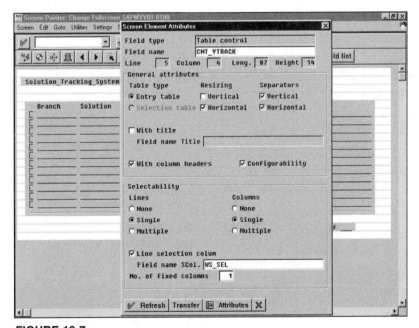

FIGURE 19-7

Table control element attributes

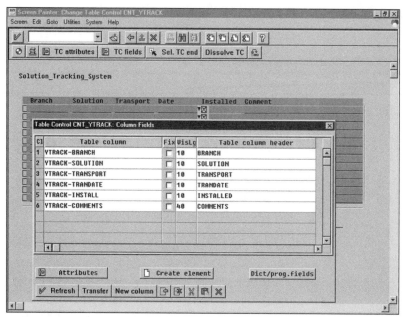

FIGURE 19-8

Table control column attributes

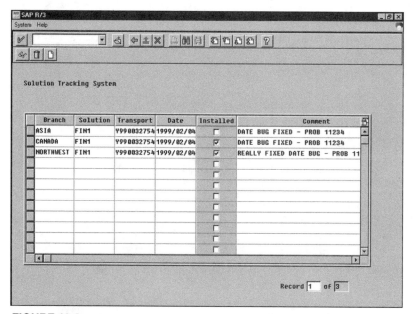

FIGURE 19-9

The completed screen with sample data

Here's the flow control for module pool SAPMYY01 Screen 0100:

```
PROCESS BEFORE OUTPUT.
  MODULE INIT_0100.
  LOOP AT INT_YTRACK WITH CONTROL CNT_YTRACK
                         CURSOR  CNT_YTRACK-TOP_LINE.
    MODULE SHOW_0100.
  ENDLOOP.
  MODULE DISP_DATA.
  MODULE STATUS_0100.
*
PROCESS AFTER INPUT.
  LOOP AT INT_YTRACK.
    MODULE GET_0100.
  ENDLOOP.
  MODULE OKCODE_0100.
```

Module Pool SAPMYY01:

```
PROGRAM SAPMYY01.
* Top - Global Data deceleration for module pool
INCLUDE MYY01TOP.
* PBO Modules
INCLUDE MYY01O10.
* PAI Modules
INCLUDE MYY01I10.
```

Include ABAP MYY01TOP which contains data declarations:

```
*_____*
*    INCLUDE MYY01TOP                                    *
*_____*


*_____Table Declaration_____*
TABLES: YTRACK.
*_____Internal Table Declaration_____*
DATA: INT_YTRACK LIKE YTRACK OCCURS 100 WITH HEADER LINE.
DATA: BEGIN OF INT_CHG_FCODE OCCURS 5,
        FCODE(4),
```

```
          END OF INT_CHG_FCODE.
*———————————————Global Data Declaration————————.*
DATA: WS_COUNT  TYPE I,       " Counter used in Table Control
      WS_CURREC(3)    ,       " Top Record Displayed
      WS_TOTREC TYPE I,       " Total number of Records
      WS_TAB_SIZE TYPE I,     " Size of Table
      WS_INT_IDX  TYPE I,     " Index pointer for Internal table
      WS_RECORD(3)    ,       " Total number of records (for display)
      WS_MODE   TYPE C,       " Current Edit Mode
      WS_INIT   TYPE C,       " First time call flag
      WS_SEL    TYPE C.       " Single line selection flag
*———————————————Control Declaration————————.*
CONTROLS CNT_YTRACK TYPE TABLEVIEW USING SCREEN 100.
```

Include ABAP MYY01O10, which contains output modules for the flow control:

```
*———————————————————————————.*
*    INCLUDE MYY01O10
*———————————————————————————.*
MODULE INIT_0100 OUTPUT.
  SORT INT_YTRACK.
  IF NOT WS_INIT IS INITIAL. EXIT. ENDIF.
  WS_INIT = 'X'.
  WS_MODE = 'D'.
  INT_CHG_FCODE = 'DIS'.
  APPEND INT_CHG_FCODE.
  INT_CHG_FCODE = 'DEL'.
  APPEND INT_CHG_FCODE.
  INT_CHG_FCODE = 'NEW'.
  APPEND INT_CHG_FCODE.
  SELECT * FROM YTRACK INTO TABLE INT_YTRACK.
ENDMODULE.

MODULE STATUS_0100 OUTPUT.
  IF WS_MODE = 'D' OR WS_MODE IS INITIAL.
      SET PF-STATUS 'MAIN' EXCLUDING INT_CHG_FCODE.
  ELSE.
```

```
          SET PF-STATUS 'MAIN' EXCLUDING 'CHG'.
      ENDIF.
      LOOP AT SCREEN.
          IF SCREEN-GROUP1 <> 'MOD'. CONTINUE. ENDIF.
          IF WS_MODE = 'D'.
                SCREEN-INPUT = '0'.
          ELSEIF SY-LOOPC <= WS_TOTREC.
                SCREEN-INPUT = '1'.
          ENDIF.
          MODIFY SCREEN.
      ENDLOOP.
ENDMODULE.


MODULE SHOW_0100 OUTPUT.
      YTRACK-BRANCH     = INT_YTRACK-BRANCH.
      YTRACK-SOLUTION   = INT_YTRACK-SOLUTION.
      YTRACK-TRANSPORT = INT_YTRACK-TRANSPORT.
      YTRACK-TRANDATE = INT_YTRACK-TRANDATE.
      YTRACK-INSTALL = INT_YTRACK-INSTALL.
      YTRACK-COMMENTS   = INT_YTRACK-COMMENTS.
ENDMODULE.


MODULE DISP_DATA OUTPUT.
      DESCRIBE TABLE INT_YTRACK LINES WS_TOTREC.
      WS_CURREC = CNT_YTRACK-TOP_LINE.
      WS_RECORD = WS_TOTREC.
ENDMODULE.
```

Include ABAP MYY01I10, which contains inputmodules for the flow control:

```
*_____*
*    INCLUDE MYY01I10                          *
*_____*
MODULE GET_0100.
* Get size of table and current internal table index.
*    ws_int_idx  = sy-stepl + cnt_ytrack-top_line - 1.
      WS_INT_IDX  = CNT_YTRACK-TOP_LINE.
```

```
          WS_TAB_SIZE = SY-LOOPC.
* exit if not in change mode
      IF WS_MODE = 'D'. EXIT. ENDIF.
* Check for selection and deletion.
      IF WS_SEL  = 'X' AND SY-UCOMM = 'DEL'.
         DELETE INT_YTRACK INDEX WS_INT_IDX.
         EXIT.
      ENDIF.
* otherwise just update the internal table
      INT_YTRACK-BRANCH    = YTRACK-BRANCH.
      INT_YTRACK-SOLUTION  = YTRACK-SOLUTION.
      INT_YTRACK-TRANSPORT = YTRACK-TRANSPORT.
      INT_YTRACK-TRANDATE  = YTRACK-TRANDATE.
      INT_YTRACK-INSTALL   = YTRACK-INSTALL.
      INT_YTRACK-COMMENTS  = YTRACK-COMMENTS.
      MODIFY INT_YTRACK INDEX WS_INT_IDX.
ENDMODULE.


MODULE OKCODE_0100.
  CASE SY-UCOMM.
    WHEN 'P+'.
        CLEAR SY-UCOMM.
        ADD WS_TAB_SIZE TO CNT_YTRACK-TOP_LINE.
        IF CNT_YTRACK-TOP_LINE > WS_TOTREC.
            CNT_YTRACK-TOP_LINE = WS_TOTREC.
        ENDIF.
    WHEN 'P++'.
        CLEAR SY-UCOMM.
        CNT_YTRACK-TOP_LINE = WS_TOTREC.
    WHEN 'P-'.
        CLEAR SY-UCOMM.
        SUBTRACT WS_TAB_SIZE FROM CNT_YTRACK-TOP_LINE.
        IF CNT_YTRACK-TOP_LINE < 1.
            CNT_YTRACK-TOP_LINE = 1.
        ENDIF.
```

```
WHEN 'P--'.

    CLEAR SY-UCOMM.

    CNT_YTRACK-TOP_LINE = 1.

WHEN 'DIS'.

    CLEAR SY-UCOMM.

    WS_MODE = 'D'.

WHEN 'CHG'.

    CLEAR SY-UCOMM.

    WS_MODE = 'C'.

WHEN 'SAVE'.

    SELECT * FROM YTRACK.

        DELETE YTRACK.

    ENDSELECT.

    INSERT YTRACK FROM TABLE INT_YTRACK.

WHEN 'NEW'.

    CLEAR INT_YTRACK.

    CNT_YTRACK-TOP_LINE =   1.

    INSERT INT_YTRACK INDEX 1.

WHEN 'EXIT'.

    CLEAR SY-UCOMM.

    LEAVE.

WHEN 'BACK'.

    CLEAR SY-UCOMM.

    LEAVE TO SCREEN 0.

WHEN OTHERS.

    CLEAR SY-UCOMM.

CNT_YTRACK-TOP_LINE = WS_CURREC.

  ENDCASE.

ENDMODULE.
```

The Final Product

Once the flow logic has been integrated with the work previously done with the Screen Painter, the result (with a bit of data) will look similar to Figure 19-9.

High Quality Table Displays

Building displays for tables involves more than just making sure that the data is displayed and that the user can edit it. Good programmers make sure that the transactions they build are easy to use and have more than the bare minimum of functionality. Adding extras to table screens requires little time and will quickly become second nature to you.

 CAUTION

If possible, do not display different screens or use different processing logic if you are processing in the foreground as opposed to calling the transaction in the background. SAP does this in many transactions but that still does not make it right for you!

Batch Input-Friendly Screens

When designing any transaction that maintains data (including tables), it is important to make sure that the screens are easy to navigate while in batch input mode. If the screens you design are difficult to use, you may find that people will bypass your screens and will update the tables directly!

Making a screen BDC friendly involves table positioning. Make sure that you have a Find or Position feature on your screen that has enough flexibility so that someone can define a unique record in the table. If you are displaying a table with three fields, such as a material number, plant, and a customer field, with the material and plant indicating a unique key, then having a position function with just material will probably be okay for online users. Such a table will display to them the material they are looking for and then they can cursor to the plant they want.

This type of search, however, will not work effectively for batch input. For a batch input program, you will want to set up both the material and plant input fields in the search function.

Another way to make screens batch input-friendly is to make sure that you can insert rows systematically into tables. SAP typically allows the user to press insert with a resulting empty second row.

Visual Attributes to Include in Transactions with Tables

In this section some features will be outlined that have no functional impact on screens but will make your transactions that contain tables better looking and easier to read.

The first thing you need to do is avoid creating multiple-line table displays. These types of displays are hard to read and can usually be avoided by transferring the data to a few single-line table displays. This enables horizontal scrolling, or where only key fields are displayed, allows the user to move to a screen with more detail.

 TIP

It is very useful to have the current page/record field as an input field even if the table is in display mode. This allows the user to position the table exactly where they want. Also, if you decide to show the current record and total records (instead of current and total pages), it is a good idea to display the record number on each line of the table display.

Sometimes there is a requirement for a two-line display to avoid having users skip back and forth between two or more screens. Figure 19-10 illustrates a two-line display with the transaction for Sales Order entry VA01. If you need to make a two-line display, distinguish the top header line from the bottom one using formatting options such as highlighting. You may also want to apply the same formatting to the data lines.

All fields in the table should be aligned properly. This means that numeric fields should be right-aligned and all other fields should be left-aligned. Column headers should have the same alignment as the column that they are describing.

Do not forget titles for the tables. A good place for the title is in the box around the table. Fields that will always be display-only should not be recessed, whereas fields that can have input should always be recessed (three-dimensional format option) even if they are currently in display-only mode. The exception to this rule is a check box, which should always be recessed (see Figure 19-11).

You may also want to tell the user what page or record they are currently on and the total number of records or pages that are in the table.

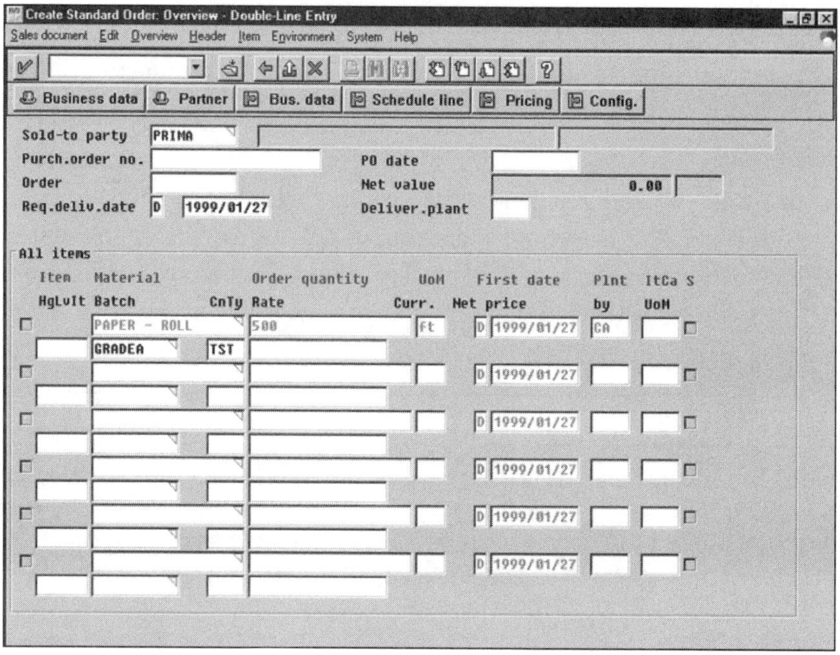

FIGURE 19-10

A two-line table display (transaction VA01)

Functional Attributes to Include in Transactions with Tables

There are many functions that you should put in transactions with tables to make them easier to use. Some of the attributes that you add will be determined by the functionality that you want in your transaction. Other attributes should be in every transaction that has a table.

Before actually starting the program development phase of a transaction containing a table, it is a very good idea to get the needs and expectations of the end users. It is easier to add all of the functions at one time than to add them individually later. You may want to ask the user to give you an example of a transaction currently in SAP that has the same functions that they want. You can then copy these functions.

The first set of attributes that should be included consists of the select all/deselect all buttons. These functions are used to select/deselect all lines for the next user

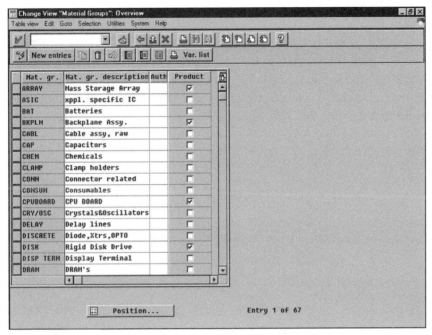

FIGURE 19-11

Preferred display attributes of a table

function (deletion, for instance). They should be included in the Edit menu along with the standard SAP buttons (refer to Figure 19-11).

Another useful set of attributes is the ability to select blocks of rows with the select block command made available through the Edit menu.

Giving the user the ability to sort the data in a variety of manners can also be a nice feature. By adding a simple sort button you may save yourself time writing reports later that simply display the data in a different sorted manner.

There are also the standard functions that nearly all table displays require: add, delete, insert, and change. When programming these, make sure that you do not allow the user to exit the screen without checking to see if they want to save their work.

Summary

Developing a transaction for the maintenance of a simple table is quite easy, especially when using the table control functionality. Table controls save the programmer from doing many of the mundane tasks that were involved with step loop programming.

Complex table maintenance and having a screen that is easy for the user to understand and use requires some work and should be designed on paper before the programming is started. Up front design and approval will save time and ensure that the end user gets what they want.

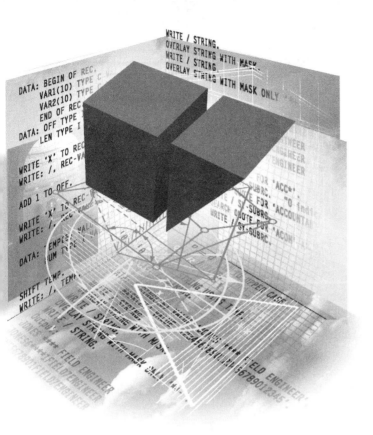

Chapter 20

Advanced
Techniques

In This Chapter

- ◆ Update and locking strategies
- ◆ Creating and using subscreens in dialog transactions
- ◆ Using TABS in transactions

Update and Locking Strategies

One of the key features of an ERP system is data integrity. This integrity is due to the fact that most of the data is located in one database, and the transactional and master data is verified and updated consistently. Of course, having hundreds of users accessing the same database can also lead to problems since several users may want to update the same record at the same time. Alternatively, some users may want to read a record while others try to update it. To get around this potential problem, programs can put locks on objects that will tell other programs that the object is about to be updated.

Locks and updates must be considered when designing any ABAP that will perform updates to the database. If locks and updates are not used or used improperly, data corruption or system performance problems may occur. To understand how to use locks and updates properly, the ABAP programmer must have an understanding of general SAP architecture, which includes all of the different pieces of hardware, the tasks running on the hardware, and how they operate together. The ABAP programmer must also understand the basic concept of transactions and Logical Units of Work (LUW).

General SAP Architecture

To effectively program in the SAP environment, it is important to understand how all of the different systems and tasks are tied together. Figure 20-1 shows a high level view of the different layers within a typical SAP environment, and Figure 20-2 shows a more detailed view of the processes and their interrelationships.

In Figure 20-2, the SAP GUI is running on the user's workstation, which is communicating with one of the application servers of the system onto which the user is logged (see Table 20-1).

Overview of SAP Architecture

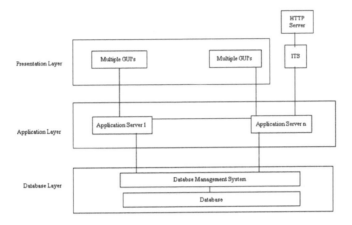

FIGURE 20-1

High level view of a typical SAP R/3 architecture

Run time Environment

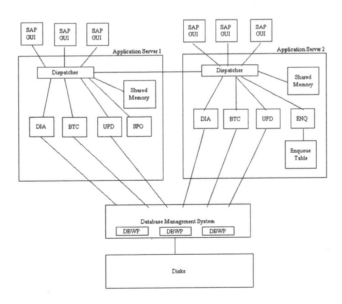

FIGURE 20-2

Process view of typical SAP R/3 run time architecture

Table 20-1

Application Server Processes

Process Type	Description
DIA	Dialog processes are tasks that handle the communications between the GUI and the rest of the SAP system. They are shared among many users and are only used for the portion of time that the ABAP is running on the user's GUI. When a GUI is using a dialog process, no other GUI can use the same process.
BTC	Background processes handle all of the background sessions on the application server.
SPO	Spooler processes handle the spool formatting requests.
UPD	Update process (V1) handles time-critical database updates. The update processes UPD and UP2 are discussed in more detail later in this chapter.
UP2	Update process (V2) handles non-time-critical database updates.
ENQ	The ENQUEUE process handles all of the SAP locks. The ENQUEUE process is discussed later in this chapter in "Locks to Ensure Data Consistency."

 NOTE

When all of the dialog processes are being used, no one can get access to that application server. The busy icon will appear until one of the processes becomes free. When in debug mode, you are taking up a full dialog session. (The dialog session is not released when you are merely looking at the code, tables, etc.) This is why it is important not to stay in debug mode too long, especially in production environments.

To view what is currently running on an application server, you can use transaction SM50 to open the Process Overview window. A list similar to that in Figure 20-3 will appear.

If database access is required from any of these processes, the requests are sent down to a database work process that, in turn, performs the actual database access. All of these processes communicate together in some form or another, but it is still

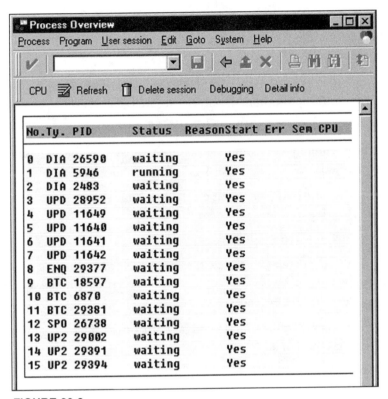

FIGURE 20-3

Overview of processes running on a typical application server

up to the ABAP programmer to ensure data integrity. You can handle all possible events by combining proper locking and update strategies within the ABAP code.

Locks to Ensure Data Consistency

In the database world, the term lock is typically used to describe the action taken by one program to tell other programs that it is about to update a record. This prevents those other programs from simultaneously attempting to write to the record.

In SAP, there are two types of locks, SAP ENQUEUE locks and database locks. Database locks are physical locks on specific, existing database entries and are automatically deleted after a COMMIT WORK is performed. They are set so that the multiple DBWPs (refer to Figure 20-2) do not try to write to the same record at the same time.

A commit that can trigger the end of a database lock can be either implicit or explicit. Implicit database commits in SAP can occur under one of the following two circumstances:

◆ At the end of a dialog step, when control changes from the Dialog Process on the application server back to the GUI;

◆ Whenever a Remote Function Call (RFC) is called or finishes

Explicit database commits are commits that are triggered by the program using one of these methods:

◆ Executing the ABAP statement COMMIT WORK. This executes a database commit work plus a series of other functions;

◆ Calling the function module DB_COMMIT

Records written to the database before either an explicit or an implicit commit is performed can be undone by performing a rollback. A database rollback basically occurs only under two circumstances:

◆ An error occurs in the program and it aborts or the program generates a message of type A or X;

◆ The ABAP command ROLLBACK is executed

SAP enqueue locks are logical locks that can encompass a single record, a combination of records, or an entire table. For details on the definition of SAP enqueue locks, refer to Chapter 10, "Lock Objects." The ENQ process controls SAP enqueue locks. There is only one ENQUEUE process per system, regardless of the number of application servers. This one process maintains the enqueue table that contains entries for all of the current SAP enqueue locks.

Enqueue locks can exist for entries that do not yet exist in the database. This allows programs to determine whether another program is trying to create the same record. For example, two users may be trying to create the same customer master record at the same time. Even if the first user has not yet saved the customer record, the enqueue lock is already in place. If a second user tries to create a customer with the same number, they will be told that the record is locked.

Enqueue locks are created by a function module call to a function named ENQUEUE_lock object name and are deleted by a function module call to a function named named DEQUEUE_lock object name. When performing these function module calls, you are actually communicating to the ENQUEUE process to update the ENQUEUE table. Locks that are currently on the system can be viewed through

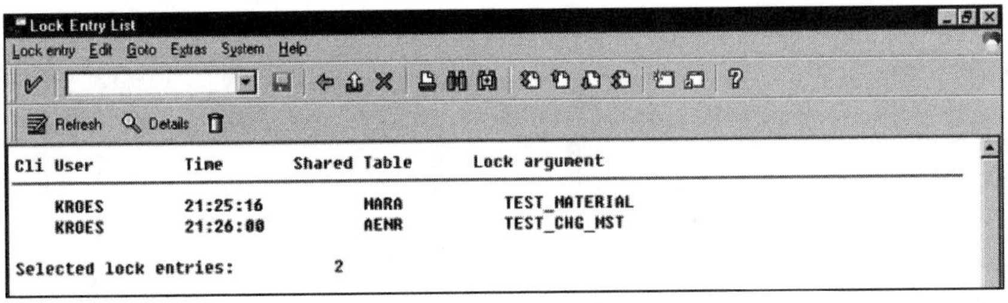

FIGURE 20-4

Transaction SM12 showing ENQUEUE locks on a system

transaction SM12 (the Lock Entry List window), an example of which is shown in Figure 20-4.

Unlike database locks, SAP enqueue locks are logical. Even if you set up an enqueue lock for an object, there is nothing to stop another program from writing to the object. This is why you should use the SAP enqueue/dequeue functions when writing ABAPs that update database tables.

Take, for example, a user in transaction MM02 who is maintaining a material master record. By using the standard SAP transaction, there is an enqueue lock on the MARA record at which the user is looking. If another user tries to update the same material master record, they will see the message that the record is locked by the first user; everything is okay, all data remains consistent, and nothing is lost. Along comes a renegade ABAP with total disregard to the SAP locking system. While the first user has the MM02 transaction open and is deciding what values to put on a screen, this program goes through and reads in the MARA record, changes a value, and then writes it back to the database. Now when the first user finishes the MM02 transaction and clicks Save, SAP will overwrite the MARA record and any change made by the renegade program will be lost.

An even worse case can occur for renegade programs that are written in the following manner:

```
TABLES: MARA.
DATA: INT_MARA LIKE MARA OCCURS 1000 WITH HEADER LINE.


SELECT * FROM MARA INTO TABLE INT_MARA
        WHERE MATNR LIKE 'A%'.
*10 minutes of processing the internal table INT_MARA.
UPDATE MARA USING TABLE INT_MARA.
COMMIT WORK.
```

If, while this program is processing the INT_MARA table, a user opens up a MM02 transaction, updates some data, and then saves, the user's input will be lost after the processing of the internal table is complete and a COMMIT WORK is performed.

There are two levels of enqueue locks, shared and exclusive. These levels are set up when the locks are defined (see Chapter 10). Shared locks are used to indicate that some other program is reading the referenced object and the object should not be changed. Multiple programs can place a shared lock on the same record.

TIP

Whenever writing an ABAP that updates a database table, always use the SAP ENQUEUE/DEQUEUE locking mechanism. Whenever creating a table in SAP, ensure that, at the same time, you also build the appropriate lock objects based on how the table falls into other LUWs.

Exclusive enqueue locks are used to tell other programs that the object is about to be changed. Only one exclusive lock can exist for an object at one time.

SAP enqueue locks should be released using a DEQUEUE function module call whenever they are no longer required. Having too many enqueue locks can degrade system performance, so make sure you use them only when necessary. All enqueue locks are released upon a call to the ABAP command COMMIT WORK or when a program finishes.

The following are some simple examples of the function module calls for ENQUEUE on a material master record:

```
* Attempt to set a shared enqueue for MARA
CALL FUNCITON 'ENQUEUE_EMMARAS'
          EXPORTING
                matnr = W_MATNR
          EXCEPTIONS
                Foreign lock   = 2
                system failure = 3.
CASE SY-SUBRC.
    WHEN '2'.
        WRITE: /001 'foreign lock on material', W_MATNR.
        EXIT.
    WHEN '3'.
```

```
        WRITE: /001 'system failure when locking', W_MATNR.
        EXIT.
ENDCASE.
.

.

* Attempt to create an exclusive lock on MARA
CALL FUNCTION 'ENQUEUE_EMMARAE'
        EXPORTING
            matnr = W_MATNR
        EXCEPTIONS
            foreign_lock   = 2
            system_failure = 3.
CASE SY-SUBRC.
    WHEN '2'.
        WRITE: /001 'foreign lock on material', w_matnr.
        EXIT.
    WHEN '3'.
        WRITE: /001 'system failure when locking', W_MATNR.
        EXIT.
ENDCASE.
```

The return codes from both the exclusive and the shared lock are the same. A FOREIGN_LOCK exception is set when another SAP lock exists that conflicts with your request. A SYSTEM_FAILURE exception is only triggered if the ENQ process has a technical problem creating the lock, such as too many entries in the enqueue table or a problem communicating to the application server that is running the ENQ process.

```
.

* Dequeueing a shared lock
CALL FUNCTION 'DEQUEUE_EMMARAS'
        EXPORTING
            matnr = W_MATNR.
```

Other than the key arguments that you want to lock (i.e. MATNR above), there are other export parameters on the ENQUEUE/DEQUEUE function module calls. The first set is identical to the arguments except that they begin with an X_. Setting this value to X means that you want to use an argument's initial value.

Another export parameter is SCOPE. This parameter needs to be filled in only if you are bundling your updates together through V1 function modules and sending them off to an update task for processing. More information on V1 and the update task can be found in "Database Updates Explained," later in this chapter. The scope parameter is used to indicate how the enqueue locks should be released, and has the valid values listed in Table 20-2.

Table 20-2

Valid Values of the Scope Parameter

Value	Purpose
1	Indicates that the lock need only be active for the length of the dialog task processing. If you use SCOPE = '1', make sure you enqueue your locks if you perform a rollback, since SAP will not do it for you.
2	This default value indicates that the lock is in place for the length of the dialog task (until the commit) and then is used by the associated update tasks. The lock will be cleared automatically by the update task. If you do not call any update tasks, the lock will not clear unless a rollback occurs, your program finishes, or you explicitly call the DEQUEUE function.
3	The same type of lock as 2, except that the lock is used by both the dialog and update tasks once a COMMIT WORK has been performed. Both processes must release a lock 3 type before it is cleared. This type of lock is used if you want to do further processing on a record after a COMMIT WORK has been performed.
WAIT	The WAIT export parameter is only associated with the ENQUEUE function module. If your program cannot wait for an enqueue lock to be established, set this value to X; otherwise set the value to anything else and the system will wait (for a few seconds) in an attempt to get the enqueue lock.

When working with locks, always use SAP's ENQUEUE/DEQUEUE locking mechanism when writing any ABAP that may update database records. There are two different kinds of locks: database and SAP. Once you understand the concept of data locks, you can organize your programs to correctly and efficiently update the data.

SAP Transaction Concept and Logical Units of Work

The SAP transaction model is discussed in Chapter 4. To recap, a transaction is a sequence of actions that logically belong together. A simple example would occur in any finance transaction where a value is subtracted from one account and added to another. The LUW here is the posting of both rows in the database. If there was a problem after only one row had been posted and the other row did not post, a data inconsistency would occur.

An SAP transaction is comprised of at least one LUW, but could be comprised of many. For instance, in month-end jobs, many financial transactions like the previous example may be processed. Each transaction is its own LUW.

Once a program or transaction has been broken down into LUWs, you can determine the proper locking strategy for the various database objects and how they relate to the user functions. After this step has been completed, it is time to proceed in updating the data in the database.

Database Updates Explained

This section covers two tightly integrated subjects. First, you will learn the different methods in which ABAP can be written to control how data is updated to the database. Second, you will learn how this process is integrated with the Update Process (refer to Figure 20-2).

Simple versus Complex Updates

A simple database update ABAP is defined as any ABAP where the database LUW is the same as the SAP LUW. This means that there can only be one screen (for transactions) and that no remote function calls or anything else can cause a database commit besides the ABAP command COMMIT WORK or the termination of the program.

In such an ABAP, the programmer can freely place database commands such as INSERT, UPDATE, MODIFY, or DELETE, anywhere in the code, since all of the operations will be performed within the same database LUW.

If there is more than one database LUW per SAP LUW, then you must group your database commands together and perform them all at once at the end of the SAP LUW. This grouping of the database commands is referred to as update bundling.

General Update Bundling

If you do not do update bundling in your code, there is no way to roll back all of the database changes for an SAP LUW. In that instance, data may already be committed at the database level due to a prior database LUW (triggered by a database commit).

SAP provides many ways of performing update bundling, including:

- ◆ Update bundling within the dialog task
- ◆ Update bundling within the update task
- ◆ Update bundling within a background process

All of these methods are set up the same way. You must tell SAP that you want to execute a subroutine or function module when the next COMMIT WORK is encountered; and you must indicate where you want the routine to run.

 CAUTION

Do not use update bundling from within a dialog module. Pass data back to the calling program through some mechanism (i.e. import/export) and perform the update bundling in the calling program. Dialog modules execute in a different roll area than the calling program, and this roll area is purged upon completion of the dialog module. There is also a problem in that update calls from dialog modules are not differentiated from those of the parent, which could cause missed update calls if done incorrectly.

Update Bundling in Dialog Task

Update bundling in the dialog task is achieved by grouping all of the database update operations (like INSERT or DELETE) in subroutines and then calling these subroutines to execute on the next COMMIT WORK:

```
. . .
PERFORM UPDATEDATA1 ON COMMIT.
PERFORM UPDATEDATA2 ON COMMIT.
COMMIT WORK.
. . .
```

The order of subroutine operation can be controlled by using the additional variant, LEVEL, on the PERFORM command with the subroutines executing from the lowest level to the highest:

```
. . .
PERFORM UPDATEDATA1 ON COMMIT LEVEL 2.
```

```
PERFORM UPDATEDATA2 ON COMMIT LEVEL 1.
COMMIT WORK.
. . .
```

After the COMMIT WORK is encountered in the above program, the UPDATEDATA2 subroutine will execute first followed by the UPDATEDATA1 subroutine.

CAUTION

Do not use COMMIT WORK or ROLLBACK WORK in subroutines that will be executed via ON COMMIT. This is misleading to anyone reading the code and can cause possible database corruption if a rollback is encountered in the middle of a subroutine.

When the subroutine is executed, the variables hold the values that were in place at the time of the commit—not the value at the time of the PERFORM statement. If you want to use the variables at the time of the call, you must use a function module, as shown in the next example. When doing this, the processing will occur in both the dialog task and the update task. Here's the sample code:

```
. . .
MARM-MATNR = 'ABC123'.
CALL FUNCTION 'UPDATEDATA' IN UPDATE TASK
     EXPORTING
     matnr = MARA-MATNR.
MARA-MATNR = 'DEF456'.
CALL FUNCTION 'UPDATEDATA' IN UPDATE TASK
     EXPORTING
     matnr = MARA-MATNR.
COMMIT WORK.
. . .
```

CAUTION

When using the PERFORM XXXX ON COMMIT, any variable used within the subroutine will contain the value at the time of the COMMIT WORK, and not the value at the time of the PERFORM.

For example:

```
. . .
MARA-MATNR = 'ABC123'.
PERFORM UPDATEDATA ON COMMIT.
MARA-MATNR = 'DEF456'.
COMMIT WORK.
. . .
FORM UPDATEDATA.
    UPDATE MARA.
ENDFORM.
```

In the example above, the value of MARA-MATNR is 'DEF456' when the subroutine is executed.

Update Bundling in Background Processes

The bundling of updates can be performed in a background process by using a function module with the IN BACKGROUND TASK option:

```
CALL FUNCTION 'SYNCDATA' IN BACKGROUND TASK DESTIONATION BAK.
```

This is typically used when you want to write data to two different systems at the same time (i.e., a development and a production system). This method of update bundling is not used commonly without the addition of the destination variant. If you do not define a destination, the result is the same as executing the function module in the update task.

Update Bundling in the Update Task

On the application servers, SAP provides a special background process that performs database updates. This special process is called the update process or update task. More details about the update process are given in the next section; for now just think of an update process as another background process.

All bundled updates performed in the update task are done via specially coded function modules. These function modules are called as shown and are triggered on the next COMMIT WORK statement.

```
CALL FUNCTION 'UPDATE123' IN UPDATE TASK.
```

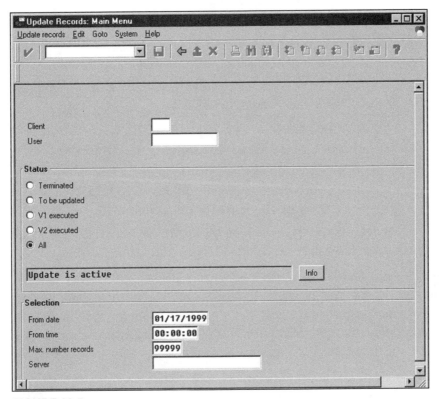

FIGURE 20-5

Selection window for transaction SM13, viewing of Update Records

The Update Task

By going to transaction SM13, the Update Records: Main Menu window, you can view the log of activity performed in the update task for a specified user ID. Before you make any changes, the initial window looks like Figure 20-5.

With the appropriate authorization, you can also restart or follow through on update calls that have terminated. Two types of functions can be sent to the update task, V1 and V2. V1 tasks are all grouped together in the same LUW, are considered to be time critical, and are higher priority than V2 function calls. The V1 and V2 designations are defined when creating the function module.

If you have a program that has several function module calls to the update task, some with V1 and some with V2 priority, and everything runs without errors, the following general sequence of update task events occurs once a commit work has been performed:

1. All dialog task forms are performed that were called ON COMMIT.
2. All V1 function modules, in the order they were called, are processed as one LUW (they all work or they all fail).
3. Release all ENQUEUE locks.
4. Return control if the commit statement has the WAIT variant.
5. Start processing V2 function modules (order of operation is not guaranteed). Each function module call has its own LUW. The background tasks are also started at this time.

When configuring the update task on the application server, the update task can be programmed to handle V1, V2, or both types of updates.

When your program performs a command like PERFORM XXXX ON COMMIT or CALL FUNCTION XXXX IN UPDATE TASK, the routines and calling program name are logged in the update task. When the next COMMIT WORK is encountered, it is the signal for the update task to start processing all events that have queued up for the program that issued the COMMIT WORK.

Requesting Local Updates

Through ABAP, you can request that processing occur locally rather than through an update task using the following ABAP command in your program:

```
SET UPDATE TASK LOCAL.
```

Updating a task locally is typically done for programs that are executed in the background, since background jobs do not get interrupts by users and usually do not have any intermediate implicit database commits (the exception being RFCs). Performance is improved since there is no extra overhead in logging function calls with the update task, nor must you wait for other processes to go through the update task. The background check can be done using the system variable SY-BATCH as follows:

```
IF NOT SY-BATCH IS INITIAL.
    SET UPDATE TASK LOCAL.
ENDIF.
```

Error Handling in the Update Task

Errors that occur while processing in the update task cannot be corrected immediately. The update task stops processing the LUW, sets the status of the call to ERR, and rolls back any processing already done in the LUW. If an error is encountered at the various stages of the update task, the following events occur:

- ◆ Error occurs while the "on commit" forms are being executed in the dialog task. Causes rollback of all data associated with the current LUW. No other forms are processed, nor will any of the functions in the update task be started.

- ◆ V1 function call. Causes a rollback of all previous V1 functions and stops the execution of any other V1 or V2 functions or background tasks. Note that a termination of a V1 function call DOES NOT roll back work from the forms that are done in the dialog task.

- ◆ V2 function call. The current LUW for this specific V2 function call are rolled back. All other V2 function calls and background processes are still allowed to proceed.

- ◆ Background task. The current LUW for this background task is rolled back. All other background processes are allowed to proceed.

Writing Function Modules to Work in the Update Task

Writing a function module for the update task is very similar to writing a normal function module (see Chapter 2 for details on the creation of normal function modules). There are, however, a few differences between the two types of function modules. The first difference is in the attribute section. As seen in Figure 20-6, the process type For Use in Update is selected along with one of its four subitems (see Table 20-3).

Table 20-3

The Four Options for Update Tasks

Option	Update Task Purpose
Start Immediately	A V1 type update with restart capability if there is a problem.
Immediate Start, No Restart	A V1 type update with no restart capability if there is a problem.
Start Delayed	A V2 type update with restart capability if there is a problem.
Collective run	A V2 type with the ability to be grouped together with other similar function modules. The collective run is started as a batch job.

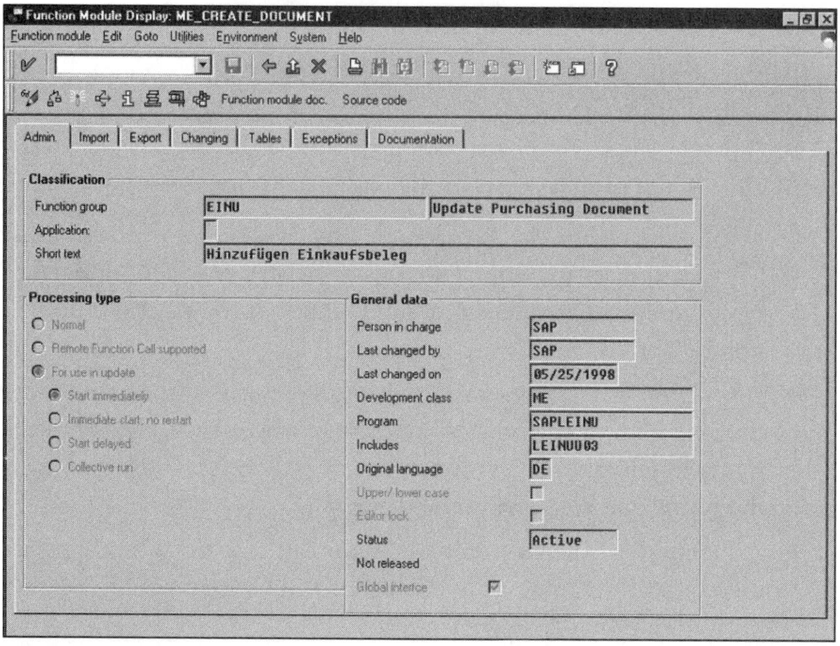

FIGURE 20-6

Attribute window for function module to be used in update task

Two other differences for update function modules exist: you cannot define return variables or exceptions, and when defining the values that you send to the function module, you must reference fields or structures defined within the SAP data dictionary.

Function modules that are written for an update task should only perform database updates. All of the data to be written out should be verified before the commit work is called.

Synchronous and Asynchronous Processing

You can control the update task to run synchronous or asynchronous to the code that triggered the commit work. This is done through the COMMIT statement, as seen in this example:

```
* Example of Synchronous Update

CALL FUNCTION 'function module' IN UPDATE TASK.

COMMIT WORK AND WAIT.

* The next statement after the commit will not
```

```
* execute until control returns to your program after
* all high priority (V1) function modules have run
* successfully.


* Example of Asynchronous Update
CALL FUNCTION 'function module' IN UPDATE TASK.
COMMI WORK.
* The next statement is executed right away even
* though the function module "update_data" may still
* be executing.
```

Rollback **Command**

A rollback can be thought of as an undo feature when it comes to database processing. When a rollback is encountered, the following events take place:

- ◆ Database rollback, including release of database locks
- ◆ Closure of all database cursors
- ◆ Deletion of all temporary sequential files (like spool objects)
- ◆ Cancellation of any subroutines that were submitted with ON COMMIT
- ◆ Cancellation of any background task functions
- ◆ Marking of all functions sent to the update task as errors

Whenever a program aborts or a message of type A or X is triggered, an automatic rollback of work is performed. A rollback can be performed manually by using the ROLLBACK WORK ABAP command.

CAUTION

Do not use the ROLLBACK WORK command in a form or function module that will be executed upon a COMMIT WORK statement. This leads to possible database corruption, since some of the records are already written out and the system might not be able to figure out which records to back out (the current commit work or the previous commit work).

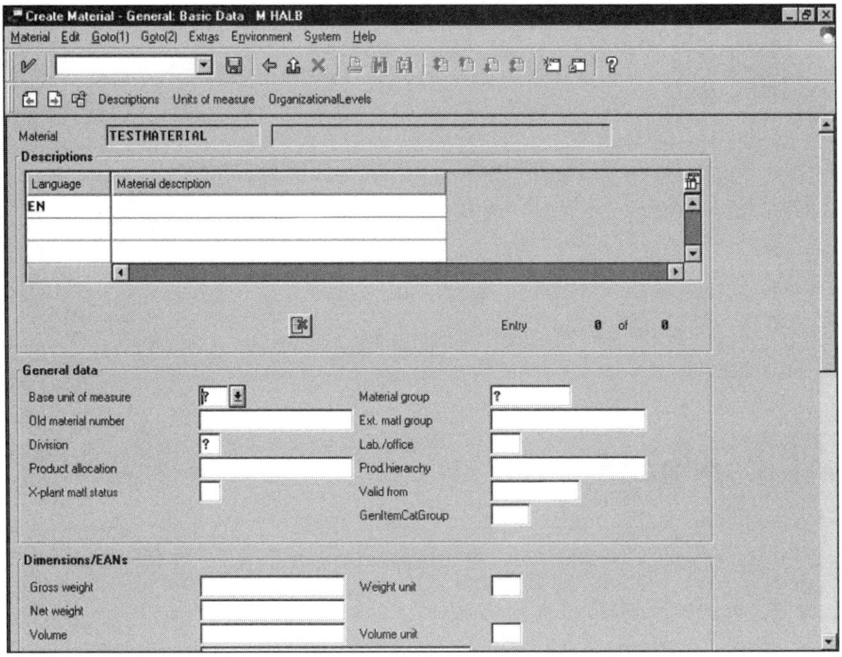

FIGURE 20-7

A dialog transaction using subscreens

Using Subscreens

Subscreens in SAP are independent windows that are displayed in other windows. An example of this is shown in Figure 20-7, which is an image from the Basic Data view of the MM01 (Create Material) transaction.

There are many advantages to developing transactions with subscreens. The first is that you can write your subscreen code once, and then use it in several places. Another is that you can control the look of the screen since you can determine which subscreen to display at run time. This allows you to make your screens customizable. As seen in Figure 20-7, you can display many subscreens within one screen, and each has its own set of fields, attributes, and flow control. SAP does not allow you to build a subscreen within a subscreen.

Creating a Subscreen

Creating a subscreen is just like creating any other screen with the Screen Painter. You start by going to the Screen Painter from the Developer Workbench and creating your new screen.

TIP

It is a good idea to place your subscreens in the same module pool as the main screen that will contain them. This way, you can share variables between the main screen and a given subscreen. If you do not do this or if your subscreen will be used in many different module pools, then you will have to transfer the data using export and import statements or parameter IDs.

When assigning attributes to the screen, make sure that you select the Subscreen radio button option, as shown in Figure 20-8.

After the attributes for the subscreen have been defined, you can use Screen Painter as you would when developing any other dialog screen, with the following exceptions:

◆ You cannot define a GUI status within a subscreen.

◆ A field named "ok-code" is not allowed in subscreens.

◆ The flow logic cannot contain an AT EXIT-COMMAND module.

◆ No cursor position logic is allowed.

When defining fields on your subscreen, remember that when the subscreen is used later, it will share its fields with all other fields on the screen, including other subscreens.

Using a Subscreen

To use a subscreen in another screen, you first must define the place where it will display. This is done using the Layout Editor in Screen Painter (Full Screen View in Screen Painter in releases prior to 4.0). Start by placing your cursor on the top left corner of the current screen where you want the subscreen to be placed, and then choose Edit | Create element | Subscreen.

SAP prompts you to select the end of the subscreen location. Place your cursor roughly where you want the bottom right corner of the subscreen to appear. It's not necessary to be precise when placing the subscreen because you can easily modify the dimensions later. Click the Area End button to set the subscreen size; the Screen Element Attributes dialog box appears, as shown in Figure 20-09.

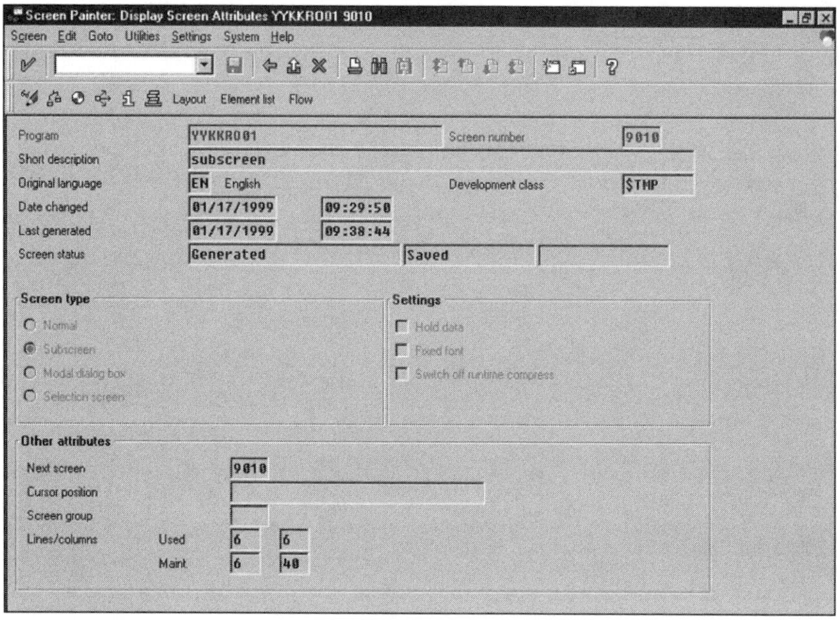

FIGURE 20-8

Attributes window for a subscreen

TIP

When setting size attributes, your subscreen must logically fit within the main screen. When you later declare the subscreen in the main screen, you will set aside a fixed amount of space for it. If your subscreen is too big, it will not be fully displayed.

Name the subscreen area in the Screen Element Attributes dialog box. Choose a short name like SUB01; it will be used in the PBO and PAI flow control. You can also change the size of the subscreen area and define how you want the window resizing function to work. After you have finished modifying the attributes, click on the close button to proceed.

Once you have the subscreen area defined, you must call the subscreen in the PBO and PAI flow logic. When these calls are performed, the respective PBO and PAI

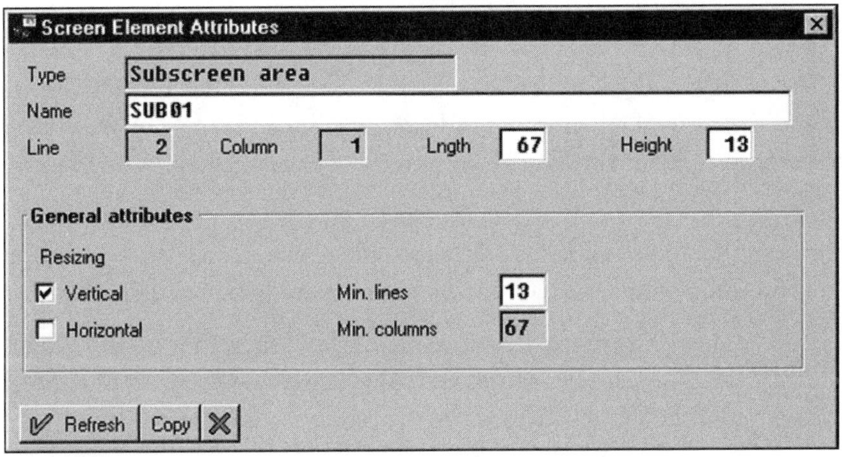

FIGURE 20-9

The Screen Element Attributes dialog box is used to set the screen element attributes for subscreen placement.

flow logic from the subscreen will be executed. Here's an example of the flow logic from the main screen, which will contain the subscreens:

```
PROCESS BEFORE OUTPUT.

. . .

CALL SUBSCREEN SUB01 INCLUDING W_SUBPROG W_SUBDYNP.

. . .


PROCESS AFTER INPUT.

. . .

CALL SUBSCREEN SUB1.

. . .
```

In this example, W_SUBPROG is a variable that will contain the name of the program containing the subscreen and W_SUBDYNP is a variable that will contain the name of the Dynpro Number of the subscreen. This allows for the subscreens to be determined at run time so that you can display different subscreens based on security profiles, data, customizations, and so on.

Using Tabstrips (in Release 4.x)

Tabstrips are a new GUI feature in SAP Release 4.0. They provide the user with an intuitive view of an entire set of logically grouped screens. A good example of the tabstrip functionality can be seen in the Create Standard Order entry screen (VA01), as shown in Figure 20-10.

The best time to use tabstrips is in applications where more than one data screen is required and where the data can be logically grouped together.

Because of the nature of tabstrips, they do not lend themselves well to applications where screens are to be processed in a certain sequence. The number or description of the tabs changes while the user is in the screen.

Creating a Tabstrip in Screen Painter

To create a tabstrip on a screen, go to the Layout Editor in the Screen Painter, position the cursor where you want to start the tabstrip, and then choose Edit | Create element | Tabstrip control.

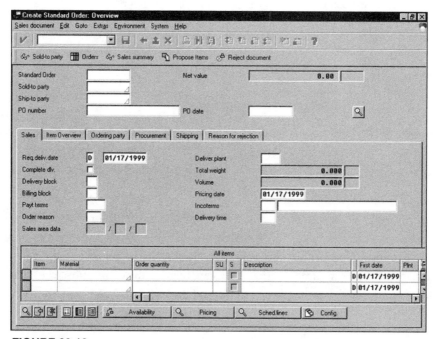

FIGURE 20-10

A screen using tabstrips (Transaction VA01)

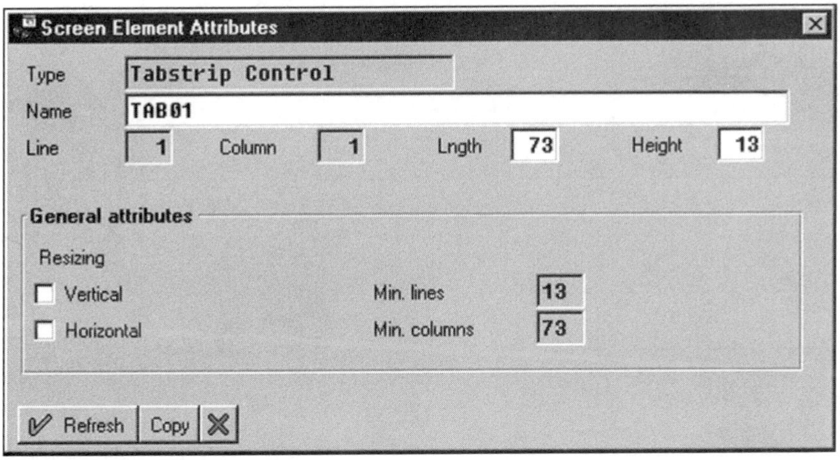

FIGURE 20-11

Screen element attributes of tabstrip TAB01

The Screen Element Attributes dialog box opens (see Figure 20-11) from where you can define the name and size of the tabstrip control. Select a short name like TAB01; this name will be used in the ABAP statement CONTROLS. Click on the close button to proceed to define the tabs within the tabstrip.

This process will give you a tabstrip with two tabs. To set up the names of the tabs and define their purpose, start by double-clicking the tabs, or their control area, and then clicking Ctrl Elements. This will take you to an element definition window similar to Figure 20-12.

The top section of the dialog box shown in Figure 20-12 contains one line for each tab that you define. Tabs are treated like push buttons, and the top section of this dialog box is used to define their functionality. Place the cursor on a new row in the Title Strip column and click the Attributes button to open a push button Element Attributes dialog box (see Figure 20-13).

From this dialog box, define both the name and function code associated with this specific tab. When finished, click Copy to return to the Tabstrip Control element definition dialog box (refer to Figure 20-12). You can now create a subscreen and associate it with the newly defined tabs.

Within the Tabstrip Control dialog box, you can define one or more subscreens. The subscreens, in turn, are allocated to the tabs themselves. The simplest form of this is to have one subscreen and associate all of the tabs against this subscreen.

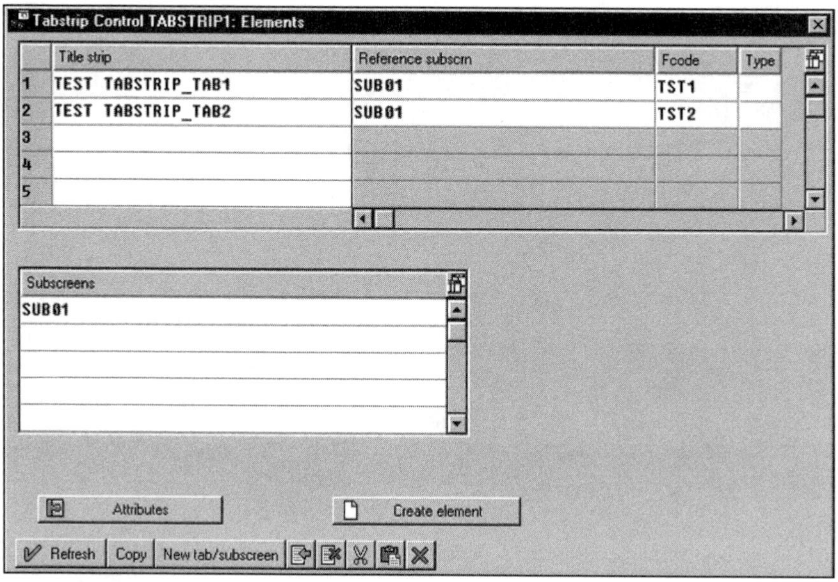

FIGURE 20-12

Control element attributes of a tabstrip

The easiest way to create a subscreen is to go to the Tabstrip Control element definition. To do so, type a new subscreen name (i.e. SUB01) in the Subscreens list and then click New Tab/Subscreen. A subscreen definition dialog box will open from where you name your subscreen and define its size. Click Copy to return to the Tabstrip Control element definition dialog box. Now, as you did for the previously defined subscreen, allocate the new subscreen to the tabs in the top portion of the screen.

Once you have created the subscreen and have allocated it to the tabs, click Copy and then click the save icon. This completes the basics of the Screen Painter side of creating a tabstrip. Now you can concentrate on handling the associated flow logic.

■ NOTE

If you plan to use Local Scrolling, you will want to define an individual subscreen area for each tab. You will also want to set the Type of each tab to P for Local GUI Functions.

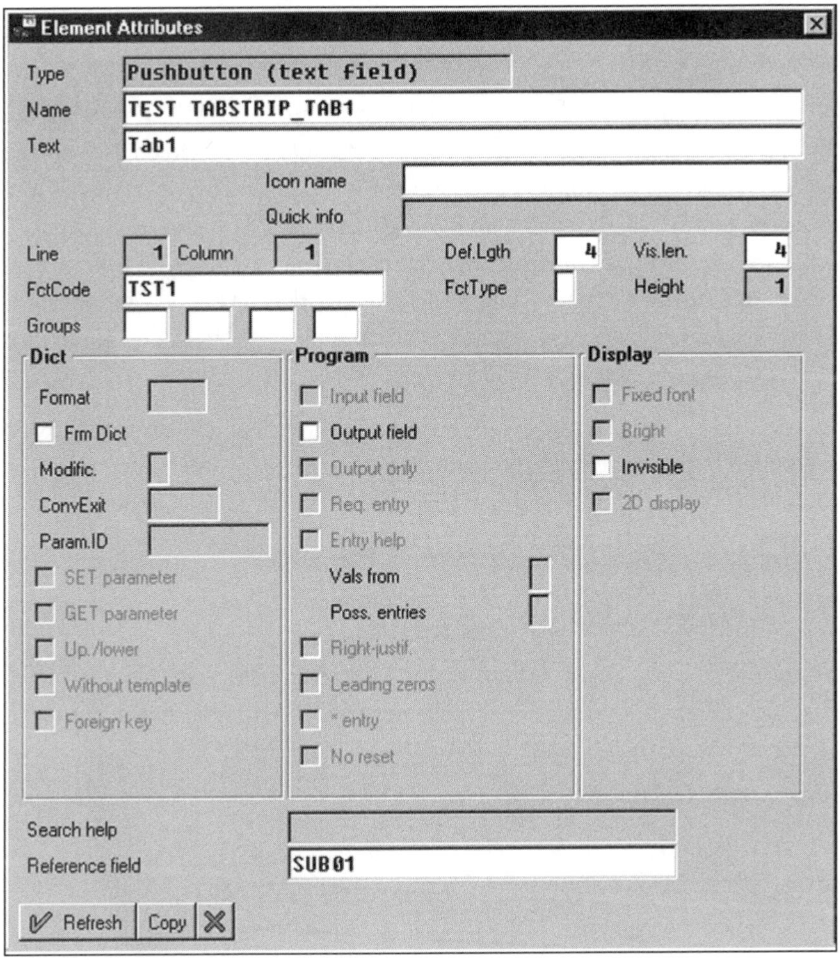

FIGURE 20-13

Single tab attributes

Flow Logic for Tab Strips

When building the flow control for screens with tabstrips, you have two choices on how the user's scrolling between the tabs will interact with the PAI and PBO events. The first method is back end scrolling. During back end scrolling, each time the user clicks on a tab, a message is sent to the application server, a PAI event is triggered for the subscreen of the old tab, and the PBO event is triggered for the new tab's subscreen. The advantage of this is that only the minimum amount of PBO/PAI activity, such as field checks, is done with each click of a tab.

The disadvantage of this method is that each time the user clicks a tab, there is communication between the presentation server and the application server.

The other scrolling method is called local scrolling. With this method, all subscreens are sent to the presentation server when the screen is displayed and there is no communication to the application server when a user presses a tab key. However, there is a drawback in that all of the PBO and PAI events for all subscreens are processed together. If the user clicks a button or enters a function code on one of the tab pages, the PAI for all of the TABS is triggered. This may take a lot of time and cause confusion for the user if a field check fails for a tab page on which the user is not currently viewing.

The method of scrolling you decide to use really depends on the nature of the transaction being coded. If the data is presented only for viewing, it probably makes sense to use local scrolling. If a lot of PAI activity is associated with each subscreen, then the back end scrolling technique is probably the best way to go.

Local GUI Scrolling Flow Logic

The flow logic for Local GUI control is very straightforward since all PBOs and PAIs are called each time. The table control, TAB01, is defined in the same manner as was the table control defined in Chapter 19:

```
CONTROLS: TAB01 TYPE TABSTRIP.


PROCESS BEFORE OUTPUT.


CALL SUBSCREEN SUB01 INCLUDING 'XXXXXXX' 'NNNN'.
CALL SUBSCREEN SUB02 INCLUDING 'XXXXXXX' 'NNNN'.
CALL SUBSCREEN SUB03 INCLUDING 'XXXXXXX' 'NNNN'.


PROCESS AFTER INPUT.


CALL SUBSCREEN SUB01.
CALL SUBSCREEN SUB02.
CALL SUBSCREEN SUB03.
```

Because the tab control element for each tab is set to P, the PAI is only executed when a user event such as a button click or save occurs.

Back End Scrolling Flow Logic

Back end flow logic is a bit more complicated since the minimum of PBO/PAI activity per tab click must be facilitated while ensuring that the overall field checks are done when functions like save are performed. Review this example and notice the difference between it and local control logic:

```
CONTROLS:    TAB01 TYPE TABSTRIP.
DATA:        DYNPRO LIKE SY-DYNPR,
                  OK_CODE LIKE SY-UCOMM.



PROCESS BEFORE OUTPUT.


* Activate first tab if this is the first time this screen is called
MODULE ENSURE_ACTIVE.
* Update the screen (since a subscreen is shared)
MODULE UPDATE_SCREEN.
* Call up appropriate subscreen
CALL SUBSCREEN SUB01 INCLUDING 'XXXXXX' DYNPRO.


PROCESS AFTER INPUT.


* Process PAI for current subscreen
CALL SUBSCREEN SUB01.
*Process the OK-CODE
MODULE OK_CODE.


*------PBO Modules---------*
MODULE ENSURE_ACTIVE OUTPUT.
If dynpro is initial.
    Dynpro = '0100'.                "First Tab dynpro number
    Tab01-activetab = 'TAB1'. "Activate first tab
Endif.
ENDMODULE.
```

```
MODULE UPDATE_SCREEN OUTPUT.
*Some screen update logic based on the value of
*TAB01-activetab.

. . .

. . .

ENDMODULE.


*——————-PAI Modules————————*
MODULE OK_CODE.


CASE OK_CODE.
           WHEN 'TAB1'.
DYNPRO = 'NNNN'. " Dynpro number for 1st tab
CLEAR OK_CODE..
                  TAB01-ACTIVETAB = OK_CODE.
           WHEN 'TAB2'.
                  DYNPRO = 'NNNN'.  "Dynpro number for 2nd tab
                  CLEAR OK_CODE.
                  TAB01-ACTIVETAB = OK_CODE.
           WHEN 'SAVE'.
                  " Special code to ensure all screens have been processed
ENDCASE.
ENDMODULE.
```

Summary

The concept of locks and updating data is very important since it affects both the integrity of the data and the performance of the transaction. Gathering all of your database updates and performing them all at one time is referred to as update bundling. With update bundling you can control both the order of the update and how the system is to react if it encounters any problems during the database update.

Subscreens and tab controls can be used to make your screens more dynamic and easier for the end user to navigate. Subscreens give you the ability to write small sections of screens with their own PBO and PAI flow control that can be used in many main screens. The subscreen that is shown in the main screen can also be determined at runtime. Tabstrips are a series of tabs that point to a subscreen. Tabstrips eliminate the need for the user to go through drop-down menus to get to a certain place in a transaction.

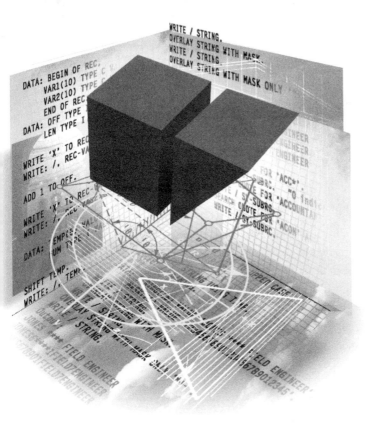

Appendix

SAP Performance Tips

In This Appendix

- ◆ SAP SQL architecture
- ◆ General SAP SQL performance tips
- ◆ Specific SAP SQL tips
- ◆ ABAP performance tips

There are few rules when it comes to improving the performance of programs in SAP. In general, a program spends most of its execution time accessing the database. Therefore, the most dramatic performance improvements you can make occur by writing correct SQL statements. Once you are confident that you have optimized your database access, you should turn your attention to the ABAP code used in your program. This appendix will offer some guidelines you can use when writing your program. Remember that there is seldom only one right answer when it comes to writing efficient code.

SAP SQL Architecture

SAP SQL has improved greatly over the years. There are a number of simple suggestions you can use that will improve performance when accessing database tables from your reports and transactions. These tips have been tested through version 4.5, but most of them apply to any version 3.0 or greater.

Partitioning logic between the application server and database server is the basic concept you must master to write effective programs with SQL. ABAP programs execute on application servers, while database tables are stored on the database server. When you execute a SQL statement in ABAP, the statement is transferred across the network to the database server. The database server performs all the necessary work to find or modify the data your SQL requests. If you are executing a SELECT statement, all of the records you requested are then moved back across the network to the application server where they are made available to your ABAP code.

This architecture means you can make decisions about where work is performed. By using very complex SQL statements, you can perform work on the database server and return only the minimum amount of data required. On the other hand, if you use simple SQL statements, you can move a large amount of data across the network and then use ABAP code to perform the work required. This trade-off between performing work on the database server and work on the application server is rarely black and white. Like most engineering problems, there is no right answer—only what works best in a given situation. Therefore, the ramifications of different options will be presented here so that you can evaluate their effectiveness for yourself.

The four variables you need to consider when partitioning logic are:

◆ Database server load

◆ Network load

◆ Application server load

◆ Application server scalability

The actions that affect these variables are reasonably straightforward. When you use complex SQL techniques such as joins or aggregates, you are increasing the load on your database server. When you use simple SQL statements to move large amounts of data across the network, you are increasing network load. Further, simple SQL statements used to process large amounts of data increase the load on the application server.

Simple SQL statements increase the load on two variables, while complex SQL statements increase the load on only one. This would suggest, at first glance, that you should always use complex SQL language. There is one other variable to consider, however—application server scalability. An R/3 system typically has only one database server, but it may have many application servers across which your ABAP programs will be spread. Therefore, if all of your programs use complex SQL statements piling load upon load on the single database server, those many application servers may be sitting idle. In addition, because SAP supports multiple application servers, it is easy to add additional servers if the load on the overall R/3 system is too great and performance is suffering. Thus, it is often best to make use of the scalability of the application servers wherever possible, even if the load on the network and any one server is increased.

Just because the potential of scaling application servers exists, loading up your programs with lots of ABAP code to make up for simple SQL is not always a good idea. You must understand the specific R/3 system for which you are coding. Some companies may have a single R/3 system that is accessed all over the world, such as a single database server located in the US that supports application servers in Asia, Europe and South America. In this setup, network bandwidth will be in scarce supply and it may be better to use very complex SQL programming so that less data is moved around the world. Another scenario might be an R/3 system running entirely on Windows NT, a common occurrence today. Currently, a single

Windows NT database server can be hard pressed to keep up with even a few application servers. Unlike UNIX database servers that can have tens or hundreds of processors and can support 15 or 20 application servers, NT databases are more limited. In this scenario, it is better to place as much of the load as possible on the application servers and not to worry about the network.

 NOTE

There is seldom a right answer when it comes to partitioning logic. It often depends entirely on your system. The best thing you can do is to test your program as much as possible under as realistic a load as possible.

General SAP SQL Performance Tips

The following are some general SQL tips valid with version 3.0 and later.

Use Field Lists with SELECT

Beginning with version 3.0, it became possible to select individual fields rather than returning all fields with the * indicator. This can have a major impact on program performance. As you know, some sap tables can have over one hundred fields, most of which are not needed in any one program. Rather than using SELECT *, you should explicitly specify only those fields you require. When you do specify fields, be sure that they are listed in the same order as they appear in the Data Dictionary. SAP is more efficient this way. There is no downside to specifying fields; it reduces the load on the database, application, and network.

Use Aggregate Functions

In addition to being able to specify an individual field, it is also possible to perform aggregate functions on fields, such as summation. Using this feature, a SELECT statement will return a single record rather than multiple records. This can be an excellent way to reduce the load on the network. Records selected from the database are transferred over the network to the application server where the program is executing. Rather than moving 10,000 records across the network to the application server where they are summed using ABAP code, it is often better to sum them in the database and then move a single value across the network. However, if used extensively, aggregates have the potential of increasing the load on the database.

Use the INNER JOIN Option Rather Than Nested Select Statements

Make use of INNER JOIN functionality, available in versions 3.0e and up (but undocumented in some earlier versions). Instead of using nested SELECT loops, which SAP does not handle well, use an INNER JOIN. INNER JOIN also reduces the load on the network because data between multiple tables is combined on the database server rather than being moved first to the application server where it must be manipulated in ABAP code. SQL statements using INNER JOIN are not especially complex and do not increase the load on the database when properly written.

Use the Correct Where Clause

Use the most restrictive WHERE clause possible. Process only those records you must and specify as many key fields as possible in your criteria. In general, databases perform better with equal conditions that are linked with AND statements.

Use SQL Trace to Evaluate SQL Statements

Use the SQL trace, ST05, to analyze the performance of your SQL statements. Look for EXEC, OPEN, and PREPARE statements that may allow use of the EXPLAIN SQL function. This will tell you how the database is processing your SQL statements and may show any indexes used to find the data.

Use Array Operations Rather Than Loops

Each time an SQL statement is executed, a load is created on the network and on the database. It is better to do more work with a single statement than little work with many statements. Therefore, use array processing where possible when executing SELECT, INSERT, and DELETE statements. In addition, be sure that common configuration and master data tables are correctly buffered.

Specific SAP SQL Tips

The following are some specific tips to help you write proper SQL statements. Compare your situation to the one described in the example and see if the example is appropriate.

Nested Selects versus Joins

One of the most important tips to improve database access is to never use nested SELECT statements. Nested SELECTs create an excessive load on both the network and database. They should be replaced with either a JOIN or, if you must process each record locally, several array SELECTs. Here is an example of a nested SELECT:

```
select vbeln auart into (vbak-vbeln, vbak-auart)
                            from vbak
                            where erdat = sy-datum.
  select posnr into vbap-posnr from vbap
                            where vbeln = vbak-vbeln.
* Process data
  endselect.
endselect.
```

The following INNER JOIN can replace the prior SELECT:

```
select v1~auart v2~posnr into (xauart, xposnr)
       from vbak as v1 inner join vbap as v2
                         on v1~vbeln  = v2~vbeln
       where v1~erdat = sy-datum.
* Process data
endselect.
```

There are times when an INNER JOIN is not appropriate because each record of data must be processed individually and it is not correct for the database to provide only the combination of records. In this case, several array SELECTs should be used to simulate the effect of nested SELECTs without the overhead of nested SELECTs, as in this example:

```
data: begin of ivbak* occurs 0,
        vbeln like vbak-vbeln,
        auart like vbak-auart,
      end of ivbak*.
data: begin of iposnr* occurs 0,
        posnr like vbap-posnr,
      end of iposnr*.


   select vbeln auart into table ivbak* from vbak
```

```
                     where erdat = sy-datum.
  loop at ivbak*.
*    process vbak records as needed
     select posnr into table iposnr* from vbap
                   where vbeln = ivbak*-vbeln.
     loop at iposnr*.
*    process vbap records as needed
     endloop.
  endloop.
```

Rather than using nested SELECT loops, array SELECTs are used to create internal tables. Nested SELECT loops are used to process data in the internal tables without experiencing the problems of nested selects.

Using Array Operations to Read Data

If you plan to store records returned from the database in an internal table, always use an array SELECT rather than a SELECT loop. This example reads data using a fast array operation:

```
select matnr werks mtvfp vrvez into table imarc
                   from marc
                   where werks in s_werks.
```

The next example performs the same function as the first, but much more slowly:

```
select matnr werks mtvfp vrvez into imarc
                   from marc
                   where werks in s_werks.
  append imarc.
endselect.
```

Using Array Operations to Modify Data

Array operations are always faster than individual SQL statements. If you want to insert a large number of records, try using the FROM TABLE option for maximum efficiency. This example illustrates how an array insert is performed:

```
insert into zccust from table icust.
```

```
A slower way to accomplish the same effect would be:
loop at icust.
  insert into zzcust values icust.
endloop.
```

Modifying Data During a Select Loop

Do not use SQL statements that modify data such as DELET, UPDATE, or INSERT within a SELECT loop where the table being modified is also the table being read. This can lead to erroneous results in the SELECT loop.

Errors When Using Large Range Tables

One of the most convenient features of SAP SQL statements is the IN operator. Using IN, the programmer can dynamically build a WHERE clause with a great deal of flexibility. It is important to understand what happens when you use IN to avoid database errors.

After a SELECT statement is executed, all records in the range table are added to the WHERE clause. This works well when the range table is small (less than 1,000 records) but as the size of the range table increases, the length of the WHERE clause increases until the length exceeds the maximum size that can be passed to the database. You can identify this error when the ABAP program terminates with a short dump that contains the error BIF_RSQL_INVALID_REQUEST.

Reading Distinct Data

There are two methods you can use to obtain data from a table that contains duplicate records. First, you can use the DISTINCT option during the SELECT to eliminate duplicates. Alternatively, you can use the ABAP command DELETE ADJACENT DUPLICATES to eliminate any duplicates in an internal table after they have been read from the database. Since the DISTINCT option forces the database to sort all records before they are returned, it is better to do the work in ABAP code.

Sorting Data

It is almost always better to sort data in ABAP using the SORT command rather than using the database ORDER BY option to read data in sorted order. The only exception is when you need the data sorted by the table's primary key. In that event, you can use the special option ORDER BY PRIMARY KEY to SORT data while selecting at no additional cost to the database. In the example that follows, data is read from the LIPS table and sorted by the primary keys, VBELN and POSNR. Use the ABAP sort command if you need this data sorted by any other fields.

```
select vbeln
        posnr
        pstyv
        ernam
        erzet
        into table ilips from lips
        where matnr in s_matnr
          and werks eq p_werks
        order by primary key.
```

Subtotaling in SQL

Using the GROUP BY option when selecting database records limits the number of records returned. This can be useful when you need to subtotal groups of records. Here is an example where the value of sales orders are subtotaled by order type. Without the SUM command, this query might return thousands of records:

```
select auart sum( netwr ) into (xauart, xtotal)
            from vbak
            where auart = 'SO'
              and erdat = sy-datum
            group by auart.
    write: / xauart, xtotal.
endselect.
```

Checking for Existence of Records

To check for the existence of any records that meet some criteria, use the UP TO option in the SELECT statement. This effectively returns only one record. Make sure you do not use *, which would unnecessarily return all fields. Here is an example:

```
select vbeln into vbak-vbeln from vbak up to 1 rows
            where auart = 'SO'
              and erdat = sy-datum.
endselect.
```

```
if sy-subrc eq 0.
* records exist!!
endif.
```

It is unimportant which field you return in the INTO clause. It is important that you do not use SELECT *, thus moving unneeded data across the network.

ABAP Performance Tips

Though most performance related issues are connected to the selection of data from the database, there are other ways to improve the performance of ABAP, such as the use of new SAP commands, effective use of internal tables, efficient program modularization techniques, and streamlined program execution.

New SAP Commands

Rather than writing code to accomplish a function, use newer ABAP commands where possible. Here is a list of efficient new commands:

- SPLIT—Parses a character string at any given delimiter (i.e. ',' or ' ').

- CONCATENATE—Combines many strings together into a single string.

- SHIFT—Shifts the contents of a string right or left. Variations of this command, such as as SHIFT LEFT DELETING LEADING SPACE or SHIFT RIGHT DELETING TRAILING SPACE, are much quicker than anything that is hand coded.

- CONDENSE—Removes extra white space in a string variable that contains multiple character strings. For example, CONDENSE command would change the string "this   is   a   test" to "this is a test". You can also add the NO-GAPS option to remove all white space from a variable, which would return "thisisatest".

- STRLEN—Returns the length of a string up to the last non-space character.

- CLEAR—Use the WITH parameter to initialize a variable to something other than its default initial state (i.e. CLEAR STR1 WITH '+').

- WRITE—Many of the newer formatting options on the WRITE command have replaced older function calls. For example, the CENTERED option replaces the function call to STRING_CENTER. This also applies to the LEFT-JUSTIFIED and RIGHT-JUSTIFIED formatting options.

Effective Use of Internal Tables

If you need to sort an internal table, use the BY parameter to identify the columns by which you want to sort. If you do not, SAP will sort all of the columns in the internal table, thus taking more time.

```
SORT INT_TAB BY COL1 COL2.
```

When you want to read a specific line from an internal table, it is much faster to use the parameter BINARY SEARCH behind the READ statement, as in this example:

READ TABLE INT_TAB WITH KEY MATNR = P_MATNR BINARY SEARCH.

When using the BINARY SEARCH parameter, it is important that the internal table is sorted in the same order as the key on which you are searching. In this instance, rather than performing a sequential search to find your record, the BINARY SEARCH parameter actually forces the READ statement to perform a type of binary tree read of the table. For large internal tables, the BINARY SEARCH parameter makes a significant difference in the time it takes to locate records. An example of how a BINARY SEARCH is executed is shown in Table A-1.

Table A-1

Binary versus Standard Read from Internal Table Looking for Key 'EEEEE'

Internal Table Contents	Records read By Seq. Read	Records read by Binary Search
AAAAA	AAAAA	DDDDD
BBBBB	BBBBB	FFFFF
CCCCC	CCCCC	EEEEE
DDDDD	DDDDD	
EEEEE	EEEEE	
FFFFFF		
GGGGG		

When possible, make use of the aggregate internal table functionality. This is useful, for example, if you want to copy one internal table to another internal table or compare two internal tables. Using aggregates, as shown below, can be much quicker than performing a LOOP/ENDLOOP series of statements.

```
INT_TAB1[] = INT_TAB2[].
```

Alternatively, use this syntax:

```
IF INT_TAB1[] = INT_TAB2[].

   ...

ENDIF.
```

If your program deals with many operations on multiple internal tables, you will want to examine the ABAP's Help text for the APPEND and INSERT commands. There are a variety of methods to insert and append entire internal tables within other internal tables that are much quicker than coding with LOOP/ENDLOOP. Two of these commands are shown in the next example:

```
INSERT LINES OF INT_TAB1 INTO INT_TAB2.
APPEND LINES OF INT_TAB1 TO INT_TAB2.
```

The command, DELETE ADJACENT DUPLICATES FROM INT_TAB, deletes identical rows from a sorted internal table. This command can also be used to look at specific fields within the internal table, which is much faster than coding a routine to do the deletion.

TIP

When processing internal tables with the loop statement, make sure to use the WHERE clause whenever possible (i.e. LOOP AT INT_TAB WHERE XXXX).

Efficient Program Modularization

When modularizing your program, use FORMS rather than FUNCTIONS whenever practical to the design of the program. A statement of PERFORM FORM XXXX requires significantly less resources and time than does a CALL FUNCTION XXXX.

Make sure that all formal parameters of your subroutines are typed, meaning the data type is listed as part of the form definition, as shown in the example below. Having the parameters typed beforehand saves a good deal of time since SAP will not do any type conversion on the parameters as they are being transferred back and forth.

```
FORM TEST1 USING VAR1    TYPE I
                    VAR2    LIKE MARA-MATNR
                    VAR3    LIKE SY-DATUM.

       . . .

ENDFORM.
```

SAP makes the exercise of typing your parameters quite easy. From the beginning screen in SE38, enter your program name and then choose Type Assignment from the Utilities menu. This program will then automatically determine the appropriate types for all form parameters and can optionally make the changes for you. You can also accomplish this operation by executing program RSPARM30.

Streamlining Program Execution

The issue of performance of programs will occur when loading data through BDC sessions. In these cases, the programmer usually does not have many available options to optimize the program that builds the data for the BDCs. One method to consider that might speed up loading of the data is to run multiple sessions of the program with each session processing a different set of records.

Another alternative to speed up BDC processing is to consider using BAPIs instead of using standard SAP transactions. Because no screen processing occurs—just the data checks—BAPIs tend to run quicker than BDC sessions. If available for your specific instance (such as with materials or assets), consider also the possibility of using one of SAP's direct load technologies.

Miscellaneous Methods to Enhance Performance

Type conversions in SAP take up a quite a bit of time. If possible, always write your code and declare variables to avoid having SAP make type conversions. If you perform a run-time analysis on your working program (transaction SE30), you can see whether any type conversions occur and what percentage of time they take of your program's overall execution.

Using a WHILE loop rather than DO/ENDDO slightly improves performance. Similarly, using CASE statements rather than IF statements may enhance your program's performance.

A large number of subroutines that are called as the result of a CASE statement should be set up with the the PERFORM XX OF .. command, as shown in this example:

```
* LOC_VAL is equal to '3' here, "FORM3" is executed.
PERFORM LOC_VAL OF FORM1
                 FORM2
                 FORM3
                 FORM4.
```

Index

A

B

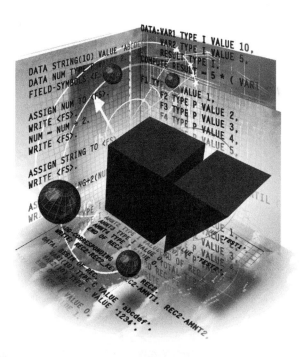
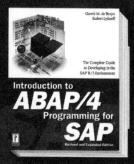

FREE SUBSCRIPTION FORM

To receive a FREE *SAP Technical Journal*, complete and return this form.

Please answer all questions, sign and date the card.

❑ **YES!** I wish to receive my FREE subscription to *SAP Technical Journal*.

❑ NO, I don't wish to subscribe

Name_____

Title_____

Company_____

Address_____

City_____ State/Province_____

Country_____ Zip/Postal Code_____

Telephone_____ Fax_____

Signature (required)_____

Date (required)_____

E-mail Address_____

1 What is your relationship to SAP? (check only one)
- 01 ❑ Customer
- 02 ❑ Third-Party vendor
- 03 ❑ Development partner
- 04 ❑ Consulting partner
- 05 ❑ Hardware partner
- 06 ❑ SAP Employee
- 07 ❑ Other_____

2 If a customer, is your R/3 System live?

Currently	Within the next 6 months
08 ❑ Yes	10 ❑ Yes
09 ❑ No	11 ❑ No

3 How many years have you been working with SAP products? (check only one)
- 12 ❑ Less than 1 year
- 13 ❑ 1 - 2 years
- 14 ❑ 2 - 5 years
- 15 ❑ Over five years

4 What is your current job function? (check only one)
- 16 ❑ Analyst/Program Analyst
- 17 ❑ Application Consultant
- 18 ❑ Application Developer
- 19 ❑ Basis Consultant
- 20 ❑ Basis Developer
- 21 ❑ Business Operations Manager
- 22 ❑ Design/Development or R&D Engineer
- 23 ❑ Network Engineer
- 24 ❑ Process Engineer
- 25 ❑ Product Manager
- 26 ❑ Quality/Reliability Manager
- 27 ❑ Software Engineer
- 28 ❑ Test Engineer
- 29 ❑ Web/Internet Professional
- 30 ❑ Other_____

5 Which SAP release(s) do you currently work with? (check ALL that apply)
- 31 ❑ R/2
- 32 ❑ R/3 3.x
- 32 ❑ R/3 2.x
- 34 ❑ R/3 4.x

6 Do you have Internet/intranet applications connected to SAP R/3?

Currently	Within the next 6 months
35 ❑ Yes	37 ❑ Yes
36 ❑ No	38 ❑ No

7 What SAP R/3 functionality do you use? (check all that apply)
- 39 ❑ Financial Accounting (FI)
- 40 ❑ Controlling (CO)
- 41 ❑ Asset Managment (AM)
- 42 ❑ Project System (PS)
- 43 ❑ Workflow (WF)
- 44 ❑ Industry Solutions (IS)
- 45 ❑ Human Resources (HR)
- 46 ❑ Plant Maintenance (PM)
- 47 ❑ Quality Management (QM)
- 48 ❑ Production Planning (PP)
- 49 ❑ Materials Management (MM)
- 50 ❑ Sales and Distribution (SD)

8 Which best describes your industry? (check only one)
- 51 ❑ Aerospace & Defense
- 52 ❑ Automotive
- 53 ❑ Banking/Insurance
- 54 ❑ Chemicals
- 55 ❑ Consumer Products
- 56 ❑ Consulting & Professional Services (please specify)_____
- 57 ❑ Computer Dealer (Reseller/Vendor)
- 58 ❑ Data Processing
- 59 ❑ Education
- 60 ❑ Entertainment/Tourism
- 61 ❑ Engineering & Construction
- 62 ❑ Healthcare
- 63 ❑ High Tech & Electronics
- 64 ❑ Media
- 65 ❑ Oil & Gas
- 66 ❑ Pharmaceuticals
- 67 ❑ Public Sector
- 68 ❑ Real Estate
- 69 ❑ Retail (not computers)
- 70 ❑ System House-Integrator or VAR/Systems/Integrators
- 71 ❑ Transportation
- 72 ❑ Telecommunications
- 73 ❑ Utilities
- 74 ❑ Other_____

9 What SAP R/3 infrastructure do you work with? (check ALL that apply)
- 75 ❑ OS/390
- 77 ❑ Windows NT
- 76 ❑ OS/400
- 78 ❑ UNIX

10 Which tools/languages do you use for SAP R/3 and SAP R/3-integrated solutions? (check ALL that apply)
- 79 ❑ ABAP
- 80 ❑ Active X
- 81 ❑ ALE
- 82 ❑ Batch
- 83 ❑ C/C ++
- 84 ❑ Cobol
- 85 ❑ COM/DCOM
- 86 ❑ CORBA
- 87 ❑ Delphi
- 88 ❑ DHTML
- 89 ❑ EDI
- 90 ❑ HTML
- 91 ❑ Java
- 92 ❑ JavaScript
- 93 ❑ PERL
- 94 ❑ PowerBuilder
- 95 ❑ SQL
- 96 ❑ Visual Basic
- 97 ❑ Other_____
- 98 ❑ None of the Above

FAX TO:
1-615-377-0525 or
SUBSCRIBE ONLINE
www.saptechjournal.com

11 What tools/topics are you interested in? (check ALL that apply)

099 ❑ Archiving
100 ❑ Application development tools
101 ❑ Application Link Enabling
102 ❑ Enterprise Management
103 ❑ Information Management
104 ❑ Internet/intranet
105 ❑ Middleware
106 ❑ Modeling
107 ❑ Performance Management
108 ❑ Reporting
109 ❑ Systems Management
110 ❑ Testing
111 ❑ Workflow
112 ❑ Other_____

12 How many total employees does your company have?

113 ❑ Under 100
114 ❑ 100 to 249
115 ❑ 250 to 499
116 ❑ 500 to 999
117 ❑ 1,000 to 4,999
118 ❑ 5,000 to 9,999
119 ❑ 10,000 or more

13 What is your company's total sales volume?

120 ❑ Under $10 million
121 ❑ $10 - $50 million
122 ❑ $50 - $250 million
123 ❑ $250 - $500 million
124 ❑ $500 million - $1 billion
125 ❑ $1 billion - $5 billion
126 ❑ Over $5 billion

Publisher reserves the right to determine qualification for free subscriptions. Terms of publication are subject to change without notice. *SAP Technical Journal* is available at no charge to qualified persons within the U.S. and Canada.

PLEASE MAKE SURE YOU'VE:

☞ **Signed and dated the form**

☞ **Filled out the form completely**

☞ **Applied postage**

☞ **Folded form in half and taped closed (do not staple)**

FOLD HERE FOR MAILING